Religion,
Public Life,
and the American Polity

Religion,
Public Life,
and the American Polity

EDITED BY LUIS E. LUGO

The University of Tennessee Press • Knoxville

Library of Congress Cataloging in Publication Data

Religion, public life, and the American polity / edited by
    Luis E. Lugo.
          p.   cm.
    Includes bibliographical references and index.
    ISBN 0-87049-830-4 (cloth: alk. paper)
    1. Church and state—United States.
    2. United States—Religion.
    3. United States—Politics and government.
    4. Freedom of religion—United States.
    I. Lugo, Luis E., 1951-
BR516.R364   1994
200' .973—dc20   93-38721
                                   CIP

‖ Contents

|| Acknowledgments

No project of this nature can be brought to a successful conclusion without the help of many people. I am particularly indebted to my colleague Corwin Smidt, who for several years has been the main inspiration and principal organizer of the Calvin Conference on Christianity and Politics. Though all members of the Political Science department contribute to these biennial events, Professor Smidt has provided the leadership necessary to make them happen. I am very grateful also to the anonymous reviewers from the University of Tennessee Press for their many helpful suggestions. Special thanks go to Professor Matthew C. Moen of the University of Maine, whose detailed and incisive comments proved invaluable. I would also like to take this opportunity to thank Meredith M. Morgan, Kimberly Scarbrough, and Stan Ivester of the University of Tennessee Press for their help and encouragement in bringing this volume to print. I am very appreciative as well of the Calvin Center for Christian Scholarship and its director, Professor Ronald A. Wells, for their generous financial support of my editorial work. Finally, I wish to express my heartfelt thanks to Maxine Comer, Debbie Romero, Kate Miller, and Donna Romanowski for their immeasurably helpful and very good natured secretarial assistance.

Religion, Public Life, and the American Polity: An Introduction

Luis E. Lugo

"Congress shall make no law respecting an establishment of religion, or prohibiting the free exercise thereof." With these two provisions, which together comprise the first freedom specified in the First Amendment to the United States Constitution, the Founders of this Republic hoped to chart a new course in the long and tortuous relationship between religion and public life. Their challenge was to move beyond toleration, itself not an insignificant advance over the widespread practice of religious persecution, toward a fuller guarantee of religious freedom. The disestablishment of a national church, commonly referred to as the separation of church and state, was the most obvious first step in that direction. In the American polity, the national government would not take upon itself the task of prejudging questions of ultimate meaning or truth either by imposing a test of religious orthodoxy on its citizens or by favoring one church at the expense of another. Here citizens would be free to decide for themselves, without the element of governmental compulsion, what church they would join or, indeed, whether they would join any church at all.

As important as the disestablishment clause is, however, it is clear that the Founders did not reduce the notion of religious freedom to a mere institutional separation between church and state. The free exercise clause that immediately follows clearly points toward a more expansive understanding of religious freedom, one that goes considerably beyond the question of church-state separation. Does it not also include the idea that citizens should be free to live out the totality of their lives in accordance with their deepest convictions? If that is indeed the case, then disestablishment cannot be made synonymous with religious freedom but must be seen instead as a basic precondition of its attainment.

It would appear, then, that by means of the First Amendment the Founders were seeking to address the narrower issue of institutional separation as well as the broader question of religious freedom. On the surface the arrangement appears simple enough, but, as we all know, its practical outworking has been anything but uncomplicated. As the present volume makes clear, two hundred years of debate have failed to produce the desired consensus on some of the most fundamental questions surrounding this issue. The problem is that although the mechanism of institutional separation is fairly straightforward, it is only a preliminary (though admittedly essential) step in securing genuine religious freedom. The obvious next question is: How is the state to accommodate the multiplicity of faiths held by its citizens, especially as these faiths take on public expression beyond the institutional church?

This question is crucial on at least two counts. In the first place, it involves a matter of simple justice. Because it is in the nature of faith commitments to seek expression beyond the more formal cultic rituals typically associated with religious practice, it would seem that any state that would truly guarantee religious liberty must necessarily extend legal protection to these public expressions as well. The claim that the state secures freedom of religion simply when it protects the right of citizens to join the church of their choice assumes a privatized notion of religious belief that most religions would find utterly unacceptable.

Beyond the matter of simple justice, the question is important for another reason. The Founders seem to have held the view, later expressed by Tocqueville and others, that religion played an indispensable role in nurturing and sustaining a healthy democracy. President Washington expressed this view in his justly famous Farewell Address. "Of all the dispositions and habits which lead to political prosperity," he declared, "religion and morality are indispensable supports." Evidently, he thought it possible for government to encourage religious expression in order, among other things, for religion to fulfill its indispensable role as a "firm prop" of this democratic polity, without the state abandoning the stance of strict neutrality that the establishment clause seems to call for. No doubt the Founders intended these two provisions of the First Amendment to complement each other, but working out that essential complementarity has proven to be a much more difficult task than they ever anticipated. The country's growing religious diversity has only sharpened the issue to an extent unimaginable to those who lived at a time when a generalized Protestant world view commanded widespread allegiance, perhaps even enjoying a quasi-established position.

The lively contemporary debate on these vital issues convinced the Department of Political Science at Calvin College to devote its 1990 biennial Conference on Christianity and Politics to the theme of "The Role of Religion in American

Public Life." The aim was to explore the historical and constitutional aspects of church-state relations in the United States, as well as the more general question of the complex ways in which religion and public life interact in a liberal democratic society such as ours. The distinguished scholars who participated in the conference were asked to contribute their thoughts on various aspects of these questions with an eye toward encouraging respectful but vigorous dialogue on this often contentious issue.

The chapters which comprise this volume initially were presented as papers at the conference or submitted in connection with it. (The Dreisbach, Guliuzza, and Stronks chapters were delivered subsequently at the 1991 convention of the American Political Science Association, held in Washington, D.C.) The thoughtful comments and irenic tone that characterized the proceedings encouraged us to share the benefits of the discussions with a wider audience. In spite of their many differences, the contributors share a profound appreciation for the signal contribution the religious freedom provisions of the First Amendment have made to the longstanding quest in the Western political tradition to define a proper relationship between religion and public life.

The main theme emerging from these chapters is the centrality and vitality of religion in American public life. So basic is this relationship that to frame the issue in the simple terms of institutional church-state separation inhibits clear thinking on the broader question of religion and politics in the United States. A less restrictive framework provides us with a better vantage point from which to examine the historical record, explore the nexus between religion and the law, and appreciate the more indirect impact of religion on the American civic conversation.

Perhaps no contemporary public policy debate better illustrates the great difficulty of achieving even genuine disagreement than the so-called church-state debate. The first obstacle one encounters along the way toward a more fruitful dialogue on the subject is the confusing array of perspectives vying for the public's attention. Unfortunately, the options are not only numerous but typically come couched in language that makes intelligent debate exceedingly difficult. It is for that reason that Carl Esbeck's chapter, "A Typology of Church-State Relations in Current American Thought," should be received as a valuable contribution. Esbeck helpfully categorizes and clearly explains the most common models of church-state relations, and in the process reduces the debate to manageable proportions. Equally important, however, is that he does so in a fair-minded way that helps set the stage for meaningful and respectful discourse. His essay amply illustrates the wisdom of Pascal's dictum that the first moral obligation is to think clearly.

Esbeck's six broadly drawn, yet distinct, categories include: strict separationism, freewill separationism, institutional separationism, structural pluralism, nonpreferentialism, and restorationism. The author carefully lays out each view and compares it with the others in terms of certain key dimensions, including, for example, its conception of the purpose of civil government and its understanding of the nature of the church. Esbeck makes no claim that his taxonomy is in any sense definitive, nor does he expect it to meet with universal approval. The value of his effort must be judged by a different standard. As he comments at the conclusion of his piece, "We need only agree at the outset that a vocabulary is required so that all citizens who care deeply about religion in America are equipped to talk with one another with less heat and more light."

A second source of confusion in this debate revolves around questions of historical interpretation. Even the most cursory look at this topic makes it abundantly clear that current discussions on the proper relationship between religion and public life are deeply rooted in a long tradition of American political reflection on the subject. Present-day advocates frequently make explicit reference to the founding documents to support their positions. And even when they do not explicitly evoke the past, they conduct the debate in terms that were set at the very founding of the Republic. That is why a look at the historical record is essential to achieving greater clarity of the subject.

Of the many statesmen who wrestled with the topic during the era of the founding, probably none were more influential in shaping the debate than James Madison and Thomas Jefferson. Accordingly, part 2 of the book examines the views of these seminal thinkers in an attempt to uncover the historical underpinnings of the contemporary church-state debate. That greater weight should be given to Madison than to any other figure is understandable given his singular contribution to the forging of a legal/constitutional framework on church-state matters.

Neal Riemer's chapter, "Madison: A Founder's Vision of Religious Liberty and Public Life," explores the nature of Madison's vision of religious liberty and public life in terms of its ethical, empirical, and prudential components. Riemer analyzes Madison's desire to go beyond toleration to genuine religious freedom, his understanding of the value of religious diversity for the preservation of religious freedom, and the importance he attached to bringing "forbearance, love, and charity" to the discussion on these vital issues. The latter emphasis, Riemer wisely suggests, could well be one of Madison's greatest contributions to the contemporary debate.

In "The Enigma of James Madison on Church and State," Charles Emmerich casts doubt on the all-too-common characterization of Madison as a strict separationist. In Emmerich's view, Madison's church-state views reflect an adherence to institutional (rather than strict) separation, as well as a desire to balance constitutional idealism with political realities. Emmerich raises several important issues that he believes could help us further clarify Madison's conception of religious liberty. Included among these are the differences between Madison and Jefferson on the subject, the question of possible changes through time in Madison's own position, and most importantly, the influence on his views of the tradition of natural law.

Along with Madison, the other key figure who helped frame the church-state debate in the early Republic was Thomas Jefferson. It is with Jefferson in particular that many today associate the doctrine of strict separation. Jefferson's contribution is examined by Daniel Dreisbach in his chapter "In Pursuit of Religious Freedom: Thomas Jefferson's Church-State Views Revisited." In an interesting exercise in historical reinterpretation, Dreisbach argues that the modern-day Supreme Court's inordinate reliance on Jefferson's celebrated *Bill for Establishing Religious Freedom* distorts the comprehensive church-state model Jefferson envisioned for his native Virginia and for the nation. His analysis of the legislative context of Jefferson's religious freedom bill leads Dreisbach to conclude that, in fact, Jefferson embraced a much more accommodating view of church-state relations than contemporary separationists are willing to acknowledge.

Dreisbach's criticism of the Supreme Court's rather selective use of historical sources leads to the more perplexing question of the general lack of consistency in recent court rulings on First Amendment religion cases. Part 3 tackles the widely acknowledged and deeply troubling question of judicial incoherence and attempts to come to terms with its likely causes as well as its potential consequences. In "The Supreme Court, the Establishment Clause, and Incoherence," Frank Guliuzza argues that the inconsistency may turn on definitional ambiguities inherent in the high court's rulings. In particular, he contends that by confusing the terms *separation* and *neutrality*, the Court has placed itself in an impossible situation. Unwilling to take the idea of separation to an extreme strict separationist position (bordering on hostility), thus precluding any degree of government accommodation toward religion, the Court has interpreted the establishment clause as requiring separation and neutrality simultaneously. Guliuzza examines the meaning and possible connections between these key terms in a concerted attempt to rescue the Court from its own incoherence.

Even more important than the possible sources of the Court's incoherence is the question of whether such incoherence does not in practice result in a kind of arbitrariness that tends to undermine the religious freedom of American citizens. Julia Stronks explores this issue in her chapter, "The Courts' Definition of Religious Activity: Protection of Diversity or Imposition of a Majority Perspective?" The important question, she suggests, is whether the courts have in fact interpreted the First Amendment's free expression of religion provision from a genuinely neutral perspective. She searches for clues to this question in court cases that have been handed down since 1965 purporting to define what is and is not (protected) religious activity. Her unsettling conclusion is that by accepting certain definitions of "religion" to the exclusion of others, federal as well as state courts have been handing down decisions that frequently result in religious discrimination against particular groups. Perhaps most troubling of all, though, is Stronks's contention that increasingly the courts are attempting to overcome this incoherence by asserting the primacy of certain state interests in freedom of religion cases. Given this alarming tendency, it is little wonder that informed observers are now warning publicly that our cherished religious liberties have been placed in considerable danger.

The courts' handling of First Amendment religion cases, however, does not begin to exhaust the many intricate connections that exist in the United States between religion and the law. Indeed, the connections are quite extensive and flow in more than one direction. John Witte's chapter examines a very specific instance in which religion has had a profound impact on the law. In "'The Three Uses of Law': Towards a Protestant Theory of Criminal Law," he argues that the Protestant theological doctrine of the uses of the moral law helped define the form, as well as the function, of modern American criminal law. He shows how the theological ideas concerning the uses of the moral law—to restrain, to condemn, and to teach—find correlative expressions in the legal doctrine of the purposes of criminal law: deterrence, retribution, and reformation. Witte believes that even as the integrating focus once provided by an older theological framework has eroded, vestiges of the traditional Protestant doctrine are still in evidence in late twentieth-century American views of crime and punishment.

Public life, of course, encompasses much more than a country's formal legal and constitutional arrangements. Perhaps even more basic is the manner in which religion interacts in more diffuse ways with the country's political culture. Accordingly, the last section of the book moves beyond the historical and legal aspects of the church-state debate to inquire about the cultural role of religion in the American liberal polity.

Robert Booth Fowler, in "Religion and Liberal Culture: Unconventional Partnership or Unhealthy Co-Dependency?" puts forth the argument that in the United States liberal culture and religion are not mere partners but greatly depend on each other for their very health and success. Religion, he contends, covers liberalism's weaknesses in several specific areas and thus helps to strengthen it. In turn, religion continues to enjoy the preferments of liberal culture, the support of liberalism's devotion to freedom, and even the benefits of liberalism's philosophical limitations, which in their own peculiar way serve to guarantee a continuing vital role for religion. Fowler acknowledges the dangers inherent in this co-dependency but is persuaded that the relationship is essentially a healthy one for both sides.

In "Politics and Eternity: The Voice of Religion in Political Discourse," Clarke Cochran engages in a very interesting exploration of how religion and politics interact in creative tension at the boundary between private and public life. His purpose is to demonstrate how religion's focus on ultimate questions like sin, death, and the fragility of public life help to sustain liberal democratic politics by holding back the forces that threaten to overwhelm it—coercion, violence, and self-interested manipulation. The danger comes, Cochran points out, when we forget that the relationship between religion and politics involves both cooperation and competition. When the tension is lost, he warns, the two either fly apart or collapse into each other, to the detriment of both.

Finally, in the concluding chapter, James Skillen reflects on some of the key issues broached in the volume and offers a critique of the various arguments from his own vantage point. Skillen is particularly concerned that we not confuse the institutional distinction between church and state, which he fully supports, with the more fundamental and indefensible dichotomy between religious and secular realms. This latter step, he argues, produces a privatized understanding of faith that is wholly incompatible with various religious traditions, and which, moreover, also tends to undermine the moral vitality of the public sphere. He believes it is not the task of the state to decide how people should practice their religion, or to impose an artificial legal distinction between sacred and secular areas of life. What is required, according to Skillen, is a properly constituted, nondiscriminatory public space in which all citizens may practice their religion freely in all areas of their lives.

Skillen is well aware that his views on the question of religious freedom are based on assumptions that are themselves deeply rooted in a distinct religious tradition not universally shared in the United States. Hence his pluralist understanding of the problem of religious freedom must also be tested in the fires of a rigorous public debate in which contending public philosophies are examined and judged. Skillen professes a desire to enter into such a debate but laments the fact that there is so little room in contemporary politics for engaging public policy questions at the level of first principles. The authors of this volume strongly share Skillen's interest in participating in a fuller and more meaningful discussion on the crucial issues relating to our first liberty. It is their sincere hope, therefore, that this volume will contribute in some small way to enhancing the civic dialogue on the role of religion in the American polity.

Part I

Contending Models
of Church–State Relations

1 || A Typology of Church-State Relations in Current American Thought

Carl H. Esbeck

Views concerning the appropriate relationship between church and state are rapidly becoming almost as numerous as America's religious sects. The Constitution's treatment of religious liberty, thought by many to be a matter long settled, has now erupted into a many-sided conflict. Not only lawyers, judges, and legal commentators are involved; historians and sociologists, theologians and ecclesiastics, political theorists and statesmen also participate in the discussion. It is part of a much larger debate over a redefinition, or for some a reclamation, of the role of religion in American public life. And the role-of-religion debate is yet a subset of the epic struggle over who will assume the mantle of cultural authority in the United States. At times this conflict focuses on discrete environments, such as public schools or ancestral lands of Native Americans. At other times it deals with broader questions such as religion's influence on economic policy, the morality of nuclear weaponry, or the direction to be taken by our foreign policy in fostering or opposing political movements in Third World nations.

The conflict is as confused as it is many sided. To the uninitiated, it seems that the issue is clearly defined as a choice between two camps: conservative religious adherents on one hand and proponents of a modernist secular society on the other, with perhaps the moderate positions notched along a line running between these polar extremes. But perplexities defy this linear model. For instance, some traditional religious groups have long made common cause with dedicated secularists in opposing many evidences of religion in civic life. So many voices are heard, so many confident but diverse assertions about how state and church should interact are made, so many lawsuits are raising novel issues, and so many seemingly conflicting court decisions are reported, that bewilderment and uncertainty beset scholars and laymen alike.

This chapter sets forth the six common positions that now model the way in which Americans are working out the problem of the relationship between church and state. One of the tools of academia is to classify, and thereby reduce, that which is complex to terms that are manageable. This alone would justify the typology attempted here, but the goal of this chapter is more ambitious. This American debate needs a vocabulary that is not "preloaded" or pejorative, so that competing groups might address one another with intelligence, fairness, and respect. At present the discourse is mired in discord. It is far too easy to lose one's way in the vilification, exaggeration, and other rhetorical devices now common and thereby perpetuate the already high degree of misunderstanding and mistrust. Thus, a secondary purpose of this chapter is to contribute to mutual understanding among variant and often contending groups.

To be sure, polemics have their place. The issue of church-state relations is emotionally charged. But there must be a time for peaceful coming together, and at present no vocabulary exists to encourage needed opportunities for respite. Moreover, without a common language enabling communication, it is difficult to know when religious liberty is truly threatened. The current alarms from all quarters (many in the company of fund-raising letters) that religious liberty is in imminent danger are little more than crisis-mongering. Such alarmism, like that of the fabled child who thrice "cried wolf," is rendering Americans tone deaf to the most subtle signals that portend genuine loss of liberty.

The effort here is not that of a historian or comparative theologian; it is the limited effort of a systematician taking a snapshot of the present. And a social taxonomy is always something of a construct. When generalizations about church-state relations are reduced to only six types, it is inevitable that some refinements are lost and that the imposed classification is, in a sense, artificial. So it is best not to regard these types as distinct and mutually exclusive views, but rather, as six tendencies in the current debate. Moreover, when one moves from the rigidity of a logical system to the rich complexity of individuals and events, it becomes evident that many persons and organizations will identify with positions held by two, or even three, of the following prototypes but not feel completely at home in any. Individuals or organizations may evidence beliefs or traits so varied that protests will issue that they are being placed into molds that are too purist for comfort. This is partially because the apparent features that enable categorization of an individual are what he or she publicly emphasizes, rather than beliefs deeply but privately held. Others may resist being classified because they have some agenda that prompts them to avow greater flexibility than this typology permits. Still others will genuinely evidence traits that are idiosyncratic. Nevertheless, this classification has the advantage of calling attention to the salient points of continuity and contention among the major players that constitute this American debate. Hence, it may also help us gain orientation as we are pressed with the immediate question of where America and, in particular, its judges and elected officials go from here.

THE TYPOLOGY

The distinctions drawn here require a temporary retreat from the intricate doctrinal analysis that is the forte of legal commentators. Differentia of consequence cannot be found merely by tinkering with the tripartite test of *Lemon* v. *Kurtzman*[1] or by fine-tuning free exercise–clause analysis.[2] These "black-letter" tests promulgated by the Supreme Court are simply the end product of deeper promptings. Thus, as a first step, analysis must reach down through the doctrinal facade lying on the surface of Supreme Court opinions concerning the religion clauses and begin to lay bare the foundational principles that undergird this debate.

Presuppositionally, a person's view of the appropriate relationship between church and state begins with one's ecclesiology (i.e., the origin and purpose of the church) and philosophy of the state (i.e., the purpose of civil government and the scope of its authority). In the present context, exploration of one of these questions cannot be performed divorced of the other. No concept of the state is value free when the question being addressed is, Which group of people and which overarching public philosophy control the power of the state? The inquiry is com-pounded because religion in the Western world has historically had a great deal to say about the values to be incorporated into society's concept of the state. A search, then, for neutral principles of law that are detached from all religious systems and that consistently yield results faithful to the First Amendment's embodiment of religious liberty is vanity. There are no such neutral principles, only juridical con-structs that align more with one presuppositional system than with others.[3]

History also has a claim on the First Amendment. America's story of emerging religious liberty is a guiding factor,[4] but it has proven not to be controlling on the courts or the commentators. It can hardly be surprising that legal solutions adopted in a time when America was overwhelmingly Protestant are today not enthusias-tically embraced by Roman Catholics, Jews, agnostics, and non-Western ethnics. History has much to teach us, particularly about mistakes that cannot be repeated without great cost.[5] Yet history is not demonstrably normative. The fundamental question for Americans today is not whether the courts have correctly construed the language of the First Amendment as it was drafted in 1789 by the First Congress assembled in New York City.[6] Nor is it what Thomas Jefferson, James Madison, or other prominent statesmen thought about church-state arrangements. Nor is it a question of whether America was a "Christian nation" in origin. At its root, one's view of church-state relations is dependent in large measure on one's theological or philosophical world view. Rightly or wrongly, historical events are cited, if at all, to make weight in support of a position held for other reasons. Only when this is admitted can we start being honest about why American views on the appropriate relationship of church and state are as varied as our religious and philosophical allegiances.

It may be said rightly that the typology is driven by establishment-clause concerns. But that is as it should be if the aim is to describe the present, for the U.S. Supreme Court and the many protagonists have been occupied (and divided) by concerns of church-state relations, as distinct from individual liberty.

Six views, broadly drawn and yet distinct, can be discerned as dominating the American debate. Here they will be called *strict separationist, freewill separationist, institutional separationist, structural pluralist, nonpreferentialist,* and *restorationist.* The terms were selected in part because they carry little or no baggage from prior use. They succinctly describe a position without either being opprobrious or giving rhetorical advantage. The views generally held by each of the six types will be compared and contrasted along the following grid:

  a. the purpose and authority of government, and the nature of the church;
  b. the juridical protection accorded religious speech;
  c. the degree of autonomy accorded a church or other religious organization;
  d. discrimination by the state in the distribution of goods and opportunities, among religious groups, and between the religious and those professing no religion; and
  e. the juridical protection accorded religious-based conscience.

A detailed comparison follows, but the chief differences between the six types are easily summarized. Strict separationists are alone in regarding religion as a private phenomenon that should little influence public affairs and matters of state. Strict separationism is the only model that fails to recognize ontological status in the law for churches and other religious organizations. To the extent that religious societies have legal defenses against state intrusion into their affairs, these defenses are merely the sum of individual rights derived from an organization's members.

Freewill separationists view the modern nation-state as strictly a human invention, rather than an entity divinely instituted. Emphasis is placed on protecting the church by separating it from the corrupting influence of civil power. Religion is voluntaristic, and church polity highly democratic. They reject the notion that the state is subject to (and a beneficiary of) any "higher law," regarding such talk as civil religion. By "civil religion" they mean a tendency toward self-righteous nationalism fueled by nativist religion.

Institutional separationists maintain that an ultimate world view transcends and unifies the state, and thus limits the state by holding it accountable to this higher law. This overarching public philosophy is properly deemed theistic and is heavily influenced by Judeo-Christian thought, as is the history and tradition of all Western nations. Nevertheless, the institutions of church and state are to be kept separate and free of mutual dependency so as to secure both individual liberty and a church free of government interference.

Structural pluralists emphasize liberty to follow one's world view, whether it be understood as religiously or philosophically based. Any juridical separation of "the religious" and "the secular" is artificial and ultimately coercive. To the extent consistent with civic order and public justice, government is to distribute goods and opportunities in a manner that does not discriminate on the basis of world and life views. Thus, religious organizations should receive the same government aid as all other nonpolitical structures. The possibility of nonstatist institutions (e.g., families, schools, businesses, unions, churches, and charities) empowering individuals to carry on lives of considerable freedom within many differentiated societal structures is celebrated as *principled pluralism.*

Nonpreferentialists would permit government to favor religion on a basis that does not prefer one religion over another. The state may aid the nonsacral activities of religious organizations. For example, all but classes in religion at a parochial school could receive state support. Unlike the prior four models, nonpreferentialists would allow the state to distribute aid to religious groups on a nondiscriminatory basis while denying aid to those professing no religious belief.

Only Restorationists would bind the state to a confession of faith and assign civic officials limited duties in defense of the dominant religion.

Strict Separationists

Strict separationists desire a secular state. By "secular" they mean a state that is decidedly nonreligious but not necessarily hostile to religion. They urge that great care be taken to insulate government and public affairs from the influence of traditional religion.[7] As a slogan, strict separationists cite the Jeffersonian metaphor of a high and impregnable wall between church and state.

Because they aspire to government unalloyed by even vestiges of religion from bygone days, strict separationists are working out the logical implications of a distinction between church and state that matches the distinction between religious and secular. Thus they argue not merely for separation of church and state, but for a separation of traditional religion from any influence on civic or public matters.

Strict separationists may be active members of a church or synagogue, devout in a particular faith, or they may profess no religious persuasion. Many are religious or ethnoreligious minorities who genuinely fear discrimination and other forms of intolerance should conservative Christian majorities be in a position to influence in any serious way matters of public law. Although others often accuse strict separationists of being antireligious or irreligious, this charge does not apply to all, or even most, strict separationists. However, being both religious and committed to strict separationism does have theological consequences. Strict separationists who hold religious beliefs are compelled to be dualistic in mind. When an individual determinedly strives to keep his public life secular, his religious life becomes increasingly consigned to that which is private. Such persons internalize the axiom that the place for religion is family, home, and church. Religion survives—indeed, for some it thrives—but as a privatized phenomenon.

A related consequence of the public-private dualism is that religion is left vulnerable to marginalization by those unsympathetic to it. For example, those professing little or no religious faith patronize it: acknowledging religion to be of therapeutic value as one way of "coping with" the complexities of modern life but viewing it as embarrassing or even offensive when believers "foist" their religion on others. The unsympathetic regard the church as little more than part of an individual's cultural identity, or worse, one's "support group."

In the public sphere, civic issues and affairs of state are to be debated and resolved in a wholly secularized medium, because religious views are effectually leached of any serious public consequence. Education, law, economics, and military defense are declared to be secular and are to be publicly debated in such terms. For a person whose religion teaches the integration of faith with the totality of life, tensions result from the imposition of such a dualistic motif. Usually it is the faith that eventually yields and is privatized.

In contrast to the other five types, strict separationists generally hold that no universal, transcendent point of reference or ethical system exists or is required for judging the state. They view higher law, if it exists at all, as indeterminate in any event. Although ethical constructs can be helpful, strict separationists hold that ultimately matters of politics and statecraft are relative. "Relative" does not mean value free, but one's choice of values is not to be judged right or wrong by reference to an external and immutable natural law. Liberal political theory[8] and pragmatic instrumentalism[9] direct their thinking.

One would think that strict separationists are protective of religious expression under the first amendment, for as a tenet of civic faith they oppose any content-based censorship of speech.[10] Nonetheless, recent cases suggest that some strict separationists, conscious of their minority status, place a lesser value on religious speech in the marketplace of ideas. Religious strife and even wars, past and present, they argue, evidence the danger of fracturing along religious lines within the civil polity. This warrants modest additional restrictions on religious expression in highly fragile environments, such as public schools, so as to prevent any misperception that government and religion are not totally separate. Fear that their children's public schooling may be affected by their minority religious status overrides their opposition to censorship.[11]

Strict separationists view churches and other religious organizations as having no institutional rights other than the derivative legal rights of their members. That is, a church qua church has no defense to governmental interference in its affairs apart from the free exercise rights of individual church members. This view is based on the jurisprudential theory, dominant among strict separationists, that only individuals can be the ultimate repose of legal rights. It follows that the state properly refused to grant religious societies ontological status and standing as rights-holders apart from their members.[12]

For strict separationists, conscience informed by religious belief is to be vigorously protected from coercive state action. They are on the forefront of litigation on behalf of religious minorities, for such groups are often the first to suffer intolerance by means of legislation adopted by the larger political community. Moreover, there is a tendency among some strict separationists to broaden this free exercise clause protection to all conscientious objectors, religious or otherwise.[13] This is done by defining "religion" broadly for free exercise clause purposes (although not for establishment-clause purposes) so as to protect any philosophically based conscience, rather than just beliefs arising from traditional religion.

When conscience is discussed, the commentary occasionally implies a common duty to not offend minority religions, as in causing a member of the political community to "feel like an outsider."[14] However, the thoughtful strict separationists concede, albeit reluctantly, that to not "give offense" ("offense" is rarely measurable by some objective standard) goes beyond the first amendment duty to refrain from state action coercive to conscience.

Freewill Separationists

Although seeking good communication between government and churches, free-will separationists desire a neutral state. By *neutral* they mean a state that doggedly avoids the use of its power to grant any benefits to, or impose burdens on, religious organizations. Freewill separationists reject the argument that it is "nonneutral" for the state to exclude religious organizations from equal participation with other private sector organizations in social welfare, entitlement, and grant programs. The pluralism they advocate is over against a state that is deeply involved with churches and their social welfare ministries. Government cannot help but affect everything it touches, including religion. This is to be avoided at all cost, they argue, if each individual is to exercise "soul freedom" in matters of faith. The phrase "a free church in a free state" encapsulates this position. Church and state, each within its own jurisdiction, is to remain completely unentangled with the other. Religion is voluntaristic (free will or "soul freedom"), and church polity highly democratic.[15]

Like strict separationists, this second type draws a dichotomy between the secular and the religious. By confining its attention to the secular realm, government maintains the desired neutrality. But the dichotomy drawn by freewill separationists is not as sharp or as absolute as that of the strict separationists. Rather, the forays of freewill separationists into public affairs have been selective or partial. Many freewill separationists have a history of political involvement in the prevention of vice and the regulation of personal morality. Their religious views have had a civic impact in matters such as regulation of gambling, pornography, and alcohol. Others have historically concentrated on peace issues. Still others have focused on labor, social welfare, and world-hunger legislation. Many from Pietistic (spiritual vs. temporal life dichotomy) and Anabaptist (faithful vs. worldly people dichotomy) backgrounds have had this sporadic political involvement, because their separationist theology has told them that "politics is dirty" and thus to be avoided on a sustained or comprehensive basis. To the extent the secular-sacred dichotomy is inconsistent, it is an inconsistency that freewill separationists have lived with for so long that they little notice.

Pluralism is a fact in America, and none in our six-part typology would deny this. However, freewill separationists regard religious pluralism as not only a fact that must be acknowledged but the desirable state of affairs. They view with favor the "rival sects" theory of how religious liberty is maintained. This concept, often attributed to James Madison, suggests that religious liberty is achieved when many religious groups freely compete, but with none dominating.[16] The model assumes that if one, or even a few, Christian denominations should become dominant, the ambition of clerics (pejoratively called *clericalism*) to promote their own church would eventually lead to loss of civil liberties for all others.

Although freewill separationists accept that religion may influence selected matters of civil government defined by them as "moral" issues, they shun any religiously generated cultural mandate to employ the offices of government to achieve ends reflective of a comprehensive world and life view. Freewill separationists do not hold that a universal, transcendent point of reference or ethical system for judging the state is required. Admittedly, as individuals they have world views, many religious in nature, that they believe transcend, and thus limit, the state. But the modern nation-state is not legally "bound" to any particular world view or public theology.[17] The state can and should be neutral toward these various religious subscriptions, for the state is not competent to determine which of these competing world views is correct. Furthermore, an overarching public theology is to be avoided as approaching a civil religion.[18] *Civil religion,* a term with multiple connotations, is used by freewill separationists in the pejorative sense of dominant religious sentiments being used to sanctify political expediencies. Where there is civil religion, the church has been prostituted to serve those moving the levers of civil power. The modern state is of human invention and instrumental, argue freewill separationists. The state is not "one nation, under God," in any sense of a particularized omnipresence legally obligating the state. Rather, through popular sovereignty (majority rule), the state is to respond to the will of its citizens, both those from the plurality of faiths and those without religious belief.[19]

Freewill separationists often prefer to posture themselves in the prophetic role. They are the ones outside the chambers of power, critiquing the state and calling it back to its true course. A prophet's role as dissenter is in contradistinction to the priestly function of a religious insider who, through self-interest, lapses into securing and conserving the existing social and political order. Freewill separationists view tension between church and state as desirable, for tension is a sign of a church that is vital and has not succumbed to the allure of political power. The role of dissenter in their story is venerated. Their literature extols them to be sojourners in the world, rather than to be of the world. The individual and his choice of faith-belief is emphasized over conformity to a church's written creed (pejoratively called *creedalism*).

Religious speech and press receive high juridical protection on a parity with, for example, expressions of political, philosophical, or artistic content, for religious faith may speak to civil affairs. However, religious believers properly influence the state "from the ground up," beginning with their own spiritual regeneration, not through an appeal to a superseding religious "higher law" or world view imposed from the top down. The latter path leads to coercion of conscience, not persuasion, and coercion yields hypocrisy, rather than an effective penetration of immoral society.

In contrast to strict separationists, freewill separationists maintain that religious organizations have distinct institutional rights, not merely the derivative free exercise rights of individual members. They reason that religious societies have a sphere in which they may operate unhindered in accordance with their understanding of their own divine origin and mission. Roger Williams's oft-repeated biblical allusion to "the garden and the wilderness" reflects the state's lack of competence in church matters.[20] State involvement only tramples the garden.

Freewill separationists would prohibit official discrimination among religious groups and, like the first four types, would disallow governmental discrimination favoring religion in general over nonreligion.[21] Finally, freewill separationists vigorously protect religious-based conscience. Only upon a showing of some truly exigent threat to public health, safety, or public order would freewill separationists allow the state to override conscience. More than any other type, freewill separationists have suffered official intolerance in America, which often attended their historic role as dissenters defying the established order.[22] Thus, they are particularly vigilant in safeguarding conscience. Those who have suffered intolerance for their beliefs, such as Seventh-day Adventists, Christian Scientists, and Jehovah's Witnesses, are often freewill separationists, as are those in the historic Baptist tradition, the Arminian tradition, the Society of Friends (Quakers), and the present-day descendants of Anabaptists,[23] such as the Mennonites, the Amish, and the Brethren.

Institutional Separationists

Institutional separationists envision a theocentric state, one in which the government's countenance regarding religion is deemed "benevolent"[24] or "wholesome."[25] The institutional separation of church and state is a model wherein both institutions are of divine ordination and are subject to the will and rule of God, who is sovereign over all things. Each institution is distinct and is designed to perform different tasks in the created order. Neither is to dominate the other, nor are they to be mutually dependent. But a functional interaction between church and state is inevitable and desirable as each pursues its own appointed duties.

Although institutional separationists may at first sound as if they tend toward theocracy, that is far from the case. The nature of this God-in-common is purposely left ambiguous. God is mentioned in public settings only in generalizations: "Supreme Being," the "Creator of us all," "Nature's God," or (as in the nation's motto) "In God We Trust."[26] Nevertheless, He is not an all-purpose, generic god. Rather, this God accords generally—if vaguely—with the personal, historical deity of Judeo-Christianity and the monotheism prevalent in the Western world.

Institutional separationists hold that a universal, transcendent point of reference or ethical system for the state exists and is required in order to secure human rights and maintain a republican structure of government.[27] Western nations, particularly the United States, are influenced by and indebted to the personal and historical concept of God within Judeo-Christianity. History is witness, maintain this third type, that of all sociopolitical constructs, only the cultural ethos derived from Judeo-Christianity has successfully (if not consistently) served as a hedge against totalitarianism. To sustain a republic, the masses must voluntarily obey the law. And in America, people obey the law, not out of self interest or to avoid punishment, but because they are influenced by values about what is just and moral.[28]

Institutional separationists admit that the United States is not "bound" to a theocentric public theology, in the sense of a particularized positive law superior to the Constitution. Nonetheless, although conceding that this overarching world view is not and should not be officially and precisely defined like a legal code, it is precedent to be followed. This is admittedly paradoxical, but nonetheless functional if one distinguishes between positive law and the source of law. Thus, America's abandonment of Judeo-Christianity as the source of law would imperil the legitimacy of republican institutions and undermine the higher law rationale for human rights.[29] Under this view, if there is no notion of the transcendent, the state has no limits to hold it in check.[30] If there is no higher appeal, one cannot truthfully say, "No state is above the law." It is no answer, according to institutional separationists, to argue that the higher appeal is to "the people." Absent firm moorings in God, they see a danger that rule by "the people," because of humanity's fallen nature, would soon slip toward tyranny by the majority.

Institutional separationists view religious speech and press as deserving high juridical protection, equal to that given political, philosophical, or artistic expression. A rule against content-based discrimination applies to all expression, because institutional separationists hold that religious values not only may, but must influence public policy. Their position, in short, is that a church separated from the state need not, indeed, must not be a silent church. Individuals of this third type believe that part of one's religious duty is preserving the good in culture and reforming the bad. They unashamedly teach a cultural mandate that arises out of their religious world and life views. Moreover, this mandate is not limited to interest-group politics or single-issue moral crusades. Rather, the commission is to integrate one's spiritual and temporal life, and to work out a comprehensive plan that may include the affirmative use of government for the well being of all citizens.

Although they agree with freewill separationists that civil religion (in the pejorative sense of that term) is harmful, institutional separationists believe that the danger of civil religion in America is presently exaggerated.[31] Admittedly, history has shown that religious people have difficulty loving both God and country without confusing the two. However, institutional separationists believe that it is still possible to avoid both denial of liberty to minority religious groups and churches' succumbing to the allure of nation worship. Given America's present situation, they view privatization of faith and the rising tides of secularism and narcissism as more imminent threats.

Institutional separationists agree with freewill separationists that civil tolerance in public discourse is important and that one should exercise restraint in the use of religiously motivated speech directed at the general *polis.* Such prudence in speech, however, must be balanced against the imperative of culture-forming religion as foundational to civil liberties, social justice, and republican virtues. Religion speaks to the totality of life; there should be no dualisms. Accordingly, institutional separationists argue that religious people must not stand mute in the face of wrongdoing that seriously threatens community order. And because their religious understanding is that faith is to be integrated with all of life, they believe that there is no subject the church may not properly address, even when others regard its views as intermeddling or socially intolerant and the issue at hand a private matter. This does not mean a politicized church; institutional separationists insist that there is an achievable balance between proclaiming eternal values and addressing the present in a practical and humble manner. Thus, they remain in the separationist camp. Although faith and life are fully integrated at the individual level, church and state maintain distinct responsibilities that should be honored as each institution fulfills its proper role.

This third type, like the second, maintains that churches and other religious organizations have ontological standing in law, rather than merely the free exercise rights derived from individual members.[32] All three separationist types join in a vigorous protection of religious-based conscience from acts of civic intolerance. Finally, like all separationist models, institutional separationists maintain that the state may neither discriminate among religious groups nor prefer religion in general over individuals professing no religious belief. Thus, institutional separationists differ from nonpreferentialists in their conviction that religious people must not ask for governmental favor or aid that is not available to all other citizens.

Structural Pluralists

Structural pluralists envision a state that is about the task of establishing and administering public justice among all individuals and institutional structures in society, including the many different confessional communities. *Religion* is equated to world view, and *pluralism* means that no individual or institutional structure is discriminatorily dealt with by the state based on his or her world view. The state is only one of many societal structures within the created order. Families, businesses, churches, schools, unions, and many other institutional structures exist and should be allowed to flourish in accordance with how they understand their providential calling. There should be no dichotomy whereby these structures are defined as either "religious" or "secular." All nonpolitical associations have their religious and secular aspects. Thus churches do not monopolize the "religious," and the state does not monopolize the "secular." Although government has a legitimate affirmative role in society, the state is limited in that it must not impose a single ideology or theological conviction on the nongovernmental structures in society. Pluralism is a matter of political respect by the state for the many world views held by the different kinds of institutions that fulfill the differentiated needs of a free society.[33]

By *pluralism* structural pluralists do not mean relativism. Rather, they characterize their view as *principled pluralism,* for it is not a denial of fixed standards or rules of right and wrong. The state is ultimately animated not by majority rule but by the conviction that the state is not the sole or final authority concerning human behavior within the nongovernmental sectors. The state is only one authority among others. Individuals acquire rights from, and owe responsibilities to, institutions other than the state, and the state is bound to respect the integrity of these diverse nonpolitical communities. Structural pluralists thus claim that it is an insufficient ontology when law takes into account only individuals, the state, and the church. Rather, many nongovernmental institutions have inherent rights. This conflicts most sharply with strict separationists, the latter ultimately reducing all of society to merely the individual and the state.

Structural pluralists argue vigorously for inherent rights for all groups, not just churches, even when that means lessening some individual rights so as to protect the autonomy of institutional structures. They maintain that their generous view of associational rights ultimately enhances individual freedom by challenging the liberal political theory of the sovereign state and radical individualism. Structural pluralists argue that if one is genuinely concerned about preserving human rights, one has more to fear from a state whose power is limited only by claims of individual autonomy. Granting autonomy to groups, including the many faith communities, permits these nongovernmental societies to counterbalance the authority of the state and provides a context for each person's exercise of freedom in a responsible manner.

Structural pluralists have a very heightened awareness of the subtle influences (they would say coercions) that occur daily when the state fails to support all institutions, governmental and nongovernmental, representing the range of world and life views. For example, they view the public school system as monopolistic and hence mildly coercive. The "common" school system, they argue, is built on the myth that there is a common American ideology that can be taught to all children without denying the free exercise of religion. But this claim that the public schools are neutral is untrue, for America is not, and never has been, homogeneous in its public philosophy and confessional beliefs. It is coercive to use the common schools to impose a single political creed on the impressionable children of an increasingly diverse American populace, argue structural pluralists. Although the state has a vital and affirmative role in educating its young people, principled pluralism dictates that government finance education in a manner that maximizes parental choice in the selection of the child's educational environment. This is not to deny the state's interest altogether, for structural pluralists agree that the state has a proper role in setting minimum curricular standards to be met by all schools.

The principal division between structural pluralists and institutional separationists is that the latter are more concerned with the danger to religion when state aid goes directly to institutions, such as schools and child care centers, op-

erated by religious organizations. Institutional separationists argue that direct
government funding of independent schools and day-care centers will inevitably
result in state interference with these religious ministries. What government pays
for, government asserts the authority to control. The current first amendment
jurisprudence simply does not admit to accepting direct government funding while
successfully contending that "separation of church and state" or "freedom of association" disallows heavy-handed conditions that attach to government dollars.[34]
The rejoinder by structural pluralists to this concern of institutional separationists
is that the state, in accord with its commitment to pluralism, can be relied on to
not abuse the power of the purse, thus respecting the institutional integrity of
religious organizations.

The sharpest point of difference between structural pluralists and nonpreferentialists is that the latter draw a dualism, which is artificial, between the "sacral"
and "secular" aspects of religious organizations. Moreover, structural pluralists
object to state benefits and opportunities for religious ministries not equally available to all others.

Structural pluralists agree with restorationists that the concept of a neutral or
value-free state is a myth, but their response is not to establish their own world view
as dominant through the power of the state. Rather, they would require the state
to respect and to equally nurture society's differentiated nongovernmental structures, as each institution goes about pursuing its own purposes as it understands
them. Whereas restorationists envision a minimalist state, structural pluralists argue
for a state that not only safeguards rights in an essentially negative role but affirmatively encourages and assists all individuals and groups to fulfill their calling.

Structural pluralists join with institutional and freewill separationists in protecting to a high degree speech and other expression of a religious content. Indeed,
structural pluralists object to the dualism implied in the distinction between religious speech and speech of political, philosophical, or artistic content. To divide
speech between the sacral and the secular is hopeless, they maintain, and ultimately
coercive.

Concerning the free exercise clause and the protection accorded religious-
based conscience, structural pluralists begin with the proposition that each person
must be allowed to define religion for himself or herself. That definition can be
traditional, nontheistic, or even a secular philosophy held as ultimate principle. For
First Amendment purposes, religion is thus equated to world view. Having accepted the claimant's understanding of religion, the courts then are to engage in

a balancing test whereby the claimant's free exercise claim is weighed against other legitimate concerns of society. Accordingly, the focus would not be on whether a claim is "religious" or "nonreligious," but rather the judgment will turn on the claimant's ability to act in accordance with his or her religious belief vis-à-vis countervailing claims of health, safety, or public order for the protection of society. The court's duty is to counterbalance these competing claims with evenhandedness toward all world and life views and with respect for the autonomy of nonpolitical institutions.

Nonpreferentialists

Nonpreferentialists desire a nonsectarian state. Unlike the secular state conceptualization of the strict separationists, however, this nonsectarianism is akin to nondenominationalism.

Nonpreferentialists emphasize that religion is crucial in the formation of virtues such as honesty, industry, thrift, charity, and sobriety. The state therefore has a strong interest in preserving and fostering religious faith. This fifth type is convinced that traditional religion is the basis for morality, that morality is vital to maintaining that critical mass of persons who are disciplined and self-governing, and that a self-regulating citizenry makes possible the open society characteristic of Western democracy. Religion is essential to the state's very self-preservation.[35] Thus, concludes the syllogism, the state may aid religion because the public interest in a stable, democratic government is thereby served.

Nonpreferentialists agree with the institutional and freewill separationists that the state is not competent to choose among religions. Unlike the separationists, however, who because of this incompetence deny direct financial aid to all religions, nonpreferentialists would permit governmental aid to religious organizations on a nonpreferential basis.[36] Symbols that have historical or cultural agreeableness, albeit religious for some, may be displayed on public property. They would achieve such results by limiting the reach of the establishment clause to only prohibiting instances of direct coercion of conscience. The view allows the state to be resistant to the expansion of religious pluralism and is less solicitous of objections by religious minorities.

The nonpreferentialist view of church-state relations bears directly on one of the major legal debates involving the establishment clause: state aid to parochial schools. They argue the dualism that religious organizations perform easily discernible sacral and secular activities, and the latter may be state-supported because no one outside the organization suffers coercion by the flow of tax money to the school. Because nonpreferentialists view such aid as constitutional, it comes as little surprise that many conservative Roman Catholics, some Protestant evangelicals, and Orthodox Jews who operate their own schools are sympathetic to the result achieved by the nonpreferentialist model. Political conservatives, even if not themselves deeply religious, are often nonpreferentialists as well.[37]

Nonpreferentialists are quick to point out two additional public benefits of a thriving religious sector. First, religious groups give citizens a sense of community in an often impersonal world. Next to the family, religious organizations are the foremost institution in society interposed between the individual and the power of the state. Religious societies are a rich source of stability and meaning in life and continuity with the past. Second, religious groups operate many worthy educational and charitable organizations. These services are delivered at less cost to the public treasury than governmental programs, and often with a quality and personal touch not achieved by governmental bureaucracy. Additionally, the availability of church-related schools affords students and parents a greater variety of choices, thus enriching culture and acting as a hedge against state monopolization of the education of impressionable children. Nonpreferentialists take the buzzwords of the separationists, such as *freedom, choice,* and *pluralism,* and turn them to their own service by arguing that educational freedom, parental choice, and pluralism in learning experiences justifies aid to parochial schools. Institutional and freewill separationists readily acknowledge the public benefits from these thriving social ministries, but are not willing to have the ministries compromised by the regulation that inevitably follows state aid.

To a large extent, nonpreferentialists echo the institutional separationists' concern that the state be limited and capable of being judged in light of a transcendent point of reference so as to check statism and make possible human rights. They also agree that the state should not discriminate among religious organizations or among individuals on the basis of differing religious beliefs.[38] However, nonpreferentialists break with all four of the prior types by permitting the state to aid religion in general over those professing no religious belief. They argue that although the First Amendment prohibits the establishment of a national church, the Founders never contemplated prohibiting government to aid religion on a nondiscriminatory basis.

Nonpreferentialists join with those types that vigorously protect religious speech and press on a basis equal with political, philosophical, or artistic expression.

They also agree in part with the view that religious organizations are legally autonomous within their sphere of operation. The state, therefore, must abstain from interfering with the inner precincts of churches. Unlike the separationist types, however, nonpreferentialists often define this sphere of operation narrowly. For example, they may well distinguish between churches and parachurch groups (e.g., charities, orphanages, day-care centers, and schools). While disallowing government interference with churches, nonpreferentialists have little objection to the regulation of parachurch organizations. They are persuaded that the receipt of state aid to the "secular" activities of parachurch organizations will not lead to government entanglement which would compromise the mission and internal governance of these organizations. This willingness to separate religious organizations into sacral and secular aspects fits with their religious-secular dualism.

Religious-based conscience is to be juridically protected absent some threat to health, safety, or public order. Nonpreferentialists are divided, however, when confronted with a claim or conscientious exemption from otherwise generally applicable and facially neutral legislation. Consider, for example, the free exercise clause claim for entitlement benefits upheld in *Thomas* v. *Review Board*.[39] Because of a sincere religious belief that he could not work on military armaments, a factory worker was discharged by his employer. The state, taking the view that the loss of employment was voluntary, denied the worker unemployment compensation. The Supreme Court held that this denial violated the worker's free exercise–clause rights to follow the dictates of religious belief without suffering a substantial burden at the hand of the state.

Some nonpreferentialists, agreeing with institutional and freewill separationists, support the Court's holding in *Thomas*. Other nonpreferentialists (mostly political conservatives) disagree, believing that the free exercise clause should relieve a religious claimant of only unavoidable burdens of conscience.[40] In the latters' view, the claimant in *Thomas* was not absolutely barred from practicing his pacifism, for the government did not force his working on armaments. So he faced no unavoidable burden, just loss of unemployment benefits if he obeyed his faith. These nonpreferentialists give greater deference to the operation of state police power. In their view, conscience is violated only when the state, without providing an alternative, prohibits an act that religious faith mandates, or when the state commands an act that faith enjoins. Disagreeing with the result in *Thomas*, they argue that the free exercise clause only commands what government cannot do, not what religious believers can demand of their government.[41]

Restorationists

Restorationists desire a confessional state. They maintain that the United States is a Christian nation, or was originally founded as one,[42] and they argue for a restoration of the nation's high view of Christianity as it existed in an earlier period.[43] Not only should the public theology of the state be explicitly Christian in creed, but much of restorationism has a "chosen people" cast to it.[44] Prayers frequently involve God's judgment or blessing upon not only individuals, but the entire nation.[45]

Restorationists argue that there is no easy dualism between the secular and the religious, and that a neutral state is not only a myth but an impossibility. The state cannot avoid being committed to some ultimate principles, and these animating principles, broadly defined, constitute the "religion" of the state. Thus, for restorationists, the only relevant question is whether the state's guiding reality is the true one. Restorationist literature is replete with warnings that the animating principles of many of America's governmental institutions is increasingly the false religion of secular humanism.

According to restorationists, a universal, transcendent point of reference for the state not only exists but is unavoidable. In the restorationist model, church and state are divinely ordained and are intended to reinforce each other in a symbiotic relationship. Although this mutual dependence is inevitable, each has a distinct role and is not to invade the jurisdiction assigned to the other within the created order. Hence, this model does not contemplate a true theocracy in the sense of a complete merger of church and state. Nor is the restorationist view Constantinian, which would entail a single benevolent head of both church and state.

Restorationists envision a government possessing primarily protectionist duties, such as law enforcement, military defense, conduct of foreign relations, and assuring public health and safety. They thus seek a minimalist state, one whose domestic authority is for the most part limited to containing the excesses of immorality. Clearly such a view eschews any direct state authority over the affairs of the church. Instead, the state is to provide a social environment in which religious claims are more plausible and conversion therefore more likely. Ideally, the state is to be a magisterial government that serves as "nursing father" to the church.

Because they assign the state a duty—albeit a mild duty that is in practice largely passive—to protect and endorse the Christian faith, the restorationist position on freedom of expression, church autonomy, and official discrimination on religious bases is different from the five other types. Restorationists would generally defend the religious speech and press of all persuasions. They would, however, restrain speech that slanders Christianity in particularly egregious circumstances, as in prosecution for open and notorious blasphemy. Under their model, government, when it exercises its powers of expression, would show official benevolence toward the Christian faith. For example, the prayers of a legislative chaplain or city council might well be overtly Christian. Official endorsement of the majority faith might also occur through enforcement of the Sabbath and government holidays coinciding with Christian holy days.

Churches and other religious organizations obviously would have institutional rights under the restorationist view. Restorationists regard official favor toward Christianity as a very different matter from governmental interference in church affairs. They insist that churches be allowed to govern themselves and control their own affairs. It is true that symbiosis between the state and Christianity would lead to numerous interactions between the state and Christian churches, and that such interaction would lead to some entanglement. Indeed, they assert, occasional friction is inevitable. Restorationists believe, however, that such friction can be held to a tolerable level.

Because restorationists envision a minimalist state, they do not contemplate a state that discriminates among religions in dispensing state aid, opportunities, tax benefits, or other governmental largess. Restorationists believe that government has very little affirmative responsibilities in domestic matter such as social welfare. Thus, discrimination in state aid would ordinarily not arise as an issue.

Finally, restorationists join all other groups in protecting to a high degree religious-based conscience, albeit out of a different rationale. Those who are not Christian are regarded as free churches or dissenters. Dissenters would have full rights of conscience under the free exercise clause, even though there would be no separation of church and state under the establishment clause as contemplated by the three separationist types. Restorationists would grant to everyone full juridical rights for religious-based conscience. At the same time, restorationists would have the relationship between church and state be a de jure approbation of Christianity. Surely, they point out, there can be full rights of conscience even when there is one established religion, for that is the settlement presently in England, Scotland, and Scandinavia. That being so, restorationists contend that their model is even less radical than that which exists elsewhere in the West. They urge no established national church, only official, if passive, benevolence toward the Christian faith.

Although the separationist types often accuse them of intolerance, in their partial defense it should be said that restorationists have no intention of engaging in religious persecution in the sense of a direct coercion of the conscience of dissenters. They recognize that conversion to Christianity, if it is to be sincere, must be voluntary. Accordingly, the state should prefer the Christian faith, which they believe would subtly encourage conversion, while refraining from acts of direct coercion toward dissenters.

CONCLUSION

Each model in this six-part typology has a different theoretical conception of what the state ought to be, ranging from wholly secular to unabashedly confessional of historic Christianity. In the area of ecclesiology, however, the six types are in greater accord. Only strict separationists and, to a lesser degree, nonpreferentialists regard the church and its ministries as a voluntary association having no autonomy from state interference apart from the free exercise rights of its individual members. Predictably, this latter two-way split in church-state theory is the source of considerable litigation today, as proponents of these various types carry the struggle concerning church autonomy into the courts. The docket of cases litigating the question of governmental interference in religious affairs is continuously growing. Curiously, there is little focus on this split, for much of the popular attention is drawn off to cases about the business of sweeping clean the public square of the symbols of a bygone Protestant hegemony. As to the latter matter, only a few symbols remain of the Protestant quasi-establishment. Now all religion is struggling to maintain a role in public matters that regards the church as something more than just another "interest group." For all its perniciousness, it can be said that the Protestant hegemony was in its day effective by half at holding secularism in check. It is now unclear whether the new regime of religious pluralism can hold its own against modernity and the positive state.

Overconfident assertions concerning sensitive and complicated matters are dangerous, especially when they concern as ancient a problem as church-state relations. No doubt some will feel slighted because their views are omitted from this social taxonomy. Others will be disturbed, believing their position is not accurately portrayed. They are invited to join this endeavor and propose needed adjustments. We need only agree at the outset that a vocabulary is required so that all citizens who care deeply about religion in America are equipped to talk with one another with less heat and more light.

NOTES

1. U.S. 602 (1971). In applying the establishment clause, the Supreme Court's current test is: (a) the law must have a secular purpose, (b) the principal or primary effect of the law must be one that neither advances nor inhibits religion, and (c) the law must not foster excessive governmental entanglement with religion. See pp. 612–13. This three-part test has come in for considerable criticism, including critical comment by several justices of the Supreme Court. See Carl Esbeck, "The Lemon Test: Should It Be Retained, Reformulated or Rejected?" *Notre Dame Journal of Law, Ethics & Public Policy* 4 (1990): 513. Indeed, recent changes in the personnel of the Court has caused many to speculate that the *Lemon* test will be overruled during the 1991 term, when deciding the case of *Lee* v. *Weisman,* cert. granted, 111 S Ct. 1305 (1991) (No. 90-1014).

2. There are four steps in every claim brought under the free exercise clause. First, the claimant must show that his religious belief is sincerely held. Second, the claimant must show that the government's action burdens his religious belief, that is, coercion of conscience is present to a degree that cannot be fairly said to be insignificant. Once the sincerity and coercion elements are demonstrated, the burden of producing evidence shifts to the government. At this point the free exercise claimant prevails unless the state can prove two elements: first, that the societal interests at stake are compelling; and second, that the state cannot achieve its purpose by means less restrictive to conscience. See *Frazee* v. *Illinois Dept. of Employment Security,* 109 S. Ct. 1514 (1989); *Thomas* v. *Review Board,* 450 U.S. 707 (1981); *Sherbert* v. *Verner,* 374 U.S. 398 (1963).

    The recent case of *Employment Division* v. *Smith,* 110 S. Ct. 1595 (1990), ostensibly overturns this time-honored four-step test, but it remains to be seen if Smith's material departure from precedent will become the standing order. Certainly alarums are sounding in high places that Smith has worked a sea change in free exercise doctrine. See, for example, Michael McConnell, "Free Exercise Revisionism and the Smith Decision," *Univ. of Chicago Law Review* 57 (1990): 1109; Douglas Laycock, "The Remnant of Free Exercise," *Supreme Court Review* (1990): 1–68. Indeed, Congress has under consideration legislation to circumvent the harsh results of the Smith decision. See Religious Freedom Restoration Act of 1991, H.R. 2797, 102d Cong., 1st sess., in 137 Cong. Rec. H5210 (26 June 1991).

3. This is why Professor Philip Kurland's *Religion and the Law: of Church and State and the Supreme Court* (Chicago: Aldine, 1962), proposing a "religion blind" state that is indifferent to whether its actions help or hinder religion, was widely criticized. See *McDaniel* v. *Paty*, 435 U.S. 618, 638–39 (1978) (Brennan, J., concurring), *Sherbert v. Verner*, 374 U.S. 398, 422 (1963) (Harlan, J., dissenting); Paul Kauper, *Religion and the Constitution* (Baton Rouge: Louisiana State Univ. Press, 1964), 15–19; Philip Pfeffer, "Religion-Blind Government," *Stanford Law Review* 15 (1963): 389.

4. Of the many historical accounts of the emergence of religious liberty in America, including the separation of church and state, some of the more responsible are William Estep, *Revolution Within The Revolution: The First Amendment in Historical Context, 1612–1789* (Grand Rapids, Mich.: Eerdmans, 1990); Thomas Curry, *The First Freedoms: Church and State in America to the Passage of the First Amendment* (Oxford: Oxford Univ. Press, 1986); William Miller, *The First Liberty: Religion and the American Republic* (New York: Knopf, 1985); A. James Reichley, *Religion in American Public Life* (Washington, D.C.: Brooking Institution, 1985); Robert Handy, *A Christian America: Protestant Hopes and Historical Realities* (Oxford: Oxford Univ. Press, 1984); Mark Noll, Nathan Hatch, and George Marsden, *The Search For Christian America* (Westchester, Ill.: Crossway Books, 1983); William Marnell, *The First Amendment: The History of Religious Freedom in America* (Garden City, N.Y.: Doubleday, 1964); Sidney Mead, *The Lively Experiment: The Shaping of Christianity in America* (New York: Harper & Row, 1963); Frank Littell, *From State Church to Pluralism* (Chicago: Aldine, 1962); Anson Stokes, *Church and State in the United States*, 3 vols. (New York: Harper, 1950); William Sweet, *Religion in Colonial America* (New York: Cooper Square, 1942); Evarts Greene, *Religion and the State: The Making and Testing of an American Tradition* (Ithaca, N.Y.: Great Seal Books, 1941); Wesley Gewehr, *The Great Awakening in Virginia, 1740–1790* (Gloucester, Mass.: Peter Smith, 1930); Charles Maxson, *The Great Awakening in the Middle Colonies* (Magnolia, Mass.: Peter Smith, 1920); Stanley Cobb, *The Rise of Religious Liberty in America* (New York: Macmillan, 1902); Michael McConnell, "The Origins and Historical Understanding of Free Exercise of Religion," *Harvard Law Review* 103 (1990): 1409.

5. See generally Richard Dunn, *The Age of Religious Wars, 1559–1689* (New York: Norton, 1970); Henry Lea, *A History of the Inquisition*, 3 vols. (New York: AMS, 1888).

6. For volumes that devote considerable attention to these debates in the First Congress, see Robert Cord, *Separation of Church and State: Historical Fact and Current Fiction* (New York: Lambeth, 1982), 3–15; Michael Malbin, *Religion and Politics: The Intentions of the Authors of the First Amendment* (Washington, D.C.: American Enterprise Institute for Public Policy Research, 1978); Chester Antieau, Arthur

Downey, and Edward Roberts, *Freedom From Federal Establishment: Formation and Early History of the First Amendment Religion Clauses* (Milwaukee: Bruce, 1964), 123–42. See also Douglas Laycock, "Nonpreferential Aid to Religion: A False Claim About Original Intent," *William & Mary Law Review* 7 (1986): 875; Rodney Smith, "Nonpreferentialism in Establishment Clause Analysis: A Response to Professor Laycock," *St. John's Law Review* 65 (1991): 245.

7. A hermetic seal between civil affairs and religion is, of course, not presently possible in America. Strict separationists readily acknowledge this; nevertheless, they advocate such absolutism as an aspirational goal:

> Those defending the strict separationist interpretation of the First Amendment's Establishment Clause recognize that the absolute separation of church and state is not possible, but what does that prove? Does the reality that no person is immortal mean that the medical and pharmaceutical profession should be abolished? Realistic separationists recognize that the absolute separation of church and state cannot be achieved, else what's a secularist heaven for? Nevertheless, that is the direction they would have constitutional law relating to the Religion Clause take, fully aware that perfection will never be reached.

Leo Pfeffer, *Religion, State and the Burger Court* (Buffalo: Prometheus, 1984), xi.

8. See William Sullivan, *Reconstructing Public Philosophy* (Berkeley and Los Angeles: Univ. of California Press, 1982), for a critique of the amoral instrumentalism of liberal political theory by an author on the political left.

9. Pragmatic instrumentalism is presently the dominant legal theory in American law. It is an amalgam of utilitarianism, sociology, and certain ideas inherited from legal realism. The principal elements of pragmatic instrumentalism postulate as follows: Law should seek to maximize the satisfaction of the wants and interests of citizens; forms of law are essentially instruments that serve goals external to law; lawmakers ought to turn mainly to social science and democratic processes in fashioning law's means and goals; valid law is whatever has been enacted or promulgated; law ultimately is reduced to predictions of official behavior; law and morals are sharply separable; forms of law should be interpreted and applied in light of social policy rather than formalistically; law accomplishes its objectives mainly through coercive force; and the use of law is to be judged mainly by its effects. See Robert Summers, *Instrumentalism and American Legal Theory* (Ithaca, N.Y.: Cornell Univ. Press, 1982).

10. See Kent Greenawalt, *Religious Convictions and Political Choice* (Oxford: Oxford Univ. Press, 1988).

11. This accounts for the persistent resistance to the Equal Access Act, 20 U.S.C. 4071–74 (1984). See *Board of Education* v. *Mergens*, 110 S. Ct. 2356 (1990), upholding the constitutionality of equal access claim of a student Bible club at a public high school. Some even fear the reintroduction of religion's role into social studies and literature curricula at public schools.

12. A good example of the clash of views concerning the ontological nature of churches
     is found in *Dayton Christian Schools, Inc.* v. *Ohio Civil Rights Commission*, 766 F.2d
     932 (6th Cir. 1985), *rev'd on other grounds*, 477 U.S. 619 (1986). *Dayton Christian*
     involved a charge of sex discrimination by a teacher who was dismissed for reli-
     gious reasons from a church-related primary school. So long as the members of a
     religious organization are united in their claim for protection from governmental
     interference, it is not necessary to determine whether religious liberty extends to
     the church qua church or, on the other hand, whether it extends to the church as a
     mere vehicle for the collective expression of individual rights. However, when, as in
     Dayton Christian, members of a church are divided and one individual's right to
     equality in employment is pitted against a church's claim of autonomy from state
     intervention, it becomes crucial to determine whether the law recognizes ontologi-
     cal status in the church. The idea that religious societies have independent consti-
     tutional value is fundamentally a denial of the proposition that rights can ulti-
     mately reside only in individuals and therefore associations have no intrinsic rights.
     See "Developments in the Law: Religion and State," *Harvard Law Review* 100
     (1987): 1606, 1740–81; and Fredrick Gedicks, "Toward a Constitutional Jurispru-
     dence of Religious Group Rights," *Wisconsin Law Review* 99 (1989): 99–169.

13. Under present Supreme Court case law, only religiously based freedom of con-
     science is protected by the free exercise clause. Dissent or acts of civil disobedience,
     however sincere or motivated by deeply held concerns, that are not grounded in
     one's religion are simply not addressed by the clause and would not demand a con-
     stitutionally required exemption from the law. See *Thomas* v. *Review Board*, 450
     U.S. 707, 713 (1981); and *Wisconsin* v. *Yoder*, 406 U.S. 205, 215–16 (1972). Com-
     pare Justice Douglas's dissent in *Gillette* v. *United States*, 401 U.S. 437, 465–66
     (1971), in which he argues that the first amendment implies a right of conscience
     whether or not religion gave rise to the deeply held belief.

14. See Richard John Neuhaus's essay on the "duty not to give offense" argument occa-
     sionally heard from strict separtionists:

> If the rule is that we must give no offense, the American people must be silent in public
> about who they are and what they believe. . . .
> What we cannot do . . . is to ask the law to muzzle others in the community because
> we are offended by what they are saying about what they believe.
> There is, of course, the danger of a tyrannical majoritarianism. That is why we have
> democracy with its institutional protections of minorities. But the minority cannot be
> protected, and should not want to be protected, from the public evidence that it is in
> fact a minority. The attempt to do that leads to what might be called tyrannical
> minoritarianism. That is what Prof. Tribe seems to be proposing when he argues that
> we should "refuse to surround public institutions with symbols of sanctity." At the same

time, he wants us to be "a country in which all the divergent streams of conscience, belief, and dissent can unite in a powerful current, one that will move us forward together, with many religious faiths but as one people." But how is this noble vision of "one people" to be publicly asserted if we exclude the language, stories and symbols that are derived from the streams of conscience, belief and religious faith affirmed by the people who are that "one people"? (Richard John Neuhaus, "Exclusions Racial and Religious," *Religion & Society Report* 3 [Feb. 1986]: 2–3)

15. See Nathan Hatch, *The Democratization of American Christianity* (New Haven: Yale Univ. Press, 1989).

16. "In a free government the security for civil rights must be the same as that for religious rights. It consists in the one case in the multiplicity of interests, and in the other in the multiplicity of sects. The degree of security in both cases will depend on the number of interests and sects" (*The Federalist* No. 51, 324 [Signet ed., 1961]). See William Miller, *The First Liberty: Religion and the American Republic* (New York: Knopf, 1985), 114–17.

17. See, for example, William Clancy, "Religion as a Source of Tension," in *Religion and the Free Society* 23 (New York: Fund for the Republic, 1958), 30: "The problems . . . for a pluralistic society are obvious. The democratic society as such is committed to no theology or ideology. . . . It is simply a civil community, its unity is purely political, consisting in 'agreement on the good of man at the level of performance without the necessity of agreement on ultimates.' Democracy has properly been described as a forum in which ultimates compete; but the competition must not become internecine; if it does the democratic community itself is shattered."

18. See Robert Linder and Richard Pierard, *Twilight of the Saints: Biblical Christianity & Civil Religion in America* (Downers Grove, Ill.: Inter-Varsity Press, 1978), 135–86.

19. For critique of the freewill separationists' apparent assumption that societal pluralism can be boundless without adverse consequences, see Francis Canavan, "The Pluralist Game," *Law & Contemporary Problems* 44 (Spring 1981): 23; and James Hitchcock, "Church, State, and Moral Values: The Limits of American Pluralism," *Law & Contemporary Problems* 44 (Spring 1981): 3.

20. See Mark Howe, *The Garden and the Wilderness: Religion and Government in American Constitutional History* (Chicago: Univ. of Chicago Press, 1965), 5–6.

21. Compare *Everson* v. *Board of Education*, 330 U.S. 1, 15 (1947): "The 'establishment of religion' clause of the First Amendment means at least this: Neither a state nor the Federal Government can set up a church. Neither can pass laws which aid one religion, *aid all religions*, or prefer one religion over another" (emphasis added). This dictum by Justice Black prohibiting even nonpreferential aid to all religions continues to carry a large majority on the Supreme Court. Compare *Grand Rapids*

School Dist. v. *Ball*, U.S. 373, 382 (1985), requiring government to "maintain a course of neutrality among religions, and between religion and non-religion," with *Wallace* v. *Jaffree*, 472 U.S. 38, 98 (1985) (Rehnquist, J., dissenting), arguing that the purpose of the establishment clause is to forbid preference of one religion over another.

22. See, for example, William Estep, *The Anabaptist Story* (Grand Rapids, Mich.: Eerdmans, 1975); William McLoughlin, *New England Dissent, 1630–1833: Baptists and the Separation of Church and State* (Cambridge: Harvard Univ. Press, 1971), chaps. 1 and 2; William McLoughlin, ed., *Isaac Backus on Church, State and Calvinism: Pamphlets, 1754–1789* (Cambridge: Belknap Press, Harvard Univ. Press, 1968).

23. See Charles Scriven, "The Reformation Radicals Ride Again," *Christianity Today* 13 (Mar. 1990): 13–15.

24. See *Walz* v. *Tax Commission*, 397 U.S. 664, 669 (1970).

25. See *School Dist.* v. *Schempp*, 374 U.S. 203, 222 (1963).

26. The most frequently quoted attribution to God is from *Zorach* v. *Clauson*, 343 (1952) (Douglas, J.): "We are a religious people whose institutions presuppose a Supreme Being."

27. The necessity of a socioreligious consensus undergirding and stabilizing the state's political power has been discussed by a number of writers. See, for example, Peter Berger, "Religious Liberty and the Paradox of Relevance," *Religion & Society Report* (Jan. 1988): 1–2; A. James Reichley, 340–60 above n. 4; Richard Neuhaus, *The Naked Public Square: Religion and Democracy in America* (Grand Rapids, Mich.: Eerdmans, 1984), 60 and 138; Robert Bellah, "Cultural Pluralism and Religious Particularism," in *Freedom of Religion in America* (Los Angeles: Univ. of Southern California Press, 1981), 33; John Courtney Murray, *We Hold These Truths* (New York: Image, 1960), 80–85; C. Dawson, *Religion and the Modern State* (New York: Sheed and Ward, 1940).

28. See Tom Tyler, *Why People Obey the Law* (New Haven, Conn.: Yale Univ. Press, 1990).

29. See Carl Henry, *Twilight of a Great Civilization* (Westchester, Ill.: Crossway Books, 1988), 145; Russell Kirk, "We Cannot Separate Christian Morals and The Rule of Law," *IMPRIMIS* (Apr. 1983), rpt. in *Christian Legal Society Quarterly* 4 (1983): 21.

30. For an excellent essay sketching seven principal themes that constitute a public philosophy, at least in the West, see Max Stackhouse, "An Ecumenist's Plea for a Public Theology," *This World* (Spring/Summer 1984): 47, 58–68. The themes are as follows: Nature is not the product of chance but is created by a God who is behind and beyond nature and is more important than nature itself; men must care for the well-being of the poor and the oppressed; each human is placed in the

world for a purpose, which we call vocation; humans are called into communities of responsibility, e.g., familial, political, and economic communities, which set forth terms and limits for our lives together; there is a transcendent and universally valid moral law; things are not as they should be in the world because of human failing and evil; and there must be religious freedom in both the voluntariness of faith and the institutional separation of church and state. The Stackhouse paper is followed by responses from five prominent and diverse students of religion, making the discourse particularly rich. See generally James Gustafson, *Ethics From a Theocentric Perspective* (Chicago: Univ. of Chicago Press, 1981); Martin Marty, *The Public Church* (New York: Cross Road, 1981); John Wilson, *Public Religion in American Culture* (Philadelphia: Temple Univ. Press, 1979); Elwyn Smith, ed., *The Religion of the Republic* (Philadelphia: Fortress Press, 1971).

31.   See Richard Neuhaus, "America in American Religious Thought," *Religion & Society Report* (Nov. 1985): 1–6.

32.   See Herbert Richardson, "Civil Religion in Theological Perspective," in *American Civil Religion* (New York: Harper & Row, 1974), 178–80.

33.   The chief theorists for structural pluralism are descendants of one strand of Reformed Protestantism, principally Dutch Calvinism. Their most distinctive characteristic is the belief that within the created order there are many institutions ordained of God. See Rockne McCarthy, James Skillen, and William Harper, *Disestablishment a Second Time: Genuine Pluralism for American Schools* (Grand Rapids, Mich.: Christian Univ. Press, 1982); Rockne McCarthy, Donald Oppewal, Walfred Peterson, and Gordon Spykman, *Society, State & Schools: A Case for Structural and Confessional Pluralism* (Grand Rapids, Mich.: Eerdmans, 1981); James Skillen, *Christians Organizing for Political Service* (Washington, D.C.: Association for Public Justice Education Foundation, 1980). For foundational works by Dutch authors, see Herman Dooyeweerd, *The Christian Idea of the State* (Nutley, N.J.: Craig Press 1968); and Abraham Kuyper, *Lectures on Calvinism* (Grand Rapids, Mich.: Eerdmans, 1931). Structural pluralism's most effective advocate is Dr. James W. Skillen, executive director of the Washington, D.C.–based Association for Public Justice, and its education fund, the Center for Public Justice.

34.   Institutional separationists, indeed, freewill separationists as well, argue that the harmful effects on religious organizations in accepting direct governmental funding are four-fold: (1) We as a people presuppose that genuine religion springs from persuasion, rather than being a by-product of state privilege in the form of government funding; (2) the state has no competence in matters of faith, and to imply that it does by allowing state regulation of a ministry uncritically exalts the state over the church; (3) religion can become a captive of nativist culture as defined by the state, and soon slide into civil religion; and (4) the ministries of the church risk

being subverted or forced into pursuing ends chosen by the state rather than by the promptings of their own faith. See Carl Esbeck, "Religion And A Neutral State: Imperative Or Impossibility?" *Cumberland Law Review* 15 (1984–85): 81–83.

35. See, for example, Louis Sirico, "The Secular Contribution of Religion to the Political Process: The First Amendment and School Aid," *Missouri Law Review* 50 (1985): 321–76; Orrin G. Hatch, "Civic Virtue: Wellspring of Liberty," *National Forum: Phi Kappa Phi Journal* 34 (Fall 1984): 34–38.

36. Justice Rehnquist, in his dissenting opinion in *Wallace* v. *Jaffree*, 472 U.S. 38, 98 (1985), espouses a nonpreferentialist view. See generally Kenneth Starr, "The Religion Clauses of the Constitution," *CLS Quarterly* 15 (Spring 1990); Robert Cord, *Separation of Church and State*, above n. 6; Malbin, *Religion and Politics*, above n. 6: Hatch, "Civic Virtue: Wellspring of Liberty," 37 above n. 35; George Goldberg, *Reconsecrating America* (Grand Rapids, Mich.: Eerdmans, 1984); Peter Ferrara, *Religion and the Constitution: A Reinterpretation* (Washington, D.C.: Child and Family Protection Institute of the Free Congress Research & Education Foundation, 1983). Compare Douglas Laycock, "Nonpreferential Aid to Religion: A False Claim About Original Intent," *William & Mary Law Review* 27 (1988): 875; with Rodney Smith, "Nonpreferentialism in Establishment Clause Analysis: A Response to Professor Laycock," *St. John's Law Review* 65 (1991): 245.

37. See J. Werner Dannhauser, "Religion and the Conservatives," *Commentary* (Dec. 1985): 51. Dannhauser makes an insightful point: conservatives who favor religion for the masses, although their own religious belief is weak or nonexistent, have embraced religion for its social utility, as distinguished from the larger question of its claims of truth (55). Accordingly, their thought is in a sense Erastian, for it justifies a publicly supported religion because of its usefulness to the state. Unlike Puritans, who came to America to set up a government that would guard the "true religion," these political conservatives hope to use religion to protect and sustain good government. This is the very thing pluralistic separationists warn against. See Frank Littell, "The Basis of Religious Liberty in Christian Belief," *Journal of Church & State* 6 (1964): 135–38. Religion does not serve the social order unless it is believed.

38. This is not a change from current Supreme Court case law. A statute that is facially neutral and has no provisions that have a disparate impact on members of different denominations is constitutional when such distinctions result from the application of secular criteria. Compare *Gillette* v. *United States*, 401 U.S. 437 (1971), upholding a classification that differentiated on the basis of religious belief, not by denominational or sect membership, with *Larson* v. *Valente*, 456 U.S. 228 (1982), holding that a charitable contributions reporting statute unlawfully discriminates against new religious movements.

39. 450 U.S. 707 (1981).

40. See, for example, Dean Kelley, "Recent Threats to Religious Liberty," in *National Forum: Phi Kappa Phi Journal* 48 (Winter 1988): 18–19, documenting this position as the one urged by President Reagan's Department of Justice); and Michael Malbin, *Religion and Politics*, 36–40 above n. 6.

41. Compare *Employment Division* v. *Smith*, 110 S. Ct. 1595 (1990), upholding the view of the politically conservative nonpreferentialists.

42. The idea has persisted in America that the United States is fundamentally a Christian republic, and that the role of the church is to build toward the time when American civilization would be fully Christian and Christian principles would triumph. For an introduction to the study of this American idea, see Handy, *A Christian America*, above n. 4: Ernest Tuveson, *Redeemer Nation: The Idea of America's Millennial Role* (Chicago: Univ. of Chicago Press, 1968); Benjamin Hart, *Faith and Freedom: The Christian Roots of American Liberty* (San Bernardino, Calif.: Here's Life Publishers, 1989).

43. One of the first books to forcefully advance the restorationist's position of a "Christian America" was Russ Walton, *One Nation Under God* (Nashville: Thomas Nelson, 1987); later came others such as Vern Hall, ed., *The Christian History of the American Revolution* (San Francisco: Foundation for American Christian Education, 1979); John Montgomery, *The Shaping of America* (Minneapolis: Bethany Fellowship, 1976). Perhaps more widely read is Francis Schaeffer, *How Should We Then Live?* (Old Tappan, N.J.: Fleming H. Revell, 1976), covering more than simply America's founding but claiming an early Christian base for the nation which Shaeffer believes is presently lost and in need of restoration. These were followed by books such as Harold Brown, *The Reconstruction of the Republic* (New Rochelle, N.Y.: Arlington House, 1977); Peter Marshall and David Manuel, *The Light and the Glory* (Old Tappan, N.J.: Fleming H. Revell, 1977); Verna Hall, ed., *The Christian History of The Constitution of the United States of America* (San Francisco: American Christian Constitutional Press, 1979); Robert Slater, *Teaching and Learning American Christian History* (San Francisco: Foundation for American Christian Education, 1980); Jerry Falwell, *Listen, America* (Garden City, N.Y.: Doubleday, 1980); Francis Schaeffer, *A Christian Manifesto* (Westchester, Ill.: Crossway Books, 1981); John Whitehead, *The Second American Revolution* (Elgin, Ill.: David C. Cook, 1982); William Stanmeyer, *Clear and Present Danger: Church and State in Post-Christian America* (Ann Arbor, Mich.: Servant Books, 1983); Benjamin Hart, *Faith and Freedom: The Christian Roots of American Liberty* (San Bernardino, Calif.: Here's Life Publishers, 1989).

44. For restorationist views that are hyper-Calvinist, or what the authors themselves term Christian *reconstructionist* or *theonomy,* see Rousas John Rushdoony, *This Independent Republic* (Fairfax, Va.: Thoburn Press, 1977); Greg Bahnsen, *By This*

Standard: The Authority of God's Law Today (Tyler, Tex.: Institute for Christian Economics, 1985); Gary North, "What is A Christian Nation?" *The Geneva Review* 47 (Sept. 1987): 47–51. Although the tone and content of the Christian reconstructionist perspective borders on triumphalism, the view appears to be to the right of many within the restorationist type. Nonetheless, their literature has been influential, especially as to the reconstructionist critique of the American situation. Their theology of the state has been less persuasive. Reconstructionists stress the uninterrupted continuity of the Old Testament's covenant between God and his chosen. They express confidence that specific civil laws can be derived or deduced from the "civil" laws of Israel. Because God is sovereign over all, and because his law is binding on all, the discontinuities between ancient Israel and a modern political order should be minimized. A helpful critique of the restorationists is Richard Neuhaus, "Why Wait for the Kingdom? The Theonomist Temptation," *First Things* 3 (May 1990): 13–21.

45. For insight into the contenting sides in this debate, consider Jerry Herbert, ed., *America, Christian or Secular?* (Portland, Oreg.: Multnomah Press, 1984):

> We can see that the proponents and critics of a Christian America emphasize different things. The critics look at America's public philosophy and are hard pressed to find anything distinctly Christian. The proponents look at the rhetoric of the founders and the courts, see the connections between America's early legal tradition and English common law, and find much that is Christian. . . .
>
> Both sides of the Christian America debate recognize the connection between how Christians perceive the founding of America and how they will act in American public life today. On the one side are Christians who perceive America's traditional consensus as being basically Christian. They would hope, of course, that America's public consensus (civil religion) might be as purely Christian as possible. But however mixed it might remain, they urge Christians to revitalize American society by working politically and legally to renew, perfect, and sustain the "Christian base" that was part of America's traditional civil religion.
>
> On the other side are Christians who perceive America's traditional civil religion to be a synthesis of Christian and non-Christian influences. They believe that there is a fundamental difference between biblical norms and values and the received norms and values of Western culture, particularly as they were given expression by the Enlightenment. They believe mixing such norms and values, as is done in American civil religion, subverts truly Christian (biblical) public action. They urge Christians to acknowledge the fundamental difference between biblical norms and the pervasive public philosophy of America's founding, and to work toward truly biblically based public and political service. (22, 25–26; footnotes omitted)

REFERENCES

Clancy, William. "Religion as a Source of Tension." In *Religion and the Free Society* 23. New York: Fund for the Republic, 1958.

Dannhauser, Werner J. "Religion and the Conservatives." *Commentary* (Dec. 1985): 51–55.

Esbeck, Carl. "The Lemon Test: Should It Be Retained, Reformulated or Rejected?" *Notre Dame Journal of Law, Ethics & Public Policy* 4 (1990): 513–48.

———. "Religion and a Neutral State: Imperative or Impossibility?" *Cumberland Law Review* 15 (1984–85): 67–88.

Greenawalt, Kent. *Religious Convictions and Political Choice.* Oxford: Oxford Univ. Press, 1988.

Hatch, Nathan. *The Democratization of American Christianity.* New Haven: Yale Univ. Press, 1989.

Henry, Carl F. H. *Twilight of a Great Civilization.* Westchester, Ill.: Crossway Books, 1988.

Herbert, Jerry, ed. *America, Christian or Secular?* Portland, Oreg.: Multnomah Press, 1984.

Howe, Mark DeWolfe. *The Garden and the Wilderness: Religion and Government in American Constitutional History.* Chicago: Univ. of Chicago Press, 1965.

Kurland, Philip. *Religion and the Law: of Church and State and the Supreme Court.* Chicago: Aldine, 1962.

Linder, Robert, and Richard Pierard. *Twilight of the Saints: Biblical Christianity & Civil Religion in America.* Downers Grove, Ill.: Inter-Varsity Press, 1978.

Miller, William Lee. *The First Liberty: Religion and the American Republic.* New York: Alfred A. Knopf, 1985.

Neuhaus, Richard John. "America in American Religious Thought." *Religion & Society Report* (Nov. 1985): 1–6.

———. "Exclusions Racial and Religious." *Religion & Society Report* 3 (Feb. 1986): 2–3.

Pfeffer, Leo. *Religion, State and the Burger Court.* Buffalo: Prometheus Books, 1984.

Richardson, Herbert. "Civil Religion in Theological Perspective." In *American Civil Religion*, ed. Russell E. Richey and Donald G. Jones. New York: Harper & Row, 1974.

Scriven, Charles. "The Reformation Radicals Ride Again." *Christianity Today* 13 (5 Mar. 1990): 13–15.

Stackhouse, Max L. "An Ecumenist's Plea for a Public Theology." *This World* (Spring/Summer 1984): 47–79.

Summers, Robert. *Instrumentalism and American Legal Theory.* Ithaca, N.Y.: Cornell Univ. Press, 1982.

Tyler, Tom R. *Why People Obey the Law.* New Haven: Yale Univ. Press, 1990.

Part II

The Founders and
the Church–State Question

2 | Madison: A Founder's Vision of Religious Liberty and Public Life

Neal Riemer

What was Madison's vision of religious liberty and public life? What is the significance of this vision? What is the relevance of this vision for contemporary America?[1]

My threefold thesis in response to these three interrelated questions is as follows: First, on the nature of Madison's vision: (1) Madison had an ethical vision of religious liberty that went far beyond mere toleration, calling for strict separation of church and state and seeing religious liberty and separation as crucial to the health of both church and state; (2) Madison had an empirical vision that saw the multiplicity and diversity of religious groups as contributing to religious freedom and to religious and political health, and he was able to extend this pluralistic insight to politics in general; and (3) Madison had a prudential vision that enabled him to work toward his goals of freedom and justice with wisdom, civility, and skill, an understanding that helped establish a valuable tone for public life in the new Republic.

Second, on the significance of this vision: (1) the ethical vision clearly advanced the cause of religious, political, and cultural freedom, enhancing the integrity, vitality, and health of both religion and the state, and of the public life that they sometimes share; (2) the empirical vision highlighted the value of pluralism and strengthened the operation of a democratic and constitutional system in both religious organizations and the state; and (3) the prudential vision established a standard of civility—of genuine respect, of nondogmatic responses, of appreciation of popular feelings, of sensible pragmatic compromise—so crucial in the ongoing dialogue on religious, political, and cultural issues that continue to agitate society.

Third, on the relevance of this vision: (1) genuine religious liberty and strict separation continue to make great sense in preserving the integrity, vitality, and health of the spiritual and secular domains; (2) Madison's commitment to pluralism and the positive value of a multiplicity and diversity of religious and other interests continues to serve as a safeguard against the dangers of religious, political, or economic monopoly; and (3) Madison's commitment to civility continues to assure the respect, wise appreciation of realities, and sagacious and nondogmatic practical response crucial for dealing with ongoing tensions, conflicts, and quarrels in religious and public life.

To develop the points in Madison's philosophy about religious liberty and public life is both to take us back to the American Enlightenment at its best and to highlight the contemporary significance and relevance of Madison's vision. In this we will see the continued vitality and validity of Madison's ethical, empirical, and prudential contributions to religious liberty and public life.

PERSECUTION, TOLERATION, AND RELIGIOUS FREEDOM

One cannot understand the philosophical underpinnings of the First Amendment, and especially of the free exercise and no establishment clauses, if one does not appreciate Madison's and the Founders' hostility to religious persecution—as well as Madison's magnificent efforts to move beyond mere toleration to genuine religious and intellectual freedom. Madison knew well the bloody history of persecution for cause of conscience. He was pained by the jailing of Baptist preachers in his native Virginia for exercising their religious convictions. He also was convinced that the connection of church and state was deadly for both religion and public life. Moreover, he clearly saw that religious toleration, based as it was on the assumption of the superiority of the dominant religious establishment toward religious dissenters, did not carry the battle on behalf of freedom far enough. Consequently, early on he adopted a strong position on the need for genuine religious liberty and a strong position on separation of church and state.

Madison's argument is excellently summarized in his 1776 amendment to George Mason's Virginia Declaration of Rights and his 1785 *Memorial and Remonstrance Against Religious Assessments,* which paved the way for the enactment in 1786 of Jefferson's Act for Establishing Religious Freedom.[2] These documents help us to understand the argument on behalf of genuine religious liberty and against church establishment, and thus help us to understand those crucial clauses of the First Amendment.

In his 1776 amendment, Madison sought to go beyond Mason's statement of religious toleration to genuine religious liberty. His amendment stated that religion is "under the direction of reason and conviction only, not of violence and compulsion"; that "all men are equally entitled to the free exercise of religion, according to the dictates of conscience"; and that "it is the mutual duty of all to practice Christian forebearance, love, and charity towards each other." Here we clearly see the language of "free exercise" that would be embodied in the First Amendment. We also note Madison's emphasis on "forebearance, love, and charity," which, I believe, strikes the important note of civility that was to characterize Madison's position.

Madison's 1787 *Memorial and Remonstrance* develops more fully the argument on behalf of genuine religious liberty and the complementary argument on the need to end church establishment and separate church and state. This argument helped to kill efforts to enact Patrick Henry's bill to require public taxes for "Teachers of the Christian Religion," and made possible the 1786 enactment of Jefferson's bill for religious freedom and church disestablishment. This bill, Madison wrote Jefferson in 1786, "extinguished forever the ambitious hope of making laws for the human mind."[3] "After Jefferson's death," Adrienne Koch writes, "Madison summed up the transcendent importance of the Act and its significance for a free society." Madison wrote: "This act . . . is certainly the strongest legal barrier that could be erected against the connection of Church and State so fatal to the liberty of both."[4]

Madison's *Memorial and Remonstrance* built on his early 1776 amendment that religion could only be based on reason and conviction, not on force and violence. He affirmed religious freedom as an "unalienable right" that could not be trespassed by the majority, in either society or the legislature. He affirmed that one must "take alarm at the first experiment on our liberties."

> We hold this prudent jealousy to be the first duty of Citizens, and one of the noblest characteristics of the late Revolution. The free men of America did not wait till usurped power had strengthened itself by exercise, and entangled the question in precedents. They saw all the consequences in the principle and they avoided the consequences by denying the principle. We revere this lesson too much soon to forget it. Who does not see that the same authority which can establish Christianity, in exclusion of all other Religions, may establish with the same ease any particular sect of Christians, in exclusion of all other Sects? that the same authority which can force a citizen to contribute three pence only of his property for the support of any one establishment, may force him to conform to any other establishment in all cases whatsoever?[5]

Madison saw Patrick Henry's bill violating the principle of equality and free (i.e., noncompulsive) support of religion. He strongly denied that the civil magistrate is a "competent Judge of Religious Truth" or could "employ Religion as an engine of Civil policy." Public monies, he argued, are "not requisite for the support of the Christian Religion." Religion can exist and flourish without support of human laws. The establishment of religion actually harms religion: "What have been its fruits? More or less in all places, pride and indolence in the Clergy, ignorance and servility in the laity, in both superstition, bigotry and persecution."

Madison further argued that establishment is "not necessary for the support of Civil Government." Indeed, established churches have harmed civil government: "What influence in fact have ecclesiastical establishments had on Civil Society? In some instances they have been seen to erect a spiritual tyranny on the ruins of the Civil authority; in many instances they have been seen upholding the thrones of political tyranny: in no instances have they been seen the guardians of the liberties of the people." Moreover, Madison argued, establishment would be seen as persecution to the "oppressed of every Nation and Religion." "It degrades from the equal rank of Citizens all those whose opinions in Religion do not bend to those of the Legislative authority." Establishment would also have a tendency to encourage religious dissenters already in America to emigrate.

In addition, Madison was convinced that Henry's bill would upset peace and order. It would "destroy that moderation and harmony which the forbearance of our laws to intermeddle with Religion has produced among its several sects." Madison reminded his readers: "Torrents of blood have been spilt in the old world, by vain attempts of the secular arm, to extinguish Religious discord by proscribing all difference in Religious opinion." He insisted that "equal and complete liberty," not proscription of religious differences, was the key to "health and prosperity" in the state. Guard, he warned, against "the first fruits of the threatened innovation." He emphasized the bill's adverse affect upon "Christian forebearance, love, and charity."

Furthermore, Madison maintained that Henry's bill would be counterproductive, that it would not extend the "light of Christianity." The bill, because obnoxious, would weaken respect for law and government. It was, moreover, not clear that a majority of citizens supported the bill. Madison concluded his argument by reiterating his 1776 view that Henry's bill was opposed to "the equal right of every citizen to the free exercise of his Religion according to the dictates of conscience."

And he warned that if this right could be swept away, then "all our fundamental rights" could be.

Unquestionably, this powerful argument informs Madison's understanding of the First Amendment. Madison sought initially to extend the protections of the First Amendment to the states. (His proposed amendment held that "no state shall violate the equal rights of conscience, or the freedom of the press or the trial by jury in criminal cases.")[6] Although he was not successful in this endeavor, it is clear that the U.S. Supreme Court in reading the protections of the Bill of Rights into the Fourteenth Amendment was acting in accordance with Madison's political philosophy.

It is important to stress that Madison saw a crucial connection between religious freedom and that intellectual, political, and cultural freedom necessary to sustain the new American Republic. Moreover, it is clear that Madison was a strong advocate of separation of church and state, not because he was hostile to religion but because he wanted to protect the integrity, vitality, and purity of both church (religion) and state (government life). He clearly wanted to resist the beginning of those governmental efforts that would involve the use of public monies for the support of religion. No one can know for sure where Madison would stand on contemporary issues such as government aid to parochial schools, prayer in the public schools, or government aid to secular projects run by religious organizations, but I believe that Madison would have been leery of such measures as being "the first experiment on our liberties." My judgment is that he would have seen "the consequences in the principle, and . . . avoided the consequences by denying the principle"; that he would have sided with Rutledge in *Everson* v. *Board of Education;* that his position on "strict neutrality" would have been Professor Freund's, not Professor Kurland's.[7] Certainly, however, he would have encouraged religious denominations to pursue their religious truth and understanding as independent forces in society, but always with "forbearance, love, and charity."

Madison's strong stance on separation of church and state is illustrated not only by his powerful argument in the *Memorial and Remonstrance* and his authorship and leadership in connection with the First Amendment but in his theoretical opposition to chaplains in Congress or the armed services, and by his reservations even about presidential proclamations on holidays such as Thanksgiving.[8] In his *Autobiography,* Madison recalled that in the First Congress he stated his disapproval of having "chaplains to congress paid out of the public Treasury." He saw such payment "as a violation of principle" and argued that "the only legitimate and becoming mode" of support for Chaplains should be "that of a voluntary contribution from the members" of Congress."[9] Furthermore, "during his Presidency, Madison agreed with Jefferson that it was against the spirit of religious freedom to proclaim any public day of thanksgiving or prayer."[10] We will return to his practical decisions on chaplains and prayer again in another section of this chapter.

Madison's dedication to religious liberty was a life-long commitment. His sustained effort to move beyond religious persecution and beyond even religious toleration is unmistakable. It is amply illustrated in his response, made in 1833, three years before his death, to a pamphlet by the Reverend Jasper Adams, then president of the College of Charleston. In his pamphlet, entitled "The Relations of Christianity to Civil Government in the United States," Adams had argued against the doctrine that "Christianity has no connection with our civil constitutions of government." Adams held that "the people of the United States have retained the Christian religion as the foundation of their civil, legal, and political institutions."[11] Thus, writes Adrienne Koch, Adams concluded that "we do indeed have a national religion, although one that is tolerant of all Christian denominations." Adams would not countenance the "pernicious" and corrupting view that religion and government had no connection with each other.[12]

In responding to this argument, which Madison felt to be an attack on his position on full and complete religious liberty, Madison came back to what he thought was the central question, which Adrienne Koch phrases as follows: "Does the Christian religion, assuming it is the best and the purest religion, require financial aid from the government?"[13] Madison reaffirmed his life-long conviction that religious organizations should rely entirely upon voluntary contributions for their support. He also reaffirmed his conviction—now buttressed by his knowledge of what had gone on before and after the American Revolution—that the effects of disestablishment and of full and complete religious freedom were salutary, both for religion and for government. He held that religion did not need the support of government. He was not persuaded by the argument that if religion was left to itself, the result would be a weakening of the moral fiber of government. "At the end of the road, as at the beginning," writes Adrienne Koch, "he was unshaken in his judgment that there was *no* empirical ground for the claim that only religion could provide a basis for social morality and good government. Genuine religiousness in a people flourishes best without official support or regulation or compulsion of any sort from government."[14]

ON RELIGIOUS DIVERSITY AND RELIGIOUS FREEDOM

The philosophical underpinnings of the First Amendment cannot be fully under-stood if we ignore Madison's empirical vision of the positive value of the multi-plicity and diversity of religious interests. As an astute political scientist, really our first articulate political pluralist, Madison recognized that paper proclamations of religious freedom and separation of church and state would not alone serve to protect these significant principles. He saw religious monopoly as a cardinal dan-ger. The existence of many religious denominations and of diverse religious beliefs guarded against that monopoly and, therefore, against church establishment.

The value of a multiplicity of religious sects for the preservation of religious liberty was a theme Madison grasped early, enunciated vigorously in 1787, and then propounded throughout his later life. Looking ahead to key aspects of Madison's broader political philosophy, of which his devotion to religious liberty and sepa-ration of church and state are a crucial part, it is not too much to say that Madison's belief in the advantages of religious pluralism, more than any other single factor, convinced him of the practical merit of his theory of the extensive republic. Merrill Peterson makes this point explicitly: "Madison's experience in the struggle for religious freedom in Virginia had also been important, for he had discovered that the principle [of religious freedom] could be best secured in a pluralistic environ-ment of competing sects, no one of which could tyrannize over the others. The theory of factions applied to the political sphere a truth drawn from the religious sphere."[15]

As early as 1774, in a letter to his Princeton friend, William Bradford, Madi-son had expressed his fears of the threat to freedom inherent in a Church of England establishment.[16] He also worried, in the battle against assessments, about a coa-lition of powerful religious denominations—for example, Episcopalians and Pres-byterians. In a letter to Jefferson in 1785, Madison had noted that "a coalition between them could alone endanger our religious rights."[17] This fear of a religious monopoly or coalition runs throughout Madison's speeches in the constitutional convention, his *Federalist* papers, his letters to Jefferson, and his speeches in the Virginia ratifying convention. In these speeches, writings, and letters we also note Madison's pluralistic premise: the multiplicity of interests—whether religious, economic, or political—would serve to guard against the danger of an unjust majority faction. This premise became a prominent feature of Madison's larger theory of the extensive republic.[18]

Madison's devotion to religious liberty was thus not only a central value in his philosophical orientation but represented a broadening of the traditional republican commitment to liberty. It also enabled him to see with unusual prescience that the principle of multiplicity of sects that operated to ensure religious liberty might also operate, in the context of a multiplicity of political, economic, and social interests, to ensure civil freedom: "Human intelligence could perceive that religious uniformity was not essential to peace and order but might militate against them, that, indeed, religious diversity might advance freedom without interfering with civil decorum and harmony."[19]

In *Federalist* No. 10, for example, Madison declared: "The influence of factious leaders may kindle a flame within their particular States, but will be unable to spread a general conflagration through the other states. A religious sect may degenerate into a political faction in part of the Confederacy; but the variety of sects dispersed over the entire face of it must secure the national councils against any danger from that source."[20] In No. 51, he wrote, "In a free government the security for civil rights must be the same as that for religious rights. It consists in the one case in the multitude of interests, and in the other in the multiplicity of sects. The degree of security in both cases will depend on the number of interests and sects; and this may be presumed to depend on the extent of country and the number of people comprehended under the same government."[21] He then stated, perhaps a little too optimistically, that "in the extended republic of the United States, and among the great variety of interests, parties, and sects which it embraces, a coalition of a majority of the whole society could seldom take place on any other principles than those of justice and the general good."[22]

In the Virginia ratifying convention, to cite another example, Madison had declared:

> If there were a majority of one sect, a bill of rights would be a poor protection for liberty. Happily for the states, they enjoy the utmost freedom of religion. This freedom arises from the multiplicity of sects, which pervades America, and which is the best and only security for religious liberty in any society. For where there is such a variety of sects, there cannot be a majority of any one sect to oppress and persecute the rest.[23]

In articulating these views about the positive value of the multiplicity and diversity of religious interests, Madison was endorsing one of Voltaire's aphorisms, which he often quoted approvingly: "If one religion only were allowed in England, the government would possibly become arbitrary; if there were but two, the people would cut each other's throats; but as there are such a multitude, they all live happy and in peace."[24]

Here I wish to emphasize that Madison's vision includes a recognition of the value of not only religious diversity but political, economic, and cultural diversity; and a recognition of the way that religious freedom and diversity reinforce political, economic, and cultural freedom. Political, economic, and cultural freedom is safest when religious freedom is safeguarded; and religious, political, economic, and cultural freedom are enhanced by multiplicity and diversity.

If, however, the multiplicity and diversity of interests in an extensive republic can function to safeguard freedom, it should also be clear that Madison presupposes the operation of other factors that contribute to freedom and the common good: representative government, federalism, requisite powers of governance, constitutional prohibitions, a fundamentally capable electorate, and separation of powers. If Madison emphasized the idea that religious interests must compete in an atmosphere of "forbearance, love, and charity," he did not ignore the importance of republican virtue informed by the best religious principles, nor did he underestimate the importance of constitutional checks against the abuse of power. Most important, of course, was Madison's conviction that certain basic freedoms—and religious freedom was such a basic freedom—must be placed beyond the reach of legislative majorities. Here Madison's ethical vision and realistic empirical vision strongly reinforce each other.

Madison did not fully and clearly develop the ways in which many religious interests, operating in a spirit of "forbearance, love, and charity," could enrich freedom, justice, prosperity, and excellence in American public life while avoiding those conflicts that threaten bitterness, hostility, hatred, disorder, and lawlessness on issues that are both religious and governmental. But there are some hints about the significance and relevance of his position to be found in his prudential vision—to which we now turn.

PRUDENTIAL STATESMANSHIP IN RELIGION, POLITICS, AND PUBLIC LIFE

Madison held strongly to beliefs in genuine religious liberty and to separation of church and state. These were life-long commitments. However, if we focus on those commitments, we must not overlook his recognition of the role that religion played in shaping moral life and in influencing political morality. His quarrel was not with the role religion could legitimately play in American public life but with the attempt of an established religion to limit religious freedom. He was clearly opposed to mere religious toleration. He was clearly opposed to government taxing people for the support of religious ideas, institutions, or practices to which they were not committed. He did not believe that there should be a chaplain for either Congress or the armed forces. He had reservations even about presidential proc-lamations of days of thanksgiving, and regretted that he had not followed Jefferson's practice of not issuing such proclamations. As president he vetoed several bills that violated the no establishment clause of the First Amendment.

Yet Madison did not act to prevent the appointment of chaplains in Con-gress—and their payment. He did, with some reservations, go along with a national proclamation of Thanksgiving. In brief, on such issues he was cognizant of con-temporary sensibilities and did not seek to overturn customary practices.

Madison's recognition of political realities calls attentions to his prudential disposition, which led him generally to be skeptical of pure theories as dogmatic and dangerous.[25] In saying this I do not intend to convey the idea that Madison would compromise his conviction that religious freedom is an unalienable right. I only mean to suggest that even on that subject he would recognize the difference between liberty and license and be willing (as in his original draft amendment to George Mason's "Virginia Declaration of Rights") to say that "all men are equally entitled to enjoy the free exercise of religion, according to the dictates of conscience . . . *Unless the preservation of equal liberty and the existence of the State are manifestly endangered.*"[26] Such an understandable qualification of religious liberty is a sensible prudential conclusion, even if we may quarrel as to the meaning and application of that qualification.

Similarly, Madison's strong position on separation of church and state did not make him into a dogmatic secular zealot unappreciative of the desire of the majority of congressmen to have a prayer offered by a congressional chaplain at, say, the opening of congressional deliberations. Prudence dictated that Madison not make a big fight on such an issue, or on the issue of a Thanksgiving Day proclamation.

In brief, Madison was firm but not fanatical in his devotion to religious liberty and separation of church and state. Thus, he clearly and unequivocally rejected the idea of religious toleration, presupposing as it does a superior religious truth con-descendingly tolerating religious error. He was suspicious of endorsing "first ex-periments on our liberties" that could lead to violations of religious liberty and separation of church and state. Here prudence dictated repudiation of "usurped power" that "strengthened itself by exercise" and "precedents." He would see "the consequences in the principle" and avoid the "consequences by denying the principle."

Bringing this analysis to bear upon the controversial issue of governmental financial aid to parochial schools, and appreciative of the difficulties of knowing with any certitude what Madison would do on current church-state issues, my judgment is that Madison's philosophy would be clearly opposed to such aid, whether through payment of parochial school teachers or through tax credits to parents who send their children to parochial schools. I am also inclined to believe— and this is a tougher call—that Madison would probably have sided with Rutledge and the dissenters in the *Everson* case. But my judgment also is that he would not object to equal and nondiscriminatory treatment for people or religious organizations when governmental activities aiding them involved such matters as police and fire protection. Moreover, he would be open to reasonable argument about government aid to religiously sponsored secular activities, especially when it was crystal clear that such aid did not involve use of public monies to advance, clearly and directly, religious purposes.

These judgments are, of course, speculative. What is not speculation, I believe, is Madison's judgment that debate be carried on in a spirit of "forbearance, love, and charity." If we are to work through our disagreements about the role of religion in public life, and about the meaning of religious liberty and separation of church and state in modern America, we need now, more than ever, to be sure that our prudential efforts to deal with thorny issues are informed by "forebearance, love, and charity."

CONCLUSION

What, finally, can we say about Madison's vision as it illuminates the philosophical underpinnings of the First Amendment, and as it illuminates the role of religion in American public life?

I find in Madison warnings against religious intolerance and acceptance of mere religious toleration. I also find in Madison a strong commitment to religious liberty and separation of church and state as crucial to both the health and vitality of religion and the state. These warnings and this commitment underlie the first clause of the First Amendment. I also see Madison clearly linking religious freedom and intellectual freedom, both of which are so crucially related to freedom of speech and press and to peaceable assembly and petition for redress of grievances. And, of course, Madison also saw the connection between religious and intellectual freedom and civic virtue and successful republican government.

I also find in Madison a clear recognition of the positive value of the multiplicity and diversity of religious groups as safeguards against religious monopoly and denial of religious liberty. Madison carried this appreciation of pluralism into the political domain and made it a cardinal premise of his political philosophy, a remarkably successful creative breakthrough in the history of politics.[27] And, clearly, political pluralism rests substantially on First Amendment freedoms.

Madison also brings to our exploration of the role of religion in American public life a prudential posture that is most appealing. He is firm in his convictions about goals to be pursued, especially religious and political liberty. He is appreciative of empirical realities—past, present, and future—and is sensitive to important contemporary concerns and habits. And he is willing to reach wise practical judgments that keep cardinal goals in mind and yet respect the concerns and habits of a variety of interests. His was a firm but nondogmatic position, deeply felt but not fanatical. Above all, he sagaciously recognized that a democratic society could not long endure if its citizens—within the framework of a pluralistic society, a sound constitutional system, and a federal republic—did not bring "forebearance, love, and charity" to religious issues and a comparable civility to political issues.

I find no barrier in Madison's political philosophy to religion's legitimate efforts to inspire, nourish, and contribute to American public life. Encouraged by his philosophy, we can address the difficult question of how religion can so inspire, nourish, and contribute without the adverse consequences of untoward religious action in public life or untoward governmental action affecting religious life.

NOTES

1. My understanding of Madison is greatly indebted to Irving Brant's splendid six-volume biography (Indianapolis: Bobbs-Merrill, 1941–61): *James Madison: The Virginia Revolutionist, 1751–1780* (1941), *James Madison: The Nationalist, 1780–1787* (1948), *James Madison: Father of the Constitution, 1787–1800* (1950), *James Madison: Secretary of State, 1800–1809* (1953), *James Madison: The President, 1809–1812* (1956), and *James Madison: Commander in Chief, 1812–1836* (1961). An excellent

one-volume biography is Ralph Ketcham, *James Madison: A Biography* (New York: Macmillan, 1970). See also the work of Robert Rutland, including a recent essay, "How Involved Was Madison in Framing the Constitution and the Bill of Rights?" in *The Political Theory of the Constitution*, ed. Kenneth W. Thompson (Lanham, Md.: Univ. Press of America, 1990). In addition, see Adrienne Koch, *Madison's "Advice to My Country"* (Princeton, N.J.: Princeton Univ. Press, 1966), esp. chap. 1 on "Liberty"; William Lee Miller, *The First Liberty: Religion and the American Republic* (New York: Knopf, 1986); and Robert S. Alley, ed., *James Madison on Religious Liberty* (Buffalo, N.Y.: Prometheus, 1985). My book-length study of Madison's political philosophy is entitled *James Madison: Creating the American Constitution* (New York: Washington Square, 1968; Washington, D.C.: Congressional Quarterly, 1986). For a volume on how issues of church and state have played out in the Supreme Court, see Robert S. Alley, ed., *The Supreme Court on Church and State* (New York: Oxford Univ. Press, 1988). For a strikingly different interpretation of Madison, see Thomas Lindsay, "James Madison on Religion and Politics: Rhetoric and Reality," *American Political Science Review* 85 (Dec. 1991): 1321–37. Lindsay argues— unconvincingly in my judgment—that Madison's argument in the *Memorial and Remonstrance against Religious Assessment* is "better understood as rhetoric than as reflecting Madison's true view," and that in fact Madison was not only hostile to religious establishment "but also to religion itself."

2. See Alley, *James Madison on Religious Liberty*, 52.

3. Qtd. in Koch, *Madison's "Advice to My Country,"* 26.

4. Ibid., 27.

5. This and subsequent quotes are from Alley, *James Madison on Religious Liberty*, 55–60.

6. Koch, *Madison's "Advice to My Country,"* 31.

7. See A. E. Dick Howard, "The Supreme Court and the Establishment of Religion," in Alley, *James Madison On Religious Liberty*, 284. See also Paul J. Weber, "Strict Neutrality: The Next Step in First Amendment Development?" in *Religion in American Politics*, ed. Charles W. Dunn (Washington, D.C.: Congressional Quarterly, 1989).

8. For Madison's larger political theory, as he developed it over a lifetime, see Riemer, *James Madison: Creating the American Constitution*. See Ralph L. Ketcham, "James Madison and Religion—A New Hypothesis," in Alley, *James Madison on Religious Liberty*, 175–96.

9. Qtd. in Koch, *Madison's "Advice to My Country,"* 32–33.

10. Ibid., 33.

11. Ibid., 36.

12. Ibid., 37.

13. Ibid., 38.
14. Ibid., 42.
15. Merrill D. Peterson, ed., *James Madison: A Biography in His own Words* (New York: Newsweek, 1974), 136. This book is based on *The Papers of James Madison,* edited first by William T. Hutchinson and William M. E. Rachal, and then by Robert A. Rutland and William M. W. Rachal.
16. See Alley, *James Madison on Religious Liberty,* 190–91.
17. Qtd. in Riemer, *James Madison: Creating the American Constitution,* 105.
18. For Madison's larger political theory, as he developed it across a lifetime, see Riemer, *James Madison: Creating the American Constitution.*
19. Riemer, *James Madison: Creating the American Constitution,* 32.
20. Alexander Hamilton, John Jay, James Madison, *The Federalist* (1787–88; rpt. New York: Modern Library, n.d.), 61–62.
21. Ibid., 339–40.
22. Ibid., 340–41.
23. Qtd. in Riemer, *James Madison: Creating the American Constitution,* 105.
24. Qtd. in Koch, *Madison's "Advice to My Country,"* 76.
25. On Madison's prudential disposition, see Riemer, *James Madison: Creating the American Constitution,* esp. 11–21.
26. Alley, *James Madison on Religious Liberty,* 52. Emphasis added.
27. On Madison and creative breakthroughs in politics, see Riemer, *The Future of the Democratic Revolution: Toward a More Prophetic Politics* (New York: Praeger, 1984), esp. 149–55.

REFERENCES

Alley, Robert S. *James Madison on Religious Liberty.* Buffalo: Prometheus Books, 1985.
Hamilton, Alexander, John Jay, and James Madison. *The Federalist* (1787–88). New York: Modern Library, n.d.
Koch, Adrienne. *Madison's "Advice to My Country."* Princeton, N.J.: Princeton Univ. Press, 1966.
Peterson, Merrill D., ed. *James Madison: A Biography in His own Words.* New York: Newsweek, 1974.
Riemer, Neal. *James Madison: Creating the American Constitution.* New York: Washington Square Press, 1968. Rev. ed. Washington, D.C.: Congressional Quarterly Press, 1986.

3 ‖ The Enigma of James Madison on Church and State

Charles J. Emmerich

When the Nazis killed Dietrich Bonhoeffer on 9 April 1945, modern Christendom lost one of its most brilliant and, some would argue, "enigmatic" theologians. The young Lutheran pastor's deep and multifaceted insights and courage in the face of Hitler's evil prompted proponents of conflicting schools of thought to trace their ideas to Bonhoeffer.[1] Just as theologians have struggled to characterize Bonhoeffer, legal scholars and political scientists interested in church and state have found James Madison somewhat of an enigma. Madison's rich political theory, worked out in a distinguished career spanning more than sixty years, has provided fertile ground for intellectual debate.[2] Scholars of fundamentally different perspectives, strict separationists as well as accommodationists, have invoked him to support their approaches.

Given the disparate interpretations of Madison, one is tempted to ask whether new endeavors to understand his convictions concerning church and state are worth the effort. Despite the current controversy over his thought, I am convinced that it is possible to discover Madison's basic convictions. The primary difficulty does not lie in ascertaining his views but in the modern distortions of his outlook to support certain ideological preferences. After making several observations about how Madison's views have been used in the law, I will discuss the way in which his church-state philosophy reflects a balance between constitutional idealism and political realism and an adherence to "institutional" rather than "strict" separation. I will then propose three areas of study that could enhance our understanding of Madison's conception of religious liberty.

I would like to thank my mentor, Arlin M. Adams, for his assistance with this article and for his faithful guidance through the years.

THE USE OF MADISON'S VIEWS IN LAW

At the outset, it is important to recognize that courts and law professors approach the study of Madison somewhat differently than historians and political scientists. It would be helpful, therefore, to review the intellectual climate in law relating to the use of history and, more specifically, the relevance of the Founders' views to constitutional law.

One of the formidable challenges faced by law professors and attorneys is to invoke history responsibly, even though they are often called upon to be advocates. The danger is that the lawyer or judge "who ventures to write the past, recent or remote, . . . [may] select for his comment only those past records which favor his side."[3] Of course, those in other disciplines are also advocates of particular ideologies or agendas. The difference is that judicial interpretations of history, particularly in constitutional law, can have immediate and far-reaching consequences for society and the coequal branches of government. In addition, the Court's institutional prestige makes it relatively easy for it to weave "synthetic strands into the tapestry of American history."[4] As a result, Mark DeWolfe Howe has warned that "the Court's distorting lessons in American intellectual history" should not be taken lightly: "A great many Americans—lawyers and non-lawyers alike—tend to think that because a majority of the justices have the power to bind us by their law they are also empowered to bind us by their history. Happily that is not the case."[5]

There is a more pressing concern, however, than whether members of the legal profession can responsibly interpret the past as an aid in construing the religion clauses. In light of the theories taught in today's law schools, it appears that many professors doubt whether history and the Founders' beliefs and practices are relevant at all in constitutional law. Current "wisdom" denigrates the study of history by asserting that it can prove nothing, be used to prove anything, or that the "dead hand" of the past holds back progress. A leading constitutional law treatise, for example, bemoans the "seemingly irresistible impulse to appeal to history when analyzing issues under the religion clauses . . . because there is no clear history as to the meaning of the clauses."[6] Another work on church and state maintains that "the historical materials themselves will not settle anything."[7] Professor Arthur Miller reflects the prevailing cynicism: "Lawyers and judges use and abuse history at will. History settles little that is worth arguing about. And as Chief Justice Hughes said, even if the history is clear, it is really not relevant."[8]

In a discussion of modern constitutional theorists, Judge Robert Bork concludes that almost all of them have repudiated originalism—the traditional approach that the Constitution should be interpreted in accordance with the intentions of its framers and ratifiers—in favor of abstruse and result-oriented theories premised on moral relativism. He asserts that "the rising flood of innovative theories signifies . . . a deep-seated malaise and, quite possibly, a state of approaching decadence."[9] To historians and political scientists, it might seem peculiar that most constitutional theorists are now, in essence, questioning the relevance of Madison's political theory to First Amendment jurisprudence.

Having summarized some of the intellectual currents in legal education, I wish to make it clear that I do not share the "innovative" and ahistorical approaches espoused by many of my colleagues. To me it appears almost self-evident that Madison's vision of religious liberty and public life is worthy of close study and important for constitutional interpretation. The study of history not only provides valuable lessons but affords "an essential framework for resolving contemporary religious freedom issues."[10] The historical materials strongly suggest, for example, that the core value of the religion clauses is liberty of conscience and that the Founders intended the establishment and free exercise clauses to be coguarantors of that value. History also yields at least four animating principles designed to foster liberty of conscience in a free society: federalism, institutional separation, accommodation, and benevolent neutrality.[11] Consequently, although the study of history may be tedious and at times perplexing, I cannot agree with legal scholars who assert that it is an essentially worthless or irrelevant endeavor.[12]

In reaching its decisions under the religion clauses, the Supreme Court has thus far ignored the ahistorical theories advanced by legal scholars. Instead, it has generally proceeded in accordance with Justice Wiley Rutledge's assertion in 1947 that "no provision of the Constitution is more closely tied to or given content by its generating history than the religious clause of the First Amendment."[13] Madison's part in this "generating history," particularly his role in the campaign to disestablish the Church of England in Virginia, has figured prominently in the Court's First Amendment jurisprudence. In the highly influential case of *Everson* v. *Board of Education*, both Justice Black for the majority and Justice Rutledge in dissent paid special homage to Madison, emphasizing his leading role in the drafting and adoption of the religion clauses and the importance of his thought as "the common unifying thread" in understanding the First Amendment's guarantee of religious liberty.[14]

Although the Court has appropriately looked to Madison for guidance, it has unfortunately done so within the narrow confines of trying to determine whether he subscribed to the nonpreferentialist thesis. According to this thesis, the Founders intended the religion clauses to prohibit preferential aid to a particular denomination but did not mean for it to forbid nondiscriminatory aid to religion. Perhaps motivated by presentist concerns, legal scholars on both sides of the nonpreferentialist debate have enlisted Madison as support and have thereby confused the courts and generated unreliable history.[15] Influenced by scholarly debate, the Court has largely limited its inquiry in establishment clause cases to determining whether the provision comprehensively bans evenhanded support for religion in general, as well as preferential treatment for a particular religious faith. In answering this question affirmatively, the Court has stressed that it "unequivocally" rejects the contention that the clause "forbids only governmental preference of one religion over another."[16] A dispassionate examination of history, I believe, supports the conclusion that Madison's political philosophy and opinions on church and state are too complex to be addressed adequately within the framework of nonpreferentialism.[17]

MADISON AS CONSTITUTIONAL IDEALIST
AND POLITICAL REALIST

One of the keys to understanding Madison's approach to church and state questions is recognizing that it embodied a tension between constitutional idealism and political realism. This tension resulted in part because Madison manifested a healthy concern for the purity and integrity of religion, as well as for that of government. More so than his anticlerical friend Jefferson, he derived his convictions from a theistic world view that affirmed liberty of conscience as a God-given right beyond the control of government. In his classic "Memorial and Remonstrance Against Religious Assessments," Madison explained that this right is inalienable because it entails "a duty towards the Creator" that is "precedent, both in order of time and in degree of obligation, to the claims of Civil Society."[18] Employing a conceptual framework similar to the two-kingdom's approach of the Reformers, Madison emphasized that a person owes allegiance first to "the Governour of the Universe" and only secondarily to temporal rulers. He contended that religion—the duty to obey the Creator in accordance with one's conscience—lies outside the cognizance of the legislature and of society at large.[19]

To preserve the integrity of both religion and government, it was necessary, according to Madison, to maintain a rigid institutional separation between church and state. In a letter written in 1822, he remarked that "a perfect separation between ecclesiastical and civil matters" should be jealously guarded, because "religion and Government will both exist in greater purity, the less they are mixed together."[20] Separation thus served a dual purpose—it prohibited government from interfering with the exercise of the conscience in religious matters and it prevented church-state alliances that lead to ecclesiastical tyranny.

As a prominent statesman, Madison grasped the problem of church and state at more than just the conceptual level. He was a political realist who realized that "paper proclamations" alone could not guarantee a society committed to religious liberty. The new Republic's multiplicity of sects played an essential role in this respect. As a practical matter, Madison reasoned that the various religious groups would keep one another in check, thereby insuring that no particular faith would gain a legally preferred status. During the debates over the federal Constitution in the Virginia ratifying convention, he stressed that there was "not a shadow of right in the general government to intermeddle with religion" and that the best security for religious freedom was in a multiplicity of sects, for "where there is such a variety of sects, there cannot be a majority of any one sect to oppress and persecute the rest." If one religion predominated, Madison explained, "a bill of rights would be a poor protection for liberty." Fortunately the nation consisted of numerous religions, and a majority of Virginians were "decidedly against any exclusive establishment."[21]

It is no surprise, then, that Madison regarded the principle of federalism as a critical—perhaps the critical—means of insuring freedom of religion. In the *Federalist Papers,* he wrote that the "accumulation of all powers, legislative, executive, and judiciary, in the same hands, whether of one, a few, or many, and whether hereditary, self-appointed, or elective, may justly be pronounced the very definition of tyranny."[22] The preservation of religious liberty depended, in short, on a successful dispersal of political power between the federal and state governments. In this regard, the Founders appeared to be virtually united in the belief that a national church patterned after the English model posed the greatest threat to freedom of religion. The principle of federalism operated to insure that an alliance of church and state at the national level would not occur.[23]

In discussing Madison's "prudential vision" of religious liberty, Neal Riemer emphasizes the Founder's strong commitment to civility in the sensitive and volatile area of church-state relations. As a political realist devoted to common sense and the importance of popular feelings, Madison was not "a dogmatic secular zealot" but a prudent advocate of institutional separation. He was, to quote Riemer, "firm but not fanatical."[24] One could only wish that modern courts would follow Madison's prudential approach in resolving cases under the religion clauses.

Not long ago, a federal district judge in Alabama issued an order stating that he would no longer open his court with, "God Save the United States and this Honorable Court." To continue to do so, he reasoned, would violate the establishment clause and would be hypocritical in light of the fact that pupils could not formally invoke the Deity in public schools. Writing tongue in cheek, Judge William Acker remarked:

> This court will continue privately to ask God's blessings on this court and on all
> other courts, recognizing that the courts need all the help they can get, divine or
> otherwise. But this court forthwith orders the discontinuance of the cruelly ironic
> and hypocritical official invocation of the Deity in its courtroom. . . . The day for
> this court to admit an inexcusable inconsistency in First Amendment jurisprudence
> is today. The awful and obvious chink in the wall of separation must be plugged,
> at least in this court's courtroom.[25]

Despite an unwavering devotion to separation of church and state, Madison probably would have regarded the "serious" issuing of such an order as zealous and imprudent.

In a revealing yet often overlooked comment, Madison stated that strictly speaking, the appointment of congressional chaplains violated the Constitution and "the pure principle of religious freedom," but that such a practice was perhaps best classified under the legal maxim "de minimis non curat lex."[26] He also suggested that the congressional chaplaincy could be explained by the Latin phrase "cum maculis quas aut incuria fudit, aut humana parum cavit natura," which literally means "with stains (moral blemishes) which either negligence poured forth or human nature guarded against too little."[27] Madison thought it best to "disarm in the same way" the allowance of military chaplains; this would prevent the practice from becoming "a political authority in matters of religion."[28] Presidential proclamations of a religious nature, he came to believe late in life, contravened the establishment clause by violating the principle of religious equality and by misusing religion for political ends.[29] This latter passage suggests that Madison was concerned more with maintaining the purity of religion than with protecting government from overbearing clerics.

In an ideal world governed by absolute principles, Madison apparently reasoned, the appointment of congressional chaplains, as well as the military chaplaincy and religious proclamations by presidents, might contravene the establishment clause. He was too astute a statesman, however, to hew to an absolutist agenda in the heated and controversial world of politics. In resolving the tension between idealism and realism in constitutional adjudication, a prudent approach must take account of human nature and *de minimis* circumstances. A politician driven by fanaticism rather than common sense, Madison recognized, could seriously harm religious liberty by alienating less devoted colleagues and by antagonizing those of different perspectives.

How would Madison respond to establishment clause challenges against "In God We Trust" on money,[30] religious symbols and slogans on government seals,[31] the depiction of religious paintings on postage stamps,[32] the wearing of sacred items by government employees while on the job,[33] or statues of religious figures on public property?[34] Given his political realism and commitment to prudence, Madison would, I suspect, regard many of these lawsuits as frivolous. Even if he thought an innocuous practice or symbol contravened the establishment clause in the strictest sense, it is my guess that Madison would consider a lawsuit, with its inherent divisiveness and toll on civility, as too great a price for an unyielding allegiance to the wall of separation.

In this respect, Leonard Levy wisely counsels fellow separationist scholars to use "a little common sense" in constitutional adjudication and to realize that "not every accommodation with religion, deriving from incidental assistance, is necessarily unconstitutional."[35] Attempts to make the wall of separation impregnable, he argues, result in "silly suits, such as those seeking to have declared unconstitutional the words 'under God' in the pledge of allegiance or in the money motto 'In God We Trust.'" Emphasizing that such litigation can be "futile and dangerously counterproductive," Levy concludes: "Separationists who cannot appreciate the principle of *de minimis* ought to appreciate a different motto—'Let sleeping dogmas lie.'"[36]

MADISON AS INSTITUTIONAL SEPARATIONIST

One of the principal difficulties with the legal literature on Madison is the confusing and inaccurate description of the Founder as a "strict" separationist. This term is generally derived from or often associated with Justice Rutledge's dissent in the *Everson* case. In sweeping language, Rutledge posited that the purpose of the religion clauses was "to create a complete and permanent separation of the spheres of religious activity and civil authority by comprehensively forbidding every form of public aid or support for religion."[37] He enlisted Madison as support for this stance, stating that the Founder opposed "any fragment of establishment" and "sought to tear out the institution not partially but root and branch, and to bar its return forever."[38]

In the legal profession, the strict separationist position is increasingly being interpreted to require not only a formal institutional separation between church and state but also the exclusion of religion from the public arena and from the ongoing debate, as Alexander Meiklejohn put it, to discover our cultural and spiritual heritage. Confessing that his own beliefs were basically nonreligious, Meiklejohn nevertheless asserted that the Constitution requires courts to acknowledge that religion plays an essential public role: "When men are trying to be self-governing, no other single factor of their experience is more important to them than the freedom of their religion or of their nonreligion. The interpreting of our spiritual beliefs is a public enterprise of the highest order."[39]

The anticlerical and privatized conception of religion advanced by Justice Rutledge in *Everson* disregards America's long and rich heritage of religious liberty. Nor is it an outlook that Madison would endorse, for he recognized "religion's legitimate efforts to inspire, nourish, and contribute to American public life."[40] The principal problem with the strict separationist position is that it contradicts the belief of virtually all the prominent Founders, including Madison, that the Republic could not survive without the moral influence supplied by religion. As John Adams declared in 1798, "Our constitution was made only for a moral and religious people. It is wholly inadequate to the government of any other."[41]

In light of the confusion engendered by the term *strict separation*, I prefer to characterize Madison as an institutional separationist committed to fostering the core value of liberty of conscience. Influenced significantly by both theological and Enlightenment concepts, he considered separation of church and state as a means for promoting religious liberty, not as an end in itself. The historical principles of federalism, neutrality, and accommodation unite with that of separation in this respect. The Founders intended these principles to serve the establishment and free exercise clauses, which they regarded as complementary coguarantors of a single end—liberty of conscience in religious matters.[42] As Justice Arthur Goldberg observed in 1963, the purpose of the clauses is "to promote and assure the fullest possible scope of religious liberty and tolerance for all and to nurture the conditions which secure the best hope of attainment of that end."[43]

Although Madison advocated separation of church and state, he did not intend for this separation to be strict, complete, or absolute in the sense that it would burden or disadvantage the exercise of religion. This point is perhaps best illustrated by the "equal-access" controversy, which raised the issue whether student religious groups are entitled to meet in public schools on the same basis as other student groups.[44] The Supreme Court first addressed this issue in 1981 in the context of public higher education. In *Widmar* v. *Vincent*,[45] a Christian student club challenged a University of Missouri policy under which school facilities were made available to all student groups except those meeting for religious purposes. Emphasizing that the university had created a forum for student expression, the Court concluded that the policy violated the general principle of the free speech clause that government may not discriminate against speech on the basis of its content. The Court specifically rejected the contention that the establishment clause required the exclusion of religious speech from university facilities open to various other groups and speakers.

The natural question after *Widmar* was whether the decision's rationale guaranteed equal access for student religious groups in public high schools. Adopting a separationist position, the lower federal courts that confronted this question declined to extend *Widmar*. Instead, they ruled that students in high school, unlike those in college, lacked the maturity to comprehend the constitutional subtleties raised by equal access and would interpret the presence of religious clubs in their schools as state endorsement of religion. In addition, courts concluded that student religious groups would cause dissension in the public schools. Troubled by these decisions and convinced that discrimination against student religious clubs was widespread, Congress passed the Equal Access Act of 1984. The act sought to end such discrimination by prohibiting public high schools with forums for noncurriculum student clubs from denying "equal access" to clubs desiring to meet for religious, political, or philosophical purposes. In *Westside Community Board of Education* v. *Mergens,* decided in 1990, the Supreme Court sustained the constitutionality of the Equal Access Act under the establishment clause. Viewing the act as a neutral measure designed to place student religious groups on the same footing as a host of secular clubs, eight justices rejected the argument that the legislation impermissibly advanced or endorsed religion.[46]

Recognizing the hazards of historical speculation, I am confident that Madison would have sided with Congress and the Supreme Court in the equal-access controversy. This conclusion finds support in Madison's commitment to the principle of equality, in his political philosophy grounded on a multiplicity of factions and interests interacting in the public arena, and in his belief that religion played an important role in sustaining the Republic. Perhaps the most revealing clue to Madison's thought with respect to equal access is the fact that he joined John Witherspoon, the only minister to sign the Declaration of Independence, in opposing state constitutional provisions that excluded clergy from holding public offices.

THREE PROPOSALS FOR FURTHER STUDY

By directing attention to Madison's effort to balance constitutional idealism and political realism and to his adherence to the principle of institutional separation, I have suggested that it is a mistake to confine the Founder's complex conception of religious liberty within modern paradigms such as strict separation, accommodation, and nonpreferentialism. To underscore this assertion and cast additional light on Madison's outlook, it would be beneficial to pursue further study along three lines: the need to differentiate the beliefs of Madison and Jefferson on church and state, the shift or change in Madison's perspective over time, and the importance of the natural law tradition in shaping Madison's concept of inalienable rights.

The Differences Between Madison and Jefferson

A great deal of confusion has resulted in the law because the Supreme Court appears to have uncritically accepted the proposition that Madison and Jefferson held the same views on church and state.[47] As a result, courts and legal scholars have attributed a Jeffersonian "wall of separation" outlook to Madison. Although a comparison of their writings reveals many common presuppositions, including the belief that liberty of conscience is an inalienable right conferred by the Creator, it also discloses significant differences.[48]

Heavily influenced by Locke and Enlightenment deism, Jefferson conceived of God in an impersonal way, manifested disdain for institutional religion and the clergy, and restrictively defined religion as a private exercise of the mind that had little relevance to public life.[49] While attending the College of New Jersey, later Princeton University, Madison studied under John Witherspoon, the college's president and a Presbyterian minister who defended orthodox Calvinism, liberty of conscience, and the public role of religion as an indispensable source of civic virtue. It is not surprising, therefore, that orthodox theology and the pietistic tradition of religious liberty significantly shaped Madison's world view.[50] In contrast to Jefferson, he thought of God in more theistic terms, eschewed harsh anticlericalism, appreciated the importance of faith in the lives of citizens, and acknowledged the essential public role played by religion. Rejecting Jefferson's Lockean and privatized conception of religion, Madison affirmed that government should be sensitive to the spiritual needs of citizens even when such needs implicated the public arena or important social duties.

A Shifting Perspective over Time

In addition to not differentiating the beliefs of Madison and Jefferson, scholars have generated confusion by assuming that the young, middle-aged, and old Madison held completely consistent views on church-state issues. Although Madison maintained a fervent and unwavering commitment to religious liberty throughout his life, he appears to have changed his mind a number of times concerning how this commitment should be expressed. To illustrate this point, it would be helpful to recount some of Madison's actions and beliefs.

As a young Virginia legislator, Madison not only sponsored Jefferson's famous "Bill for Establishing Religious Freedom" but also introduced a number of overtly religious bills resulting from Jefferson's revisions of the state's colonial laws. Among these were a bill preserving the property rights of the Anglican church during its gradual disestablishment, a bill imposing harsh penalties for disturbing religious worship or laboring on the Sabbath, a bill requiring all ministers to observe state appointed days of public fasting and thanksgiving, and a bill incorporating Old Testament Levitical laws concerning prohibited marriages.[51]

While serving in the First Congress, Madison sat on a committee that recommended the appointment of paid chaplains for the House and Senate. In addition, there is no evidence that he disapproved of the First Congress' resolution urging George Washington to declare a national day of public thanksgiving and prayer. During his two terms as president, Madison voiced no opposition to the appointment of congressional and military chaplains, permitted the appropriation of federal money for teaching religion and morality to Native Americans, and issued four proclamations recommending days of prayer and thanksgiving. Later in life, however, he expressed the belief that strictly speaking, the establishment clause prohibited presidential religious proclamations and congressional and military chaplains.[52]

The apparent inconsistencies in Madison's actions or views need not trouble us. Some can probably be explained in terms of the principle of federalism, the idea that the states possessed authority in the area of church and state not possessed by the federal government. This might account for Madison's sponsorship of religious bills at the state level. Other "discrepancies," such as the question of chaplaincies and religious proclamations, might fall under Madison's "prudential vision"; they might illustrate the fact that a leader in the thick of war, economic crises, and other troubles would be unwise to relentlessly pursue an absolutist agenda.

Perhaps most important in understanding Madison over time is that he exhibited a common characteristic of humans—he simply changed his mind. This fact might supply the best explanation for his change or shift as a young legislator who supported—or at least did not oppose—military and legislative chaplains and religious proclamations, to an elder statesman who found all of these incompatible with the establishment clause. In a tribute that could apply equally to Madison, Alexander Bickel praised Justice Hugo Black by observing that men and women "engaged in a life of doing, not of scholarly contemplation and system-building" do not leave behind "a wholly coherent and self-consistent philosophy of law and politics, or of the Constitution, or even of a single large subject of constitutional adjudication." Scholars commit "some injustice," Bickel asserted, when they "attempt to draw from such lives a coherent, self-consistent view of the system that underlay the life work."[53]

Madison and Natural Law

To grasp Madison's contribution to political thought, it is necessary to place him in the political and philosophical milieu at America's founding. What strikes me most about the legal commentary is that it attempts to understand Madison's stances on church-state issues without adequately comprehending his world view or without recognizing that his presuppositions differ, often times radically, from those espoused by many modern scholars. Like virtually all the Founders, Madison embraced a theory of natural law informed by various sources, most prominent among them, the Bible, covenant theology, the common law, the Enlightenment, and Scottish common sense realism.[54] To appreciate what Madison and the other Founders meant by "inalienable rights," it is therefore necessary to explore the

British natural law tradition as shaped by Blackstone and other writers who were widely read in the colonies.

Although denigrated by legal scholars for much of this century, natural law enjoyed a brief resurgence after the Nuremberg trials and most recently captured public attention with the nomination of Clarence Thomas to the Supreme Court. Upon learning that Judge Thomas believed in the natural law principles underlying the Declaration of Independence and other historical documents, law professors such as Laurence Tribe of Harvard expressed alarm, decrying Thomas's jurisprudence as "troubling" and as a threat to democratic government. What is troubling is not Thomas's allegiance to "the venerable concept of 'natural law'" but the arrogance of his critics who claim to speak for the American legal tradition.[55] Even a cursory examination of this tradition reveals that natural law provided the philosophical underpinnings for American law from the settlement of Virginia in 1607 until recent times. From the standpoint of history, it is legal positivism and its progeny that are an aberration.

Natural law has played a prominent role in human thought and history for thousands of years.[56] It has a distinguished and multifaceted past and stands as a constant reminder that law, as a part of ethics, is accountable to the concept of justice. Although the natural law tradition consists of various theoretical strands, it rests in its theological manifestations on a number of propositions: (1) there is a sovereign God whose nature and attributes can be known, at least in part, through reason and revelation; (2) God has established a well-ordered universe governed by immutable moral principles; (3) man is a rational creature capable of discovering and applying these principles, which form the basis for natural law; (4) in order for a human rule to be regarded as law, and therefore entitled to obedience, it must correspond to a minimum degree with natural law, which is the embodiment of justice; and (5) law is more than a command backed by force, it is a subset of ethics designed to restrain evil, promote order, and foster certain forms of virtue.[57]

In his *Commentaries on the Laws of England*, probably the most widely used legal commentary in the colonies, Sir William Blackstone posited that the natural law derived its content from divine law, which was discoverable in its purest form through revelation and in a less reliable way through reason. The natural law, Blackstone emphasized, applied "in all countries, and at all times" and imposed an obligation superior to all human claims. As a result, the enactments of sovereign states derived their legitimacy from the natural law—"no human laws are of any validity, if contrary to this [law], and such of them as are valid derive all their force, and all their authority, mediately or immediately, from this original."[58]

The American Founders generally embraced the five propositions set forth above, and although they disagreed with Blackstone's concept of parliamentary sovereignty and many of his political views, they agreed with his description of the natural law. Working within this jurisprudential framework, the Founders emphasized the "natural rights" of citizens in the context of a Lockean social compact. These rights, wrote John Dickinson in 1766, derive not from kings and Parliaments but from "a higher source—from the King of kings, and Lord of all the earth." In an eloquent summary of prevailing thought, Dickinson declared: "They are created in us by the decrees of Providence, which establish the laws of our nature. They are born with us; exist with us; and cannot be taken from us by any human power without taking our lives. In short, they are founded on the immutable maxims of reason and justice."[59]

Most prominent among these natural or inalienable rights was liberty of conscience, a duty to obey the Creator that took precedence over the duties owed to civil society. In a proposed draft of the religious liberty guarantee of the Virginia Declaration of Rights, Madison underscored the supremacy of this duty, asserting that "all men are equally entitled to enjoy the free exercise of religion, according to the dictates of conscience, unpunished and unrestrained by the magistrate, Unless the preservation of equal liberty and the existence of the State are manifestly endangered."[60] In other words, Madison considered the right to practice one's religion in accordance with conscience to be so fundamental that civil rulers lacked authority to interfere with it unless the state's survival was clearly at stake.

To demonstrate how radically this perspective differs from current understandings of religious freedom, one need only look at the Supreme Court's 1990 decision in *Employment Division* v. *Smith*.[61] The Court took a rather routine case involving the extent of Oregon's obligation to accommodate a concededly religious ingestion of peyote and used it to announce a new free exercise standard at odds with precedent, history, and sound constitutional policy. Prior to *Smith*, the Court had applied the "compelling state interest" test enunciated in *Sherbert* v. *Verner*.[62] Under this standard, a law that burdened a sincerely held religious practice was invalidated as unconstitutional unless the government could demonstrate that the law advanced a compelling state interest and that it employed a means "narrowly tailored" to achieve that end.

Speaking for a majority of five in *Smith*, Justice Scalia relegated the *Sherbert* test to a narrow set of circumstances and eviscerated the free exercise clause by adopting a standard known as the secular regulation rule. According to this rule, the government has no constitutional duty to exempt a religious person from the requirements of "an otherwise valid law prohibiting conduct that the State is free to regulate. " Claiming that the *Sherbert* test "contradict[ed] both constitutional tradition and common sense," the Court reasoned that to uniformly apply the test in a religiously pluralistic society would be "courting anarchy."[64] It would be "a constitutional anomaly," Justice Scalia stated, to recognize "a private right to ignore generally applicable laws."[65] If such a right to religious exemption is to exist, he added, it must be left to the political process and the legislatures, not to the courts. The majority in *Smith* declared in closing, "We cannot afford the luxury of deeming *presumptively invalid,* as applied to the religious objector, every regulation of conduct that does not protect an interest of the highest order."[66]

How would Madison respond to the *Smith* decision? I have little doubt that he would echo the words of Justice O'Connor that the decision "is incompatible with our Nation's fundamental commitment to individual religious liberty."[67] While leading scholars have justifiably criticized *Smith* on constitutional grounds,[68] the principal difficulty with the decision lies at a deeper level touching philosophical and political presuppositions. Modern scholars and courts invariably address religious freedom issues from the perspective of statism, that is, they assume the sovereignty of the state over virtually all areas of life and then ask, to what extent if at all must the state tolerate religious practices that impinge upon its authority. Even those advocating a constitutional duty to accommodate religious belief are tinged by statist premises, for they usually begin their analyses by positing governmental dominion over religion. Such an outlook reduces religious liberty to a "privilege" or "luxury" dependent on the benevolence of government. One is reminded of Thomas Paine's comment that toleration is the counterfeit of intolerance: "Both are despotisms. The one assumes to itself the right of withholding Liberty of Conscience, and the other of granting it. The one is the Pope armed with fire and faggot, and the other is the Pope selling or granting indulgences."[69]

Understood in light of the British natural law tradition and the concept of inalienable rights, Madison's outlook on religious liberty would, I suspect, make many courts uneasy. Regarding liberty of conscience as a God-given right superior to almost all claims of government, Madison would phrase the issue in terms of how much a religious citizen needs to "accommodate" the state's interest in promoting the common good. In other words, to what extent does the believer have a duty to share God's domain—the conscience and the religious duties it imposes—with Caesar? Viewed from this perspective, it is understandable that Madison imposed an exceedingly high burden on the state to justify an infringement of religious freedom; he asserted that government must demonstrate that its existence is "manifestly endangered" before it could punish or restrain the free exercise of religion. Thus, Madison's standard arguably exceeded that imposed by the *Sherbert* test, which required only that the state demonstrate a compelling governmental interest or an aim of the highest order.

To Justice Scalia's disquieting remark that accommodations of religion are the sole province of the legislature, Madison would respond with a rudimentary lesson in political theory, namely that legislation generally reflects the policy preferences of majority factions that often are insensitive to minority rights. Thus the *Smith* Court's solution to the plight of small religions with different or unique beliefs is in most instances no solution at all. The Founders placed liberty of conscience and other inalienable rights in the Constitution to confirm their conviction, derived from natural law, that the power of the state is not limitless. They distrusted centralized authority, particularly the legislative branch, and realized that a dangerous propensity of democracies was the persecution of minorities by overbearing majority factions. The Bill of Rights, entrusted to the care of an unelected branch, was meant to be a charter of natural rights and as such to stand as a barrier between citizens, acting individually and communally, and the majoritarian abuses that constitute tyranny. Its "very purpose," as Justice Robert Jackson so eloquently stated, "was to withdraw certain subjects from the vicissitudes of political controversy, to place them beyond the reach of majorities and officials and to establish them as legal principles to be applied by the courts."[70] By subordinating religion to governmental power, the *Smith* Court dishonored the Anglo-American heritage of religious liberty and abdicated its role as the guardian of our most cherished right.

CONCLUSION

Like the German theologian Dietrich Bonhoeffer, James Madison was not only a brilliant thinker who developed a sophisticated world view but a man of action who forged ideas on the anvil of human experience. Studying the life and thought of such a dynamic leader can be a formidable task. Those who appreciate the lessons of history, however, recognize that it is an essential and rewarding endeavor. I hope that this chapter will take us a little further down the road in understanding this eminent Founder.

Perhaps the most important point is the necessity of placing Madison's concept of liberty of conscience within the framework of the Anglo-American tradition of natural law. This suggestion will undoubtedly trouble scholars who disdain historical inquiry and who adopt the positivist tenets that morality is grounded in utility rather than in immutable principles, that ethical inquiry and law are separate, that religion is not a necessary source for morality, that religion is a private matter and should be excluded from public life, and that the solution for social ills is to expand the role of government rather than to foster civic virtue. It is odd that, even though Madison rejected all of these tenets, modern revisionist scholars somehow claim him as a champion of the secular state and of a diminished role for religion. Such a Madison, however, is the creation of academic folklore, not the Founder of history.

NOTES

1. Traditional Lutheran scholars as well as the "God is dead" theologians, Thomas Altizer and William Hamilton, have appealed to Bonhoeffer for support. Altizer and Hamilton, for example, formulated their views by seizing on reflections taken from letters and papers written by Bonhoeffer while in prison. For a helpful overview of Bonhoeffer's theology, see William E. Hordern, *A Layman's Guide to Protestant Theology*, rev. ed. (New York: Macmillan, 1968), 210–29.

2. The definitive biography of Madison is the six-volume work by Irving Brant, *James Madison* (Indianapolis: Bobbs-Merrill, 1941–61). Scholarly one-volume biographies include Ralph L. Ketcham, *James Madison: A Biography* (New York: Macmillan, 1970), and Robert A. Rutland, *James Madison: The Founding Father* (New York: Macmillan, 1987). Neal Riemer discusses Madison's political theory in *James Madison: Creating the American Constitution* (Washington, D.C.: Congressional Quarterly, 1986). Madison's beliefs on church and state are explored at length in Robert S. Alley, ed., *James Madison on Religious Liberty* (Buffalo: Prometheus, 1985). For a brief discussion of the views of Madison and other Founders on religious liberty, see Arlin M. Adams and Charles J. Emmerich, *A Nation Dedicated to Religious Liberty: The Constitutional Heritage of the Religion Clauses* (Philadelphia: Univ. of Pennsylvania Press, 1990), 21–31.

3. Arthur Sutherland, "Historians, Lawyers, and 'Establishment of Religion,'" in *Religion and the Public Order*, ed. Donald Giannella (Villanova, Penn.: Villanova Univ. Press, 1969), 5: 27.

4. Mark DeWolfe Howe, *The Garden and the Wilderness: Religion and Government in American Constitutional History* (Chicago: Univ. of Chicago Press, 1965), 4.

5. Ibid., 5.

6. John E. Nowak, Ronald D. Rotunda, and J. Nelson Young, *Constitutional Law*, 2d ed. (Minneapolis: West Publishing, 1983), 1029–30.

7. Richard E. Morgan, *The Supreme Court and Religion* (New York: Free Press, 1972), 186.

8. Arthur S. Miller, "An Inquiry into the Relevance of the Intentions of the Founding Fathers, with Special Emphasis Upon the Doctrine of Separation of Powers," *Arkansas Law Review* 27 (1973): 583, 598.

9. Robert H. Bork, *The Tempting of America: The Political Seduction of the Law* (New York: Simon & Schuster, 1990), 133.

10. See Adams and Emmerich, *A Nation Dedicated to Religious Liberty*, 94.

11. Ibid., 32–73.

12. For an excellent example of the way in which history can illuminate the understanding of the Constitution, see Michael W. McConnell, "The Origins and Historical Understanding of Free Exercise of Religion," *Harvard Law Review* 103 (1990): 1409–1517.

13. *Everson* v. *Board of Education*, 330 U.S. 1, 33 (1947) (Rutledge, J., dissenting). Thus the Court deemed the practices of the Founders virtually dispositive in sustaining Nebraska's legislative chaplaincy against an establishment clause challenge. See *Marsh* v. *Chambers*, 463 U.S. 783, 794–95 (1983). Similarly, the Court accorded great weight to tradition in upholding New York's tax exemption for church property. See *Walz* v. *Tax Commission*, 397 U.S. 664, 677–80 (1970).

14. See *Everson* v. *Board of Education*, 330 U.S. at 13; also at 39 (Rutledge, J., dissenting). Several prominent legal scholars have criticized the Court for relying too heavily on Madison in interpreting the First Amendment. See Edward S. Corwin, "The Supreme Court as National School Board," *Law and Contemporary Problems* 14 (1949): 3, 13 (asserting that Justice Rutledge's reliance on Madison was "obviously excessive"); John Courtney Murray, "Law or Prepossessions?," *Law and Contemporary Problems* 14 (1949): 23, 27 (arguing that the religion clauses do not incorporate Madison's "total personal ideology"); Paul G. Kauper, "*Everson* v. *Board of Education*: A Product of the Judicial Will," *Arizona Law Review* 15 (1973): 307, 318–19 ("It would be a mistake . . . to interpret the establishment clause wholly in terms of what Madison and Jefferson thought.").

15. Robert Cord, an accommodationist, argues that the Founders, including Madison, adhered to the nonpreferentialist thesis. See Robert L. Cord, *Separation of Church and State: Historical Fact and Current Fiction* (New York: Lambeth, 1982). For a lengthy criticism of the thesis by a prominent separationist, see Leonard W. Levy,

The Establishment Clause: Religion and the First Amendment (New York: Macmillan, 1986). A helpful discussion of how advocates from the two camps enlist support from Madison is contained in Daniel L. Dreisbach, *Real Threat and Mere Shadow: Religious Liberty and the First Amendment* (Westchester, Ill.: Crossway, 1987), 135–58.

16. *Abington School District* v. *Schempp*, 374 U.S. 203, 216 (1963). Only recently has a justice adopted the view that the Founders intended the establishment clause to embody the nonpreferentialist principle. See *Wallace* v. *Jaffree*, 472 U.S. 38, 91–114 (1985) (Rehnquist, J., dissenting).

17. See Adams and Emmerich, *A Nation Dedicated to Religious Liberty*, 19 (questioning "whether the rich and diverse history of the religion clauses can be reduced to such a simplistic formula"). Riemer's chapter in this volume provides a better model for structuring debate than the nonpreferentialist thesis. His three-pronged approach better accounts for the complexity of Madison's thought and thus provides a superior analytical tool for grasping the full import of the Founder's beliefs.

18. Madison, "Memorial and Remonstrance Against Religious Assessments," c. 20 June 1785, in *The Papers of James Madison*, eds. William T. Hutchinson and William M. Rachal, et al. (Chicago: Univ. of Chicago Press, 1962), 8: 299.

19. Ibid.

20. Madison to Edward Livingston, 10 July 1822, in *The Writings of James Madison*, ed. Gaillard Hunt (New York: G. Putnam's Sons, 1910), 9: 102.

21. Madison, speech in the Virginia Ratifying Convention, 12 June 1788, in *The Debates in the Several State Conventions on the Adoption of the Federal Constitution*, ed. Jonathan Elliott (2d ed. 1836; rpt. New York: Burt Franklin, 1888), 3: 330.

22. *The Federalist*, No. 47, ed. Benjamin Wright (Cambridge: Harvard Univ. Press, 1961), 336.

23. For a discussion of the Founders' conception of federalism and the importance of this principle in maintaining religious liberty, see Adams and Emmerich, *A Nation Dedicated to Religious Liberty*, 43–51.

24. Riemer, "Madison: A Founder's Vision," chap. 2, above.

25. "Memorandum Opinion and Standing Rule for the Courtroom of William M. Acker, Jr." (Unpublished opinion issued on 22 Aug. 1990 by Judge Acker, for the Northern District of the United States District Court of Alabama), 5.

26. Elizabeth Fleet, ed., "Madison's 'Detached Memoranda,'" *William and Mary Quarterly*, 3d ser., 3 (Oct. 1946): 558–59. The maxim means "the law does not concern itself with trivial matters."

27. Ibid., 559. I would like to thank Arthur Rupprecht, Professor of Ancient Languages at Wheaton College, for translating this phrase.

28. Fleet, "Madison's 'Detatched Memoranda,'" 559.

29. See ibid., 560–62.

30. See *Aronow* v. *United States,* 432 F.2d 242 (9th Cir. 1970) (holding that the federal statutes requiring "In God We Trust" on money do not violate the establishment clause).

31. See *Friedman* v. *Board of County Commissioners,* 781 F.2d 777 (10th Cir. 1985) (*en banc*) (concluding that a New Mexico county seal bearing a Latin cross impermissibly advances Christianity in violation of the establishment clause).

32. See *Protestants and Other Americans United for Separation of Church and State* v. *O'Brien,* 272 F. Supp. 712 (D.D.C. 1967) (dismissing the suit on procedural grounds but expressing the view that issuance of a stamp depicting Hans Memling's famous painting, "Madonna and Child with Angels," does not contravene the establishment clause), reversed on procedural grounds, *Protestants and Other Americans United* v. *Watson,* 407 F.2d 1264 (D.C. Cir. 1968).

33. See *O'Hair* v. *Paine,* 312 F. Supp. 434 (W.D. Tex. 1969) (stating that the establishment clause does not disallow astronauts from wearing religious items while on a space mission), affirmed on procedural grounds, *O'Hair* v. *Paine,* 432 F.2d 66, 67 (5th Cir. 1970).

34. See *State ex rel. Singelmann* v. *Morrison,* 57 So.2d 238 (La. Ct. App.), certiorari denied, 57 So. 238 (La. 1952) (considering a challenge against the erection on public property of a statue of a prominent canonized nun).

35. Levy, *The Establishment Clause,* 176.

36. Ibid., 176–77.

37. *Everson* v. *Board of Education,* 330 U.S. at 31–32 (Rutledge, J., dissenting).

38. Ibid., 40.

39. Alexander Meiklejohn, "Educational Cooperation Between Church and State," *Law and Contemporary Problems* 14 (1949): 61, 67.

40. Riemer, "Madison: A Founder's Vision," chap. 2, above.

41. Adams to a unit of the Massachusetts militia, 11 Oct. 1798, *The Works of John Adams,* ed. Charles F. Adams (Boston: Little, Brown, 1854), 9: 229.

42. This approach is defended at length in Adams and Emmerich, *A Nation Dedicated to Religious Liberty,* 32–73.

43. *Abington School District* v. *Schempp,* 374 U.S. 203, 305 (Goldberg, J., concurring).

44. See Adams and Emmerich, *A Nation Dedicated to Religious Liberty,* 75–82 (analyzing the equal-access controversy in light of the historical principles designed to promote religious liberty).

45. 454 U.S. 263 (1981).

46. 493 U.S. 1014 (1990).

47. For an insightful discussion of the friendship between the two Founders, see Adrienne Koch, *Jefferson and Madison: The Great Collaboration* (Oxford: Oxford Univ. Press, 1950).

48. A helpful comparison of the views of Jefferson and Madison on religious freedom is contained in McConnell, "The Origins and Historical Understanding," 1449–55.

49. Jefferson's restrictive conception of religious freedom is emphasized in David Little, "Thomas Jefferson's Religious Views and Their Influence on the Supreme Court's Interpretation of the First Amendment," *Catholic Univ. Law Review* 26 (1976): 57.

50. Stressing his training under Witherspoon, one scholar described Madison as "perhaps the most theologically knowledgeable president the nation ever had." Dreisbach, *Real Threat and Mere Shadow*, 136. The pietistic or evangelical position, espoused by Roger Williams, William Penn, and Isaac Backus, emphasized that God had appointed two distinct kinds of government—temporal and spiritual. Regarding "religious liberty as vital to authentic faith and the purity of the church," advocates of this position condemned governmental interference with religion and worked tirelessly against established churches. See Adams and Emmerich, *A Nation Dedicated to Religious Liberty*, 28.

51. See Dreisbach, *Real Threat and Mere Shadow*, 118–22.

52. Ibid., 149–57.

53. Alexander M. Bickel, *The Morality of Consent* (New Haven: Yale Univ. Press, 1975), 10–11.

54. See Richard B. Morris, "The Judeo-Christian Foundation of the American Political System," in Alley, *James Madison on Religious Liberty*, 112–13.

55. See Michael W. McConnell, "Trashing Natural Law," *New York Times*, 16 Aug. 1991, late edition, sec. A, p. 23.

56. See generally A. P. d'Entreves, *Natural Law: An Introduction to Legal Philosophy*, 2d rev. ed. (London: Hutchinson, 1970), and Edward S. Corwin, *The "Higher Law" Background of American Constitutional Law* (Ithaca: Cornell Univ. Press, 1955). For a leading work on the political and philosophical beliefs of the Founders, see Bernard Bailyn, *The Ideological Origins of the American Revolution* (Cambridge: Harvard Univ. Press, 1967).

57. This is my own distillation of natural law theory, derived largely from A. P. d'Entreves, *Natural Law*.

58. William Blackstone, *Commentaries on the Laws of England* (1778), in *The Sovereignty of the Law*, ed. Gareth Jones (Toronto: Univ. of Toronto Press, 1973), 18.

59. John Dickinson, "An Address to the Committee of Correspondence in Barbados" (1766), in *The Writings of John Dickinson*, ed. Paul L. Ford (Philadelphia: Memoirs of the Historical Society of Pennsylvania, 1895), 14: 261–62.

60. Alley, *James Madison on Religious Liberty*, 52.

61. 494 U.S. 872 (1990).

62. 374 U.S. 398 (1963).

63. *Employment Division* v. *Smith* 494 U.S. at 878–79. For a discussion of the secular

regulation rule, see David Manwaring, *Render Unto Caesar: The Flag-Salute Controversy* (Chicago: Univ. of Chicago Press, 1962), 48–55.

64. *Employment Division* v. *Smith,* 494 U.S. at 888.
65. Ibid., 886.
66. Ibid., 888 (emphasis in original).
67. Ibid., 891 (O'Connor, J., concurring).
68. See Douglas Laycock, "The Remnants of Free Exercise," *Supreme Court Review* (1990), 1; Michael W. McConnell, "Free Exercise Revisionism and the Smith Decision," *University of Chicago Law Review* 57 (1990): 1109.
69. Thomas Paine, *Rights of Man* (1791), in *The Writings of Thomas Paine,* ed. Moncure D. Conway (New York: G. Putnam's Sons, 1894), 2: 325.
70. *West Virginia Board of Education* v. *Barnette,* 319 U.S. 624, 638 (1943).

REFERENCES

Acker, William M., Jr. "Memorandum Opinion and Standing Rule for the Courtroom of William M. Acker, Jr." Unpublished opinion issued on 22 Aug. 1990 for the Northern District of the United States District Court of Alabama.

Adams, Charles F. *The Works of John Adams.* Vol. 9. Boston: Little, Brown, 1854.

Bickel, Alexander M. *The Morality of Consent.* New Haven: Yale Univ. Press, 1975.

Blackstone, William. *Commentaries on the Laws of England.* In *The Sovereignty of the Law,* ed. Gareth Jones. 1778. Rpt. Toronto: Univ. of Toronto Press, 1973.

Bork, Robert H. *The Tempting of America: The Political Seduction of the Law.* New York: Simon & Schuster, 1990.

Dickinson, John. "An Address to the Committee of Correspondence in Barbados." In *The Writings of John Dickinson.* Vol. 14, ed. Paul L. Ford. 1799. Rpt. Philadelphia: Memoirs of the Historical Society of Pennsylvania, 1895.

Dreisbach, Daniel L. *Real Threat and Mere Shadow: Religious Liberty and the First Amendment.* Westchester, Ill.: Crossway Books, 1987.

Fleet, Elizabeth, ed. "Madison's 'Detached Memoranda.'" *William and Mary Quarterly,* 3d ser. 3 (Oct. 1946): 534–68.

Howe, Mark DeWolfe. *The Garden and the Wilderness: Religion and Government in American Constitutional History.* Chicago: Univ. of Chicago Press, 1965.

Levy, Leonard W. *The Establishment Clause: Religion and the First Amendment.* New York: Macmillan, 1986.

Madison, James. Letter to Edward Livingston, 10 July 1822. In *The Writings of James Madison.* Vol. 9, ed. Gaillard Hunt. New York: G. P. Putnam's Sons, 1910.

————. "Memorial and Remonstrance Against Religious Assessments" (c. 20 June 1785). In *The Papers of James Madison*. Vol. 8, eds. William T. Hutchinson, William M. Rachal, et al. Chicago: Univ. of Chicago Press, 1962.

————. Speech in the Virginia Ratifying Convention (12 June 1788). In *The Debates in the Several State Conventions on the Adoption of the Federal Constitution*. Vol. 3, ed. Jonathan Elliott. 2d ed. 1836. Rpt. New York: Burt Franklin, 1888.

Meiklejohn, Alexander. "Educational Cooperation Between Church and State." *Law and Contemporary Problems* 14 (1949): 61–72.

Miller, Arthur S. "An Inquiry into the Relevance of the Intentions of the Founding Fathers, with Special Emphasis Upon the Doctrine of Separation of Powers." *Arkansas Law Review* 27 (1973): 583–602.

Morgan, Richard E. *The Supreme Court and Religion*. New York: Free Press, 1972.

Nowak, John E., Ronald D. Rotunda, and J. Nelson Young. *Constitutional Law*. 2d ed. Minneapolis: West Publishing, 1983.

Paine, Thomas. *Rights of Man*. In *The Writings of Thomas Paine*. Vol. 2, ed. Moncure D. Conway. New York: G. P. Putnam's Sons, 1894.

Sutherland, Arthur. "Historians, Lawyers, and 'Establishment of Religion.'" In *Religion and the Public Order*. Vol. 5, ed. Donald Giannella. Villanova, Pa.: Villanova Univ. Press, 1969.

Wright, Benjamin, ed. *The Federalist* No. 47. Cambridge: Harvard Univ. Press, 1961.

4 ‖ In Pursuit of Religious Freedom: Thomas Jefferson's Church-State Views Revisited

Daniel L. Dreisbach

In 1777 Thomas Jefferson drafted "A Bill for Establishing Religious Freedom," one of the most venerated political documents in American history. This was one measure in an ambitious revision of the laws of Virginia commenced following the political separation from England. The statute provided in its brief enabling clauses that

> no man shall be compelled to frequent or support any religious worship, place, or ministry whatsoever, nor shall be enforced, restrained, molested, or burthened in his body or goods, nor shall otherwise suffer on account of his religious opinions or belief; but that all men shall be free to profess, and by argument to maintain, their opinions in matters of religion, and that the same shall in no wise diminish, enlarge, or affect their civil capacities.[1]

The religious freedom bill is a passionate affirmation of intellectual and spiritual independence that, in many respects, resembles Jefferson's better-known Declaration of Independence.[2] "More than a statute," wrote Merrill D. Peterson, "it was an eloquent manifesto of the sanctity of the human mind and spirit."[3] James Madison grandly proclaimed that the bill's passage "extinguished for ever the ambitious hope of making laws for the human mind."[4]

The bill failed to gain passage when it was first introduced in the Virginia legislature in 1779. Despite its eloquence and the growing stature of its author, it proved too radical for the times.[5] By the mid-1780s, church-state issues had once again begun to agitate the public mind. In the autumn session of 1784, the Virginia legislature received numerous petitions requesting an assessment that would require all citizens to pay an annual tax for the support of teachers of the Christian religion. These petitions told of nations that had fallen because of the demise of religion and described the alarming decline of morals in the Commonwealth.[6]

Research for this article was supported by grants from the Virginia Historical Society and the Religion & Public Policy Research Fund.

Proponents of a general assessment, including George Washington and John Marshall, rallied behind the dominant personality in the legislature, Patrick Henry.[7] Henry supported legislation that would have imposed a modest property tax for the support of Christian clergymen.[8] James Madison, who opposed the measure, successfully moved to postpone final action on Henry's bill until the next legislative session in 1785.[9] In the interval, Madison labored diligently to mobilize opposition to the assessment, writing his celebrated *Memorial and Remonstrance Against Religious Assessments.*[10] The ground swell of anti-assessment sentiment[11]— orchestrated in part by Madison's "Remonstrance"—settled the fate of Henry's bill, which died quietly in committee after only brief consideration in the autumn of 1785.[12] Enthused by this victory, Madison brushed the dust off Jefferson's bill for religious freedom and guided it to passage in January 1786.[13]

The dramatic disestablishment struggle in revolutionary Virginia that culminated in the enactment of Jefferson's bill had a profound impact on church-state developments across the fledgling nation and arguably influenced the formulation of the First Amendment religion provisions. The religious freedom bill is, indeed, an eloquent expression of the author's devotion to religious liberty. Detached from its legislative and political context, however, it fails to capture Jefferson's versatile vision for church-state relations. The argument of this chapter is that the bill must be interpreted in light of Jefferson's complete legislative strategy for redefining church-state arrangements in Virginia. The religious freedom bill, in fact, was only the first of five consecutive bills in Virginia's revised code addressing issues of concern to organized religion. These bills, which were framed by Jefferson and sponsored by Madison in the Virginia legislature, provide critical qualifications of the scope and meaning of the "Bill for Establishing Religious Freedom" and give us a more accurate picture of Jefferson's church-state model. Taken together, they do not indicate a strict separationist arrangement; rather, they suggest a model that was intended to facilitate limited church-state cooperation in support of uninhibited religious belief and expression.

HISTORICAL AND JUDICIAL INTERPRETATIONS OF THE VIRGINIA STATUTE

Biographers of Jefferson and students of church-state relations in revolutionary Virginia have typically described the religious freedom bill as the culmination of

Jefferson's efforts to erect "an unbreachable wall of separation between Church and
State and make religious opinions forever private and sacrosanct from intrusion."[14]
Virginia historian Hamilton James Eckenrode viewed passage of the statute even
more broadly as the event that "marked the end of the conservative effort to check
and control the growth of democracy and the spread of liberal ideas."[15] The concepts enshrined in Jefferson's bill, it is frequently argued, found eventual expression
and ultimate influence in the subsequently enacted First Amendment religion
clauses.[16]

The United States Supreme Court has long relied on American history, especially the bitter disestablishment struggle in revolutionary Virginia, to inform its
interpretation of the First Amendment religion clauses.[17] Indeed, if there is one
constant in the confused arena of church-state law, it is that judges—regardless of
their legal opinion—consistently have appealed to history to buttress their respective interpretations of the religion clauses. As Justice Rutledge observed:

> No provision of the Constitution is more closely tied to or given content by its
> generating history than the religious clause of the First Amendment. It is at once
> the refined product and the terse summation of that history. The history includes
> not only Madison's authorship and the proceedings before the First Congress, but
> also the long and intensive struggle for religious freedom in America, more espe-
> cially in Virginia, of which the Amendment was the direct culmination. In the
> documents of the times, particularly of Madison, who was leader in the Virginia
> struggle before he became the Amendment's sponsor, but also in the writings of
> Jefferson and others and in the issues which engendered them is to be found irre-
> futable confirmation of the Amendment's sweeping content.[18]

It was not until the landmark case of *Everson* v. *Board of Education* (1947) that the
Supreme Court offered its first comprehensive interpretation of the constitutional
pronouncement on church-state relations. *Everson* was the "beginning of an impressive and influential body of [church-state] case law."[19] A divided Supreme
Court upheld the constitutionality of state reimbursements to parents for money
expended in the transportation of their children to and from parochial schools.
Despite its holding, the Court declared that the "First Amendment has erected a
wall between church and state [that] must be kept high and impregnable."[20]

More important than the holding itself was the separationist rhetoric used
lavishly in both majority and minority opinions and the Court's extensive reliance

on selected historical events and documents to buttress its broad construction of the First Amendment nonestablishment provision.[21] In defining the establishment clause, Justice Black, writing for a slender majority of five justices, declared: "Neither a state nor the Federal Government can set up a church. Neither can pass laws which aid one religion, aid all religions, or prefer one religion over another."[22] In even more sweeping terms, Justice Rutledge asserted in a minority opinion that the First Amendment's purpose was "to uproot" all religious establishments and "to create a complete and permanent separation of the spheres of religious activity and civil authority by comprehensively forbidding every form of public aid or support for religion."[23]

In their efforts to interpret the establishment clause, the *Everson* Court and virtually all subsequent courts have turned most frequently to the words and deeds of Jefferson and Madison, not only because they led the disestablishment struggle in their native Virginia but because their idea of the proper church-state arrangement is thought to be expressive of the purposes of the First Amendment.[24] In particular, the Supreme Court, as well as lower federal and state courts, have invoked Jefferson's "Bill for Establishing Religious Freedom" and Madison's "Memorial and Remonstrance" to inform their church-state pronouncements.[25]

These documents and the disestablishment movement in Virginia that inspired them, the justices have instructed, confirm that the two Virginians advocated a sweeping separation between church and state. In *Committee for Public Education and Religious Liberty* v. *Nyquist*, for example, Justice Powell recounted how the "debate over the relationship between Church and State" in Virginia—the controversy generated by Patrick Henry's general assessment plan in particular—inspired "Madison's Memorial and Remonstrance, recognized today as one of the cornerstones of the First Amendment's guarantee of government neutrality toward religion," which, in turn, set the stage for "Thomas Jefferson's Bill for Establishing Religious Freedom . . . [and] Virginia's first acknowledgement of the principle of total separation of Church and State."[26] Powell merely echoed the historical assertions of Justices Black and Rutledge in *Everson.*[27]

The modern Supreme Court, like most historians, has concluded that the struggle for religious liberty in revolutionary Virginia—Jefferson's religious freedom bill in particular—found equivalent expression in the subsequently enacted First Amendment religion clauses.[28] However, an inordinate reliance on Jefferson's celebrated bill, detached from its legislative context, misrepresents the versatile church-state model Jefferson envisioned for his native Commonwealth and the nation. Collectively, what the five religion bills from Virginia's revised code suggest is that Jefferson embraced a more accommodating view of church-state relations than the separationist model attributed to him in conventional judicial interpretations of his famous bill. Insofar as the Supreme Court has relied on an erroneous conception of Jefferson's church-state views to inform its First Amendment analysis, its legal pronouncements may lack analytical merit and historical validity.[29]

The legislative initiative that produced the revised code of Virginia, including Jefferson's celebrated bill and the succeeding four proposals addressing religious concerns, thus merits further historical scrutiny. Of particular importance is the collective impact of the five bills on conventional interpretations of Jefferson's vision for church-state relations.

THE REVISION OF THE LAWS OF VIRGINIA

Conventional interpretations of the "Bill for Establishing Religious Freedom" have mistaken Jefferson's overall model for church-state relations by taking his celebrated bill out of its proper legislative context. The bill was only one of 126 measures in a revision of the laws of Virginia prompted by the Commonwealth's political separation from England. The adoption of the Declaration of Independence on 4 July 1776 not only signaled political separation from the English Crown but severed the colonies' formal legal links with the mother country. Thus it seemed desirable, indeed necessary, to bring the laws of the individual colonies into conformity with republican principles and to strip the existing legal codes of remaining vestiges of monarchical rule.[30]

For many in the colonies, political independence was the end toward which the American "rebellion" was directed; but for Jefferson and his more forward looking colleagues, it was only the beginning.[31] "When I left Congress, in '76," Jefferson wrote in his *Autobiography*, "it was in the persuasion that our whole code must be reviewed, adapted to our republican form of government; and . . . it should be corrected, in all its parts, with a single eye to reason, and the good of those for whose government it was framed."[32] The patriots' objectives, Jefferson believed, could not be counted accomplished until the newly independent, fledgling states were placed on republican legal foundations. Accordingly, on 12 October 1776, Jefferson introduced a proposal in the Virginia legislature to revise the Commonwealth's legal code,[33] which passed on 26 October.[34] The legislature appointed a committee of prominent Virginians, chaired by Jefferson, to "revise, alter, amend, repeal, or introduce all or any of the said laws" of the Commonwealth.[35] In addition to Jefferson, the committee appointed on 5 November 1776, included Edmund Pendleton, George Wythe, George Mason and Thomas Ludwell Lee.[36]

Despite this formidable brain trust, it was soon apparent that the thirty three year-old Jefferson would assume the lion's share of the work in framing the revised code. Jefferson recounted in his *Autobiography* that when the committee

> proceeded to the distribution of the work, Mr. Mason excused himself, as, being no lawyer, he felt himself unqualified for the work, and he resigned soon after. Mr. Lee excused himself on the same ground, and died, indeed, in a short time. The other two gentlemen, therefore, and myself divided the work among us.[37]

Much of the work initially assigned to Lee and Mason eventually fell to Jefferson, and Pendleton's contributions were relatively minor.[38] Clearly, no one took a more prominent role in the legal reforms than Jefferson, and, in the final analysis, no one had more influence on Virginia law.[39]

The Committee of Revisors convened in Fredericksburg on 13 January 1777 to set forth their objectives and distribute the work among themselves. They first considered "whether [they] should propose to abolish the whole existing system of laws, and prepare a new and complete Institute, or preserve the general system, and only modify it to the present state of things."[40] Ironically, Jefferson—never one to dodge a momentous challenge such as composing a "new Institute, like those of Justinian and Bracton, or that of Blackstone"[41]—advocated alterations only, whereas the usually more conservative Pendleton pressed for sweeping changes.[42] Jefferson's view prevailed, largely because a radical restructuring of the code would undoubtedly have proven to be an "arduous undertaking," requiring "vast research, . . . great consideration and judgment" and would, in all probability, have exceeded the committee's legislative mandate.[43]

According to Jefferson's account, the revised code—especially the bills abolishing the laws of entail and primogeniture and promoting general education and religious freedom—was purposed to structure "a system by which every fibre would be eradicated of ancient or future aristocracy; and a foundation laid for a government truly republican."[44] A further objective, in Jefferson's words, was "to leave out everything obsolete or improper, insert what was wanting, and reduce the whole [code] within as moderate a compass as it would bear, and to the plain language of common sense, divested of the verbiage, the barbarous tautologies and redundancies which render the British statutes unintelligible."[45] After agreeing to a general plan of action, the committee members distributed the work among themselves.[46] Jefferson, according to his biographer Dumas Malone, specifically assumed responsibility for drafting the bills pertaining to crimes and punishment, descents, education, and religion.[47]

Two years later, in February 1779, Wythe and Jefferson reconvened in Williamsburg. Meeting on a daily basis, they examined drafts of the revised code "sentence by sentence, scrutinizing and amending, until [they] had agreed on the whole."[48] On 18 June 1779, the speaker laid before the House of Delegates a report on the revisal submitted by Jefferson (who recently had been elevated to the governor's office) and Wythe.[49] The revisors had prepared 126 bills, the titles of which were included in an accompanying catalog.[50] Several bills thought to have immediate application were extracted from the revised code and promptly enacted. Most of the revisal, however, was shelved for the next half decade. The uncertainties and pressures of war during this period distracted the legislators from considering the revisal as a whole.

On 31 October 1785, Madison revived Jefferson's dream of seeing the revised code enacted as a whole when he introduced in the Virginia legislature 118 of the bills contained in the *Report of the Revisors* that had not yet been enacted into law.[51] Thirty-five bills were adopted at this session of the legislature and another 23 were eventually passed in the autumn 1786 session.[52] It became apparent, however, that despite Madison's commitment to the revisal and Jefferson's desire to see the code enacted as whole, the legislature had no intention of acting on it as a united body of law. Instead, select bills were considered and voted upon in a piecemeal fashion.

In the autumn of 1785, Jefferson was the American minister in France. Nevertheless, he remained influential in the legislative strategy to enact these bills, with James Madison acting as the chief sponsor. By the mid-1780s, Madison had become a respected and influential figure in the legislature, and so successful was his handling of the revised code that under his legislative guidance nearly half of the bills were eventually enacted without significant amendment.

The most celebrated bill in the revisal, Jefferson's "Bill for Establishing Religious Freedom," was debated in the legislature in December 1785 and signed into law in January 1786.[53] This was Bill No. 82 of the revised code and only the first of five consecutive bills addressing religious concerns. Jefferson himself assumed responsibility for drafting the bills dealing with religious issues. Taken as a whole, these five bills do not make a convincing argument for the modern Supreme Court's construction of a "high and impregnable" wall of separation between church and state.[54] Rather, they suggest a flexible church-state model that fosters cooperation between religious interests and the civil government and proscribes governmental interference with freedom of religious beliefs. In short, they illustrate that Jefferson's ultimate objective was less separation of church and state than the fullest possible expression of religious belief and opinion.

JEFFERSON'S FIVE RELIGION BILLS

Bill No. 82

Bill No. 82 of the revisal, the Virginia "Statute for Establishing Religious Freedom,"[55] is clearly one of the most profound and influential documents in American political history.[56] Jefferson counted it supreme among his contributions to the Commonwealth and the nation, selecting his authorship of the statute as one of three achievements he wanted memorialized on his gravestone.[57] The document is passionate and artfully crafted, and for more than two centuries has proven to be a manifesto for intellectual freedom, not only in Virginia but across the nation and around the world.[58] The arguments advanced in the bill have been woven into the fabric of American political thought, and in the course of time the conventional interpretation of the bill has been adopted as the orthodox principle of American church-state relations.[59]

The prevailing interpretation of Bill No. 82, as previously indicated, is that in its "sweeping language Jefferson sought to create an unbreachable wall of separation between Church and State and make religious opinions forever private and sacrosanct from intrusion."[60] The bill, however, did not expressly advocate a sweeping separation between religion and the state. Indeed, as Harvard legal historian Mark DeWolfe Howe emphasized, Bill No. 82 did not "in its enacting clauses explicitly prohibit establishment."[61] Rather, Jefferson's bill, drawing inspiration from Locke's *A Letter Concerning Toleration*,[62] was more narrowly drawn to terminate compelled religious attendance or observance and remove penalties for dissenters who publicly expressed their religious opinions.

The Virginia statute for religious freedom consists of three sections. The first is the eloquent preamble (four times the length of the act itself), which sets forth in passionate terms the following reasons for the measure:[63] First, "Almighty God hath created the mind free" and willed "that free it shall remain."[64] Jefferson maintained that the mind of man was, by the intrinsic free-ranging nature and individual variety deliberately created in it by God, not intended to be coerced into intellectual conformity. "The holy author of our religion, who being lord both of body and mind," he argued, chose that religion should be propagated by reason and not by coercion.[65] Second, "legislators and rulers, civil as well as ecclesiastical," have impiously "assumed dominion over the faith of others," and because of their own fallibility and use of coercion have "established and maintained false religions over the greatest part of the world."[66] Third, it is "sinful and tyrannical" to compel a man to support a religion "which he disbelieves and abhors."[67] It is also an infringement on his freedom of choice to force him to support a "teacher of his own religious persuasion," because this inhibits the free encouragement of the minister whose moral pattern and righteousness the citizen finds most persuasive and worthy of support.[68] Fourth, "civil rights have no dependance on our religious opinions, any more than our opinions in physics or geometry"; and, therefore, imposing religious qualifications for civil office deprives the citizen of his "natural right" and tends to corrupt religion by bribery to obtain purely external conformity.[69] Fifth, it is undesirable to use civil magistrates to suppress the propagation of opinions and principles, even of allegedly false tenets, because "truth is great and . . . has nothing to fear from the conflict" with error "unless by human interposition disarmed of her natural weapons, free argument and debate."[70] Jefferson concluded that "it is time enough" for officers of civil government "to interfere when principles break out into overt acts against peace and good order."[71]

The statute's second section, the operative portion, enacted the following provisions: In the Commonwealth of Virginia no man shall (1) be compelled by civil government to attend or support any religious worship, place or ministry, nor (2) be punished or restrained by the Commonwealth on account of his religious beliefs; but, on the contrary, every man shall (3) be free to profess and contend for his religious beliefs, and (4) such activity shall in no way affect his civil capacities.[72]

The statute's third, and final, section acknowledged that any subsequent legislature has the authority to repeal the statute, but declared that if it does so, such action will be an infringement of natural rights.[73] "In the corpus of Jefferson's work," one commentator observed, "there is no equal in terms of binding future generations."[74]

Significantly, Jefferson's statute was not neutral toward religion.[75] The existence of "Almighty God" who "hath created the mind free" and willed "that free it shall remain,"[76] he reasoned, provided the rationale for governmental recognition of religious freedom.[77] The statute, which presumed a "Creator" involved in human affairs,[78] fell short of advocating an absolute principle that civil government and religion may never interact in a cooperative manner. This statutory recognition of the deity and Jefferson's assertion that religious liberty is derived from the "plan of the holy author of our religion"[79] offends many strict separationists today and arguably renders the measure constitutionally suspect under prevailing establishment clause analysis.[80] As one modern jurist opined, "If all endorsement by the state of Christian beliefs is forbidden, then any state that today enacted Jefferson's Bill for Establishing Religious Freedom would be violating the Establishment Clause!"[81] Jefferson's bill did not advocate, in the modern sense at least, a strict separation between religion and civil government, nor was it a blueprint for a wholly secular state. It was a bold and eloquent affirmation of the individual's right to worship God, or not, according to the dictates of conscience, free from governmental interference or discrimination.

Bill No. 83

The second consecutive revised bill of importance to the religious establishment, Bill No. 83, was entitled "A Bill for Saving the Property of the Church Heretofore by Law Established."[82] Although never formally enacted,[83] Bill No. 83, in the words of a nineteenth-century biographer of Jefferson, "somewhat mitigated" the radical perception of Bill No. 82 held by some conservative backers of the established church.[84]

The bill, in essential parts, reserved to members of the Anglican church all property in its legal possession. Legal title and control of church assets, however, were to be transferred from the formal vestries to resident parish members who would be obligated to use the resources to support the ministry, but would be the sole judges of the conditions of such application. "This bill," according to one nineteenth-century commentator, "seems to have aimed to steer between a violation of vested rights, and using property for other purposes voluntarily devoted to religious objects by its owners—and the arming of a hierarchical body with perpetual power to use a fund contributed by *all* denominations for the exclusive support of a particular *class of tenets*."[85]

The purpose of Bill No. 83 was to protect the property interests of the Anglican church, which had recently lost its tax subsidies,[86] and to ensure that the church could use its resources to meet any outstanding contractual obligations.

Reflecting democratic reforms of the time, the bill, in effect, shifted control of church assets from formal, and often self-serving and absentee, vestries to resident parish members, thus further weakening the established ecclesiastical hierarchy. In this sense, the measure may have encouraged resident parishioners to take a more active role in local church governance and attendant religious concerns. Nonetheless, the measure sought specifically to preserve the property interests of the "church heretofore by law established." Insofar as the bill benefited one sect exclusively, it would arguably violate the *Everson* Court's prohibition on "laws which aid one religion, aid all religions, or prefer one religion over another."[87] Viewed in this light, Bill No. 83 is difficult to reconcile with a strict separationist interpretation of Bill No. 82 or the First Amendment.

Bill No. 84

On 31 October 1785, Madison introduced the third consecutive revised bill dealing with religion, which was entitled "A Bill for Punishing Disturbers of Religious Worship and Sabbath Breakers."[88] The evidence indicates that this bill, enacted on 27 November 1786 in a slightly amended form, also was penned by Jefferson.[89]

The bill, in essential parts, exempted clergymen from being arrested while conducting religious services in any place of worship.[90] The measure also authorized severe punishments, including imprisonment and amercement, for disturbers of public worship or citizens laboring on Sunday. The bill's third paragraph, which undoubtedly offends modern judicial sensibilities, stated:

> If any person on Sunday shall himself be found labouring at his own or any other trade or calling, or shall employ his apprentices, servants or slaves in labour, or other business, except it be in the ordinary houshold [*sic*] offices of daily necessity, or other work of necessity or charity, he shall forfeit the sum of ten shillings for every such offence, deeming every apprentice, servant, or slave so employed, and every day he shall be so employed as constituting a distinct offence.[91]

The bill was designed to benefit adherents of all denominations by preserving the sanctity of religious worship. It did not, however, expressly require church attendance in order to avoid punishment for Sabbath breaking.

Bill No. 84 was not merely a "blue law." Rather, it was an affirmation of civil government's responsibility to protect the formal act of worship.[92] It provided that a "minister of the gospel" shall not be arrested while performing a religious meeting, and services of divine worship shall not be disrupted by private citizens or interrupted by public officials. Civil government, in short, was foreclosed from disturbing citizens in the peaceful expression of their religious beliefs. Jefferson, it seems, believed that a society's commitment to religious freedom was served when civil government took affirmative steps to protect citizens from external disruptions during the act of worship.

The title of Bill No. 84 unequivocally states that the measure was written to punish individuals who worked on the Sabbath.[93] The religious intent of the bill is clear, made obvious by use of the word *Sabbath,* as compared with a religiously neutral term such as *Sunday.* The word *Sabbath* reflects the Judeo-Christian tradition of commemorating the Lord's "day of rest"[94] and the fourth commandment requiring that that day be kept free from secular defilement.[95] Jefferson's choice of *Sabbath* suggests that the measure was inspired by religious concerns, as opposed to wholly neutral purposes such as promoting recreation and rest from secular employment.[96] In short, there is no indication that the sponsors of this legislation advanced the bill for the secular purpose of lessening the burdens on exploited laborers, in the same way progressive social legislation earlier this century limited the number or working hours in a day.[97]

Bill No. 84 and Sunday closing laws in general arguably discriminate against individuals who choose not to preserve the sanctity of the "day of rest" observed by practitioners of the Christian faith.[98] Acknowledgment of the Christian Sabbath in the official calendar and its preservation by law conflicts with a separationist ban on state support for organized religion or its activities. Modern advocates of church-state separation have criticized Sunday legislation less restrictive than Bill No. 84 as a breach in the "wall of separation."

Bill No. 84, however, is consistent with Jefferson's life-long commitment to protecting the right of citizens to express their religious beliefs and opinions peacefully. His principal objective was to preserve the sanctity of worship and freedom of religious expression by deterring those who might seek to disrupt such activities. Bill No. 84 also suggests that Jefferson's desire to separate church and state, compelling though it may have been, was merely a means of achieving the fullest possible freedom of religious expression. If religious liberty was realized in its richest sense through cooperation between the state and the church, then Jefferson, it would seem, endorsed such a limited union.

Bill No. 85

The fourth in the series of five bills addressing religious concerns was a proposal entitled "A Bill for Appointing Days of Public Fasting and Thanksgiving."[99] This legislation, like the preceding bills, apparently was drafted by Jefferson and introduced in the Virginia legislature by Madison on 31 October 1785.[100]

Bill No. 85 authorized the governor or chief magistrate of the Commonwealth, with the advice of the council, to designate days for thanksgiving and fasting and to notify the public by proclamation. Far from simply granting the governor power to appoint "days of public fasting and humiliation, or thanksgiving," the bill issued the following punitive provision:

> Every minister of the gospel shall on each day so to be appointed, attend and perform divine service and preach a sermon, or discourse, suited to the occasion, in his church, on pain of forfeiting fifty pounds for every failure, not having a reasonable excuse.[101]

Although Bill No. 85 was never enacted, it was sponsored by Madison, and a surviving manuscript copy of the bill bears a notation in the "clerk's hand" indicating that the bill was "endorsed" by Thomas Jefferson.[102] The final disposition of this proposal is unimportant to the present discussion. The relevant consideration here is that Jefferson and Madison jointly sponsored a bill that is difficult to reconcile with the strict separationist church-state model frequently attributed to Jefferson.[103] Bill No. 85 graphically illustrates how extensive judicial reliance on the Virginia statute for religious freedom—to the exclusion of Jefferson and Madison's other legislative contributions to the revisal—has misrepresented the views of the two Virginians on church-state relations.

Another declaration of Jefferson's pertaining to thanksgiving day proclamations is often cited by strict separationist commentators as confirmation of his separationist predilection. This, too, has mistaken his views on such proclamations. As president of the United States, Jefferson steadfastly refused to declare a national day of fasting and thanksgiving. In a celebrated letter to the Danbury Baptist Association of Connecticut, which had requested such a proclamation, he wrote:

> Believing with you that religion is a matter which lies solely between man and his God, that he owes account to none other for his faith or his worship, that the legislative powers of government reach actions only, and not opinions, I contemplate with sovereign reverence that act of the whole American people which declared

that their legislature should "make no law respecting an establishment of religion, or prohibiting the free exercise thereof," thus building a wall of separation between Church and State.[104]

Jefferson thereby erected the famous "wall of separation" that has become a persistent theme of modern church-state analyses.[105] Indeed, the *Everson* Court indicated that the wall metaphor informed its interpretation of the establishment clause.[106]

Although Jefferson's wall metaphor is frequently invoked by the modern judiciary, his "Bill for Appointing Days of Public Fasting and Thanksgiving" is largely ignored. The *Everson* Court either was unaware of or disregarded Jefferson and Madison's joint sponsorship of Bill No. 85—a significant omission given the Court's reliance on Bill No. 82 and the Danbury letter.[107] Reference to Bill No. 85, authorizing the official designation of days for religious observances, arguably tempers the rhetoric of Bill No. 82 and undermines the Court's contention that the public actions of Jefferson and Madison substantiate the strict separationist interpretation of the religion clauses.

Because Bill No. 85 was written more than a decade before the religion clauses were added to the federal Constitution, one could argue that Jefferson's sponsorship of the bill is less relevant to his understanding of the First Amendment than the Danbury letter, which was written long after the First Amendment and which purports to interpret the religion clauses. Although this argument has merit from a chronological perspective, one cannot ignore the fact that the Supreme Court has stated that the words and acts of Jefferson and Madison in their native Virginia, prior to the drafting of the First Amendment, are expressive of the purposes of the religion clauses and give content and meaning to the First Amendment. If the religious freedom bill, written long before the First Amendment, is thought to have influenced the original understanding of the religion clauses, it seems plausible that Bill No. 85, written contemporaneously with Bill No. 82, also may have modestly informed the understanding of church-state relations in the early Republic. In any case, Bill No. 85 illustrates that Jefferson and Madison, contrary to many strict separationists, did not consistently advocate absolute separation throughout their public careers.[108]

In marked contrast to the separationist imagery of the Danbury letter, in the colonial and state government settings Jefferson demonstrated an accommodationist inclination on the religious proclamation issue. For example, as a member of the

House of Burgesses, on 24 May 1774, he participated in drafting and enacting a resolution designating a "Day of Fasting, Humiliation, and Prayer."[109] Jefferson recounted in his *Autobiography:*

> We were under conviction of the necessity of arousing our people from the leth-
> argy into which they had fallen, as to passing events [the Boston port bill]; and
> thought that the appointment of a day of general fasting and prayer would be most
> likely to call up and alarm their attention. . . . [W]e cooked up a resolution . . . for
> appointing the 1st day of June, on which the portbill was to commence, for a day
> of fasting, humiliation, and prayer, to implore Heaven to avert from us the evils of
> civil war, to inspire us with firmness in support of our rights, and to turn the
> hearts of the King and Parliament to moderation and justice.[110]

Jefferson seemed pleased with this accommodation between religion and the state in May 1774 through a "cooked up" religious proclamation cynically issued to excite a public reaction against England. This political use of a solemn religious act took place only a few years before he wrote "A Bill for Establishing Religious Free-dom."[111] Moreover, in 1779, when Jefferson was governor of Virginia, he issued a proclamation decreeing a day "of publick and solemn thanksgiving and prayer to Almighty God."[112] This proclamation was issued after Jefferson had written Bill No. 82. The 1774 and 1779 religious proclamations, as well as Bill No. 85, did not figure in the *Everson* Court's examination of Jefferson's church-state views.

A major question remains: How is Jefferson's record in Virginia to be recon-ciled with the Danbury letter? A careful study of Jefferson's actions throughout his public career suggests that he believed, as a matter of federalism, the national government should avoid exercising authority in religious matters, whereas state governments were free to accommodate religious exercises as they saw fit.[113] A perusal of the Danbury letter reveals that Jefferson was not addressing the broader issue of separation of religion and civil government (both federal and state); rather, he was examining the narrower issue of whether a separation between the entire federal government and religion was required by the First Amendment. The ques-tion presented, in other words, concerned whether the First Amendment restricted only the Congress in matters respecting an establishment of religion, or whether the prohibition extended to the coequal branches of the federal government, thereby denying the executive branch the prerogative to issue religious proclamations.

The Danbury letter specifically placed the wall of separation between the federal regime and ecclesiastical establishments, not between religion and all civil government. This interpretation is buttressed by Jefferson's second inaugural address:

> In matters of religion, I have considered that its free exercise is placed by the constitution independent of the powers of the general [federal] government. I have therefore undertaken, on no occasion, to prescribe the religious exercises suited to it; but have left them, as the constitution found them, under the direction and discipline of State or Church authorities acknowledged by the several religious societies.[114]

Jefferson concluded that although state governments had the authority to act on matters pertaining to religion, such power was denied the entire federal regime, including the executive branch. Accordingly, Jefferson would have seen no contradiction between authoring a religious proclamation to be issued by state authorities and refusing to issue a similar proclamation as the federal chief executive.[115]

Jefferson's commitment to protecting the public's recognition and expression of religious beliefs apparently encompassed statutory authorization for state representatives to designate days for religious observances and to sanction such observances in the official calendar. Bills No. 84 and 85, taken together, illustrate a church–state model wherein the church, although separated institutionally from civil government, could unite its mission with the state to encourage "religious morality" in society[116] and the free and public expression of religious beliefs. Jefferson's notion of church–state separation was flexible and could be relaxed where cooperation between church and state fostered uninhibited religious expression, including public expression through official religious proclamations. These two bills were no less consistent with Jefferson's church–state model than the principles outlined in his celebrated statute for religious freedom.

Bill No. 86

The last of the five consecutive bills touching upon a religious concern was entitled "A Bill Annulling Marriages Prohibited by the Levitical Law, and Appointing the Mode of Solemnizing Lawful Marriage."[117] As the title indicates, the bill is pertinent to the present discussion in that it ostensibly enacted biblical law by reference:

> Be it enacted by the General Assembly, that marriages prohibited by the Levitical law shall be null; and persons marrying contrary to that prohibition, and cohabiting

as man and wife, convicted thereof in the General Court, shall be amerced, from time to time, until they separate.[118]

This bill was presented to the legislature by Madison on 31 October 1785, along with the preceding four bills.[119] Bill No. 86 passed the second reading in the legislature, but no final action was taken on it.[120]

The bill required couples wishing to live together as man and wife to obtain a marriage license and declare marriage vows in the presence of witnesses. Despite its reference to the Pentateuch, the bill significantly omitted any requirement that marriage ceremonies be performed under ecclesiastical authority. The exclusive authority of clergy in the established church to perform legally sanctioned marriages had been a source of bitter criticism in colonial and revolutionary Virginia from the rapidly growing nonconformist (and unlicensed) religious sects. In this sense, the bill may have further weakened the disintegrating monopoly formerly held by the officially established church.

The union of biblical authority and the reformed legal code of Virginia is significant in the light of modern establishment clause jurisprudence. The judiciary, in recent years, has warned of the dangers of a close identification or "symbolic union" of the powers of civil government with religious institutions. The Supreme Court has counseled that if such an identification conveys a message of government endorsement or disapproval of religion, a core purpose of the nonestablishment provision has been violated.[121] The adoption of biblical law by reference in the revised code represents at least a "symbolic union" of religion and the state that the Supreme Court today arguably would find unconstitutional.[122]

A NEW PERSPECTIVE ON JEFFERSON'S CHURCH-STATE VIEWS

A perusal of the existing scholarship confirms that most historians of revolutionary Virginia and the First Amendment, as well as biographers of Jefferson, have neglected Jefferson's role in framing Bills No. 83 to 86 of the revised code.[123] They have, instead, focused on Bill No. 82 and the wall of separation Jefferson constructed in the Danbury letter. Similarly, although commentators have devoted considerable attention to Madison's legislative sponsorship of Bill No. 82, they have overlooked the fact that Madison, acting in concert with Jefferson, introduced in the Virginia legislature Jefferson's bills for punishing "disturbers of religious worship and Sabbath breakers" and for "appointing days of public fasting and thanksgiving."

The paucity of comment on Bills No. 83 to 86 by students of Jefferson and his times is interesting. Justice Rutledge's *Everson* opinion reveals that the Court knew the legislative history of the revised code and Jefferson's contribution to it as "chairman of the revising committee and chief draftsman."[124] Nonetheless, the Court declined to examine Bill No. 82 in its full legislative context. At least two general questions are raised by this pattern of omission. First, why have so many commentaries on Bill No. 82 examined the measure without reference to Bills No. 83 to 86? Second, are there unifying principles or themes of Jefferson's church-state views that offer a coherent framework for interpreting the five revised bills addressing religious concerns?

There is no dispute that Bill No. 82 is the preeminent of the five bills discussed here and deserves the attention it has received. Jefferson clearly considered the measure the most important of the proposals in the revised code. Moreover, Jefferson counted the struggle for religious freedom in Virginia—which inspired Bill No. 82—among the severest contests of his public life.[125] These facts alone may account for the attention afforded Bill No. 82, to the near exclusion of the four succeeding measures.

Another, more uncomfortable, explanation concerns the inclination of modern commentators to revise the Jefferson image to serve contemporary political objectives or conform to modern ideals. As architect of the wall of separation and author of Bill No. 82, Jefferson "appears most congenial to modern eyes. It is here," an admiring biographer proclaims, "that he takes his rightful position with the great liberating influences of all time."[126] This flattering perception of Jefferson may explain, in part, why many commentators have been unwilling to challenge the conventional view of Jefferson and Madison as libertarian champions of strict separation between church and state. Traditional portrayals of the two Virginians are inconsistent with their sponsorship of bills that imposed penalties on "disturbers of religious worship," "Sabbath breakers," and "ministers of the gospel" who failed to perform services on days appointed for fasting and thanksgiving. Accordingly, the tendency is great to disregard facts that conflict with, or at least complicate, modern idealizations of Jefferson.[127]

A few historians have acknowledged that, taken together, the revised bills addressing religious concerns present a more relaxed model of church-state relations than that proposed by modern proponents of the Jeffersonian wall. Healey, for example, argues that Bills No. 84 and 85 expose the myth that after Jefferson wrote the "Bill for Establishing Religious Freedom," he disavowed all wedding of church and state and espoused the "most rigid separation" between civil and ecclesiastical institutions.[128] Similarly, Gurley concludes that "Jefferson, as proved by his actions, did not hold to such a rigid view of complete separation of Church and State as some modern secularists have read into his famous 'wall of separation' metaphor."[129]

Many modern commentators, however, have disregarded Jefferson's complete work on the revised code, despite the fact that many studies devote considerable attention to Bill No. 82. For example, in his acclaimed book *The First Liberty: Religion and the American Republic* (1986), Miller devotes nearly seventy-five pages to a detailed examination of "A Bill for Establishing Religious Freedom." He writes eloquently of the bill as the embodiment of truth, reason, and civilization. He acknowledges that the "same Assembly that passed Jefferson's religious liberty bill also passed a statute requiring the observance of Sunday as a day of rest" (Bill No. 84).[130] However, Miller reflects briefly on Bill No. 84 not to place Jefferson's church-state views in a context broader than that suggested by reference to Bill No. 82 alone but to illustrate that despite passage of Jefferson's religious freedom bill in 1786, enlightened views on church-state separation did not yet prevail in the Virginia legislature. In other words, Bill No. 84, in Miller's opinion, was the work of a reactionary remnant in the legislature. He was apparently unaware that the bill punishing Sabbath breakers was not simply the product of reactionary elements in the legislature, but emanated from Jefferson himself.

The most significant question raised by Bills No. 83 to 86 concerns their relation to Jefferson's overall vision for church-state relations. The bills reflect a church-state arrangement seemingly inconsistent with the strict separationist model frequently attributed to Jefferson. What are the unifying principles or themes of Jefferson's church-state views that may provide a coherent framework in which to interpret these revised bills?

As a preliminary consideration, one could argue that Bills No. 83 to 86 are merely aberrations in Jefferson's otherwise constant devotion to the principle of complete independence of religion and civil government and do not reflect Jefferson's mature thinking on church-state relations as set forth in Bill No. 82 and the Danbury letter. Some commentators have suggested that Jefferson and Madison reluctantly sponsored accommodationist bills in the revisal they did not wholly endorse, perhaps to garner legislative backing for the separationist agenda they enthusiastically supported.[131] True, both Jefferson and Madison were consummate politicians skilled in the gentle art of compromise and coalition building, which often necessitates sacrificing stated positions to secure greater objectives, bolster coalitions, or advance future political objectives.[132] It is difficult to accept, however, that a principled Jefferson or Madison would have acceded to a statutory regime antithetical to the sweeping separation between church and state they purportedly embraced.[133] Political compromises on such vital issues concerning church-state arrangements in the Commonwealth would have been out of character for both Jefferson and Madison, whose passionate devotion and adherence to principle on church-state matters are well known.[134]

There are recurring principles and themes in Jefferson's political thought that offer explanations for some apparent inconsistencies in his church-state views. For example, a persistent theme of Jefferson's pronouncements on church-state relations is a commitment to the principle of federalism. The First Amendment prohibited the federal government from making laws respecting an establishment of religion or abridging civil and religious liberties, but the states reserved competent jurisdiction in such matters. Accordingly, although Jefferson thought government-sponsored activities and laws fostering religion at the federal level (such as designating days for public fasting and thanksgiving) were unconstitutional, he saw no contradiction in permitting or even encouraging such practices at the state level.[135] Limited state cooperation with religious institutions, Jefferson believed, was desirable if it advanced freedom of religious belief and expression. Jefferson's church-state views, especially the Danbury letter, have been frequently misunderstood by commentators who fail to comprehend that his wall of separation was less an instrument for a general separation of religious influences from all civil institutions than an affirmation of the principle of federalism.

The central pillar of Jefferson's church-state model and the unifying theme of Bills No. 82 to 86 is an unflagging devotion to freedom of religious belief and expression. Separation of church and state was not an end in itself; rather, it was a means toward achieving religious freedom. If free and uninhibited religious exercise was fostered through a limited interaction between church and state, Jefferson endorsed such a cooperative arrangement. The wall he constructed was not between religion and civil government generally, but between religious freedom and the powers of the general government.

Jefferson's wall was intended to foster an environment in which freedom of religious belief and expression could flourish. His driving motivation was to place the rights of conscience beyond the control of men and statist institutions. Freedom of opinion, he believed, was violated by the establishment of a specific church. Whenever the state enforced belief in doctrine, it also burdened true religion, Jefferson thought. And whenever the church relied on civil government for financial support, it tended to become a parasite on society. Thus, Jefferson believed that state churches, as a rule, corrupted civil government and religion, inhibited the emergence of truth by discouraging competition in the marketplace of ideas, and, as far as he could tell, brought no improvement in the morals of society. No concept, therefore, better communicated his personal idea of what was best for religion and best for society than the graphic wall metaphor.

True, Jefferson viewed the concepts of religious freedom and church-state separation as dependent principles. Religious freedom could not endure, he thought, as long as civil government was party to or adopted a specific religious dogma; and government could not disengage itself from sectarian quarrels except in a milieu of social and intellectual freedom. Therefore, Jefferson believed an institutional separation of church and state was the preferred means of achieving religious freedom.[136] But the wall was only useful insofar as it advanced the end of religious freedom. If that end was best served by a limited, strategic union of church and state, Jefferson, it seems, was willing to breach the wall.

CONCLUSION

Jefferson has cast a long shadow across the nation's political landscape. Indeed, few figures have had a greater impact on American political thought. The First Amendment pronouncements on church-state relations are, perhaps, the most innovative features of the American experiment, and few dispute they reflect Jefferson's genius. His wall metaphor is an enduring theme of modern church-state law, and the ideas expounded in the "Bill for Establishing Religious Freedom" have been woven into the fabric of American thought.

This chapter does not argue that the religious freedom bill inaccurately represents Jefferson's church-state views, nor does it suggest that Bill No. 82 is undeserving of its honored reputation in American political thought. Rather, it argues that Jefferson's imprint on Bills No. 83 to 86 modifies conventional interpretations of Bill No. 82 and qualifies the strict separationist church-state model the *Everson* opinions attributed to Jefferson. Near exclusive reliance on Bill No. 82 to illustrate Jefferson's vision for American church-state relations has distorted the historical understanding of the Jeffersonian model for church-state relations.

For a century and a half, the Jefferson image has been shaped and reshaped to serve contemporary political objectives or to conform to modern ideals.[137] The record of church-state relations in revolutionary Virginia, given the Supreme Court's continuing reliance on this history to inform First Amendment doctrine, is similarly susceptible to manipulation by "law office historians"[138] and ideologues with partisan goals. The gloss, unfortunately, often obscures the true historical Jefferson and his contribution to church-state developments in the Commonwealth and the nation. The Supreme Court's failure to reference Bills No. 83 to 86, despite its extensive reliance on Bill No. 82, calls into question the legitimacy of its selective use of history to inform legal doctrine. "By superficial and purposive interpretations of the past," Howe has lamented, "the Court has dishonored the arts of the historian and degraded the talents of the lawyer."[139]

The judiciary, perhaps, has embarked on a misguided search for consistency in Jefferson's church-state views. Jefferson never endeavored to articulate a comprehensive, systematic theory of American church-state relations, although he had much to say on the subject. Moreover, his public declarations and private ruminations over a long career are not free of contradiction, as is arguably illustrated by his contributions to the revisal. Yet a constant theme of devotion to freedom of conscience in religious belief emerges from Jefferson's public life. The wall of separation Jefferson espoused was not so much an end in itself as it was a means toward achieving the end of religious freedom, broadly defined.[140] Too often students of Jefferson have viewed the wall in isolation, separated from the liberty it was intended to engender. Jefferson and Madison jointly sponsored five bills in Virginia's revised code that collectively demonstrate that neither man believed, in practice, in a high and impregnable wall of separation between church and state. These bills suggest that both men endeavored to protect and encourage public and private expressions of religious belief. True, they objected to the establishment of an official church and to state practices infringing on religious freedom, such as compelled tax support for teachers of an officially preferred religion. The wall, however, was never meant to effect a complete and absolute separation between church and state prohibiting all religious influence in state-sponsored activities and laws.

Jefferson's chief aim was to foster freedom of religious expression, and if that objective was best served through statutory cooperation between church and state, he appeared willing to endorse it. To Jefferson, religious liberty meant that the civil authority must refrain from interfering with an individual's religion except to protect the individual in the enjoyment of the right to worship God, or not, according to the dictates of one's conscience.

NOTES

1. William Waller Hening, ed., *The Statutes at Large; Being a Collection of all the Laws of Virginia, From the First Session of the Legislature, in the Year 1619* (Richmond: J. & G. Cochran, 1823), 12: 86 (hereafter cited as *Statutes at Large*); *Virginia Code, Annotated* (repl. vol. 1986), sec. 57-1. Jefferson's bill is reprinted in Julian Boyd, ed., *The Papers of Thomas Jefferson* (Princeton: Princeton Univ. Press, 1950), 2: 545–47 (hereafter cited as *Papers of Thomas Jefferson*).

2. See William B. Huntley, "Jefferson's Public and Private Religion," *South Atlantic Quarterly* 79 (1980): 299 (the "language of [Jefferson's bill] resembles that of the Declaration of Independence"); Willibald M. Plöchl, "Thomas Jefferson, Author of the Statute of Virginia for Religious Freedom," *Jurist* 3 (1943): 219 ("If the Declaration of Independence was a declaration against political tyranny, his Statute of Religious Freedom may be called the correlative Declaration against the suppression of free mind and conscience.").

3. Merrill D. Peterson, *Thomas Jefferson and the New Nation* (New York: Oxford Univ. Press, 1970), 134.

4. James Madison to Thomas Jefferson, 22 Jan. 1786, *The Papers of James Madison*, ed. Robert A. Rutland and William M. E. Rachal (Chicago: Univ. of Chicago Press, 1973), 8: 474.

5. William Lee Miller, *The First Liberty: Religion and the American Republic* (New York: Knopf, 1986), 18.

6. For a description of the petitions and arguments circulated in support of a general assessment, see Hamilton James Eckenrode, *Separation of Church and State in Virginia: A Study in the Development of the Revolution* (Richmond: Davis Bottom, 1910), 75–76, 83–84, 88–90, 111–13; Thomas E. Buckley, *Church and State in Revolutionary Virginia, 1776–1787* (Charlottesville: Univ. Press of Virginia, 1977), 74, 80–81, 90, 94–95, 98–99, 141–47.

7. For a list of prominent Virginians in favor of a general assessment, see Gerard V. Bradley, *Church-State Relationships in America* (Westport, Conn.: Greenwood Press, 1987), 38.

8. The general assessment proposal Henry supported, "A Bill Establishing a Provision

for Teachers of the Christian Religion," is reprinted in *Everson* v. *Board of Education*, 330 U.S. 1, 72–74 (1947) (appendix to Rutledge, J., dissenting).

9. *Journal of the House of Delegates of the Commonwealth of Virginia*, 24 Dec. 1784 (Richmond: Thomas W. White, 1828), 82 (hereafter cited as *Journal of the House of Delegates*).

10. For the text of Madison's "Memorial and Remonstrance" and accompanying editorial notes, see *Papers of James Madison* 8: 295–306.

11. For a general description of the rise of anti-assessment sentiment in the Commonwealth, see Eckenrode, *Separation of Church and State in Virginia*, 95–98, 103–13; Buckley, *Church and State in Revolutionary Virginia*, 97–105, 113–17, 130–40, 147–55; Rhys Isaac, "'The Rage of Malice of the Old Serpent Devil': The Dissenters and the Making and Remaking of the Virginia Statute for Religious Freedom," in *The Virginia Statute for Religious Freedom: Its Evolution and Consequences in American History*, ed. Merrill D. Peterson and Robert C. Vaughan (New York: Cambridge Univ. Press, 1988), 146–56 (hereafter cited as *Virginia Statute*).

12. William Henry Foote, *Sketches of Virginia, Historical and Biographical* (Philadelphia: William S. Martien, 1850), 431. Katherine L. Brown disputes Foote's account of the demise of Henry's bill in the autumn 1785 session of the legislature. See "The Role of Presbyterian Dissent in Colonial and Revolutionary Virginia, 1740–1785" (Ph.D. diss., Johns Hopkins Univ., 1969), 392.

13. For a complete legislative history of the enactment of the religious freedom bill, see Eckenrode, *Separation of Church and State in Virginia*, 113–15; Buckley, *Church and State in Revolutionary Virginia*, 155–65; Marvin K. Singleton, "Colonial Virginia as First Amendment Matrix: Henry, Madison, and Assessment Establishment," *Journal of Church and State* 8 (1966): 344.

14. Nathan Schachner, *Thomas Jefferson: A Biography*, 2 vols. (New York: Appleton-Century-Crofts, 1951), 1: 160.

15. Eckenrode, *Separation of Church and State in Virginia*, 116.

16. Merrill D. Peterson, for example, has asserted that "the principles of the [Virginia Statute for Religious Freedom] entered into the United States Constitution by way of the First Amendment." Editors' preface to *Virginia Statute*, ix.

17. See, e.g., *Reynolds* v. *United States*, 98 U.S. 145, 162–64 (1878).

18. *Everson* v. *Board of Education*, 330 U.S. 1, 33–34 (1947) (Rutledge, J., dissenting) (citations omitted).

19. Paul G. Kauper, "*Everson* v. *Board of Education:* A Product of the Judicial Will," *Arizona Law Review* 15 (1973): 307. Arthur E. Sutherland has similarly noted that Everson "has become the most influential single announcement of the American law of church and state." Sutherland, "Establishment According to Engel," *Harvard Law Review* 76 (1962): 31.

20. *Everson* v. *Board of Education*, 330 U.S. at 18.

21. A significant feature of the Everson opinions was the total lack of confrontation between the basic historical assumptions underlying the majority and minority opinions. Justice Black, for the Court, and Justices Jackson, Rutledge, Frankfurter, and Burton, in dissent, were unanimous in their description of the disestablishment movement in revolutionary Virginia and separationist interpretation of the establishment clause. See Daniel L. Dreisbach, *Real Threat and Mere Shadow: Religious Liberty and the First Amendment* (Westchester, Ill.: Crossway Books, 1987), 233–34 n. 10.

22. *Everson* v. *Board of Education*, 330 U.S. at 15.

23. Ibid., at 31–32 (Rutledge, J., dissenting).

24. Comment, "The Supreme Court, The First Amendment, and Religion in the Public Schools," *Columbia Law Review* 63 (1963): 79. See also A. E. Dick Howard, "The Supreme Court and the Serpentine Wall," in *Virginia Statute*, 315 ("Tracing the events in Virginia that led to Madison's drafting of the 'Memorial and Remonstrance' and to the enactment of Jefferson's Bill for Establishing Religious Liberty, [Justice] Black concluded [in Everson] that the First Amendment was meant to provide 'the same protection against governmental intrusion on religious liberty as the Virginia statute.'") (quoting *Everson* v. *Board of Education*, 330 U.S. at 13); Arlin M. Adams and Charles J. Emmerich, "A Heritage of Religious Liberty," *Univ. of Pennsylvania Law Review* 137 (1989): 1572 n. 54 ("No other historical episode has influenced the Supreme Court's interpretation of the religion clauses more than the Virginia struggle. References to it abound in the Justices' opinions in religious liberty cases."); Gerard V. Bradley, "Imagining the Past and Remembering the Future: The Supreme Court's History of the Establishment Clause," *Connecticut Law Review* 18 (1986): 832 ("Justice Black essentially reduced the religion clauses to a federal codification of Thomas Jefferson's 'Bill for Establishing Religious Freedom,' the denouement of the 1784–85 Virginia controversy over public stipends for Protestant clergymen.").

Significantly, both Justices Black and Rutledge in their respective Everson opinions devoted considerable space to recounting the church-state controversy in colonial and revolutionary Virginia, yet they virtually ignored the legislative history of the First Amendment religion clauses. The proper interpretation of the establishment clause was, after all, at issue in Everson. It would seem that the legislative history of the First Amendment, not the disestablishment controversy in revolutionary Virginia, should have been the focus of the Court's historical review. Furthermore, as one legal historian argues, if the "object is to understand what was meant by 'an establishment of religion' at the time of the framing of the Bill of Rights, the histories of the other states are equally important, notwithstanding the stature and influence of Jefferson and Madison as individuals." Leonard W. Levy, *The Establishment Clause: Religion and the First Amendment* (New York: Macmillan, 1986), 60.

25. For a list of state and federal judicial opinions that cite these documents, see Daniel L. Dreisbach, "Thomas Jefferson and Bills Number 82–86 of the Revision of the Laws of Virginia, 1776–1786: New Light on the Jeffersonian Model of Church-State Relations," *North Carolina Law Review* 69 (1990): 173–75 nn. 77–83.

26. *Committee for Public Education and Religious Liberty* v. *Nyquist*, 413 U.S. 756, 770–71 n. 28 (1973).

27. *Everson* v. *Board of Education*, 330 U.S. at 13 ("This Court has previously recognized that the provisions of the First Amendment . . . had the same objective and were intended to provide the same protection against governmental intrusion on religious liberty as the Virginia statute [for religious liberty]."). See also at 39–40 (Rutledge, J., dissenting) (the great documents of the "Virginia struggle for religious liberty . . . became the warp and woof of our constitutional tradition" of church-state separation).

28. A. E. Dick Howard has opined that "the United States Supreme Court has taken the Virginia Bill [for Religious Freedom] and the First Amendment to be coextensive and has acknowledged the intended wall of separation implicit in both." *Commentaries on the Constitution of Virginia*, 2 vols. (Charlottesville: Univ. Press of Virginia, 1974), 1: 293.

29. Justice Rehnquist similarly observed: "It is impossible to build sound constitutional doctrine upon a mistaken understanding of constitutional history." *Wallace* v. *Jaffree*, 472 U.S. 38, 92 (1985) (Rehnquist, J., dissenting).

30. For a description of how various new American states handled this legal transition, see A. E. Dick Howard, *The Road from Runnymeade: Magna Carta and Constitutionalism in America* (Charlottesville: Univ. Press of Virginia, 1968), 241–47.

31. Peterson, *Thomas Jefferson and the New Nation*, 100.

32. Thomas Jefferson, *Autobiography,* in *The Life and Selected Writings of Thomas Jefferson,* ed. Adrienne Koch and William Peden (New York: Modern Library, Random House, 1944), 44.

33. *Journal of the House of Delegates of Virginia. Anno Domini, 1776,* 12 Oct. 1776 (Richmond: Samuel Shepherd, 1828), 10.

34. Ibid., 26 Oct. 1776, 28.

35. Hening, *Statutes at Large* (1821), 9: 175–77; *Papers of Thomas Jefferson* 1: 562–63.

36. *Journal of the House of Delegates,* 5 Nov. 1776, 41.

37. Jefferson, *Autobiography,* 45.

38. Editorial note in *Papers of Thomas Jefferson* 2: 316, 320. The remaining members of

the Committee of Revisors, Jefferson, Wythe, and Pendleton, met in Williamsburg in February 1779 to review the progress made on the revision as a whole. Pendleton apparently was called home from the meeting, and he authorized Jefferson and Wythe to consider his vote in agreement with any decisions they reached. Jefferson and Wythe unhappily discovered that the bills Pendleton had prepared failed to conform to the general plan and style agreed upon. Instead of clarifying and simplifying the language of the old statutes, Pendleton had merely copied the old statutes, eliminating only the provisions obviously inapplicable to the new republican government. Jefferson and Wythe thought it necessary to re-write Pendleton's portion of the assignment in order to present a uniform code. Jefferson assumed much of the work previously assigned to Pendleton, further enhancing his personal imprint on the revised laws. Claude G. Bowers, *The Young Jefferson, 1743–1789* (Boston: Houghton Mifflin, 1945), 180.

39. Noble E. Cunningham, Jr., *In Pursuit of Reason: The Life of Thomas Jefferson* (Baton Rouge: Louisiana State Univ. Press, 1987), 54.

40. Jefferson, *Autobiography*, 44.

41. Ibid.

42. See Henry S. Randall, *The Life of Thomas Jefferson*, 3 vols. (New York: Derby and Jackson, 1858), 1: 208.

43. Jefferson, *Autobiography*, 44–45. Edward Dumbauld argues that replacing the old legal system with an entirely new code would have been a bold move beyond the intent of the legislature. See *Thomas Jefferson and the Law* (Norman: Univ. of Oklahoma Press, 1978), 133–34.

44. Jefferson, *Autobiography*, 51.

45. Thomas Jefferson to Skelton Jones, 28 July 1809, *The Writings of Thomas Jefferson*, ed. Andrew A. Lipscomb and Albert Ellery Bergh (Washington, D.C.: Thomas Jefferson Memorial Association, 1905), 12: 299.

46. Jefferson was given the task of reforming the whole field of the common law and statutes of England down to the foundation of the Virginia Colony in 1607. The British statutes from 1607 to the end of the colonial era were assigned to Wythe, and the laws of the Commonwealth during the same period were assigned to Pendleton.

47. Dumas Malone, *Jefferson the Virginian* (Boston: Little, Brown, 1948), 262.

48. Jefferson, *Autobiography*, 46.

49. *Journal of the House of Delegates*, 18 June 1779, 56–57.

50. The revisal was printed in 1784 by order of the House of Delegates. See *Report of the Committee of Revisors Appointed by the General Assembly of Virginia in MDCCLXXVI* (Richmond: Dixon & Holt, 1784) (hereafter cited as *Report of the Revisors*). The most complete legislative and documentary history of the revisal is

found in *Papers of Thomas Jefferson* 2: 305–665. Julian Boyd's editorial notes constitute the most thorough study of the revised code conducted to date. Boyd examined the legislative documents in laborious detail, attributing authorship of the revised bills to various members of the Committee of Revisors.

51. *Journal of the House of Delegates,* 31 Oct. 1785, 12–15.

52. See Dumbauld, *Thomas Jefferson and the Law,* 137; editorial note in *Papers of James
Madison* 8: 389–402; editorial note in *Papers of Thomas Jefferson* 2: 322.

53. On 31 October 1785, Madison reintroduced in the Virginia House of Delegates
Bill No. 82 from the revised code—"A Bill for Establishing Religious Freedom."
See *Journal of the House of Delegates,* 31 Oct. 1785, 12–15. The measure was specifically brought to the attention of the House on 14 December. The committee of
the whole debated the bill the following day. On 16 December it was moved that
Jefferson's trenchant preamble be struck entirely and replaced by Article XVI of the
Virginia Declaration of Rights. This motion was defeated by a vote of thirty-eight
to sixty-six, and the bill was ordered to be engrossed and read the third, and final,
time. The engrossed bill was read on 17 December and passed by a convincing
majority of seventy-four to twenty. See *Journal of the House of Delegates,* 14–17 Dec.
1785, 92–96.

The bill was read in the Senate for the first time on Saturday, 17 December
1785. See *Journal of the Senate of the Commonwealth of Virginia,* 17 Dec. 1785
(Richmond: Thomas W. White, 1827), 54 (hereafter cited as *Journal of the Senate*).
The Senate read the bill a second time on 19 December and sent it to a committee
of the whole for further consideration. See *Journal of the Senate,* 56. When the Senate took up the bill again on Friday, 23 December 1785, it voted to replace the
preamble with Article XVI of the Virginia Declaration of Rights. See *Journal of the
Senate,* 61. The bill was read for the third time, passed and returned to the House
of Delegates.

The House, once again, rejected the amendment altering Jefferson's preamble.
See *Journal of the House of Delegates,* 29 Dec. 1785, 117; *Journal of the Senate,* 30
Dec. 1785, 67. Unable to reconcile differences between the House and Senate versions of the bill, a conference committee was formed early in the new year. See
Journal of the Senate, 9 Jan. 1786, 81. On 16 January 1786, the House considered
and, perhaps reluctantly, accepted relatively minor Senate amendments. See *Journal
of the House of Delegates,* 143–44; *Journal of the Senate,* 92. The speaker signed the
act on 19 January 1786. See *Journal of the House of Delegates,* 148.

54. *Everson* v. *Board of Education,* 330 U.S. at 18.

55. *Report of the Revisors,* 58–59. The bill is reprinted in *Papers of Thomas Jefferson* 2:
545–47; Hening, *Statutes at Large* 12: 84–86.

56. Harvard historian Bernard Bailyn described the bill as "the most important docu-

ment in American history, bar none." Quoted in James H. Smylie, "Jefferson's Statute for Religious Freedom: The Hanover Presbytery Memorials, 1776–1786," *American Presbyterians Journal of Presbyterian History* 63 (1985): 355.

57. See Paul Leicester Ford, ed., *The Writings of Thomas Jefferson*, 10 vols. (New York: G. Putnam's Sons, 1899), 10: 396.

58. See *Bond v. Bond*, 144 W.Va. 478, 492, 109 S.E.2d 16, 23 (1959) ("The Virginia Statute of Religious Freedom . . . is said to have formed a model for statutes and constitutional provisions throughout the land."). In a letter to Madison, written shortly after the bill was enacted, Jefferson proudly reported that "the Virginia act for religious freedom has been received with infinite approbation in Europe, and propagated with enthusiasm. . . . It has been translated into French and Italian, has been sent to most of the courts of Europe, and has been the best evidence of the falsehood of those reports which stated us to be in anarchy. It is inserted in the new 'Encyclopédie,' and is appearing in most of the publications respecting America." Thomas Jefferson to James Madison, 16 Dec. 1786, *Life and Selected Writings of Thomas Jefferson*, 408–9. For a general survey of the legacy of Jefferson's religious freedom bill in Virginia and the nation, see Cushing Strout, "Jeffersonian Religious Liberty and American Pluralism," in *Virginia Statute*, 201–35.

59. C. Randolph Benson notes that Jefferson's church-state views "in the course of time became the official American position." Benson, *Thomas Jefferson as Social Scientist* (Rutherford, N.J.: Fairleigh Dickinson Univ. Press, 1971), 190–91.

60. Schachner, *Thomas Jefferson: A Biography* 1: 160.

61. Mark DeWolfe Howe, *The Garden and the Wilderness: Religion and Government in American Constitutional History* (Chicago: Univ. of Chicago Press, 1965), 44.

62. For a concise summary of John Locke's influence on the development of American theories of religious freedom, see Michael W. McConnell, "The Origins and Historical Understanding of Free Exercise of Religion," *Harvard Law Review* 103 (1990): 1430–35, 1443–55. Locke's influence on Jefferson's religious freedom bill is well documented. It is important to note, however, that Jefferson went beyond Locke's policy of toleration and advocated complete religious liberty, not only for Christian denominations but for all religious sects. See Charles B. Sanford, *The Religious Life of Thomas Jefferson* (Charlottesville: Univ. Press of Virginia, 1984), 28. For an examination of Locke's influence on Bill No. 82, see Sanford Kessler, "Locke's Influence on Jefferson's 'Bill for Establishing Religious Freedom,'" *Journal of Church and State* 25 (1983): 231; S. Gerald Sandler, "Lockean Ideas in Thomas Jefferson's Bill for Establishing Religious Freedom," *Journal of the History of Ideas* 21 (1960): 110.

63. The following summary draws from commentary provided in Leo Pfeffer, *Church, State, and Freedom* (Boston: Beacon Press, 1953), 101–2; Sanford, *The Religious Life of Thomas Jefferson*, 29–30; and Plöchl, "Thomas Jefferson," 217–18, 220.

64. *Report of the Revisors*, 58; *Papers of Thomas Jefferson* 2: 545. Jefferson's words "that free it shall remain" were deleted from the preamble by Senate amendment on 16 January 1786.

65. *Report of the Revisors*, 58; *Papers of Thomas Jefferson* 2: 545; Hening, *Statutes at Large* 12: 84.

66. *Report of the Revisors*, 58; *Papers of Thomas Jefferson* 2: 545; Hening, *Statutes at Large* 12: 84–85.

67. *Report of the Revisors*, 58; *Papers of Thomas Jefferson* 2: 545. Jefferson's words "and abhors" were deleted from the preamble by Senate amendment on 16 January 1786.

68. *Report of the Revisors*, 58; *Papers of Thomas Jefferson* 2: 545; Hening, *Statutes at Large* 12: 85.

69. *Report of the Revisors*, 58; *Papers of Thomas Jefferson* 2: 545–46; Hening, *Statutes at Large* 12: 85.

70. *Report of the Revisors*, 58; *Papers of Thomas Jefferson* 2: 546; Hening, *Statutes at Large* 12: 85.

71. *Report of the Revisors*, 58; *Papers of Thomas Jefferson* 2: 546; Hening, *Statutes at Large* 12: 85.

72. *Report of the Revisors*, 58; *Papers of Thomas Jefferson* 2: 546; Hening, *Statutes at Large* 12: 86.

73. *Report of the Revisors*, 59; *Papers of Thomas Jefferson* 2: 546–47; Hening, *Statutes at Large* 12: 86.

74. Thomas E. Buckley, "The Political Theology of Thomas Jefferson," in *Virginia Statute*, 92. William Lee Miller similarly observed that "one can discover in this last paragraph the un-Jeffersonian desire, suppressed but real, to bind the future." Miller, *The First Liberty*, 63.

75. See Benjamin Hart, *Faith & Freedom* (Dallas: Lewis and Stanley, 1988), 341–42 (Jefferson's "bill justifies itself on Protestant theological principles"); Buckley, "The Political Theology of Thomas Jefferson," in *Virginia Statute*, 93 ("the statute is not neutral toward religion. . . . [It] presupposes a belief in God."); *American Jewish Congress* v. *City of Chicago*, 827 F.2d 120, 135 (7th Cir. 1987) (Easterbrook, C. J., dissenting) ("The preamble to the bill is itself an exercise in religious persuasion."); Steven D. Smith, "Separation and the 'Secular': Reconstructing the Disestablishment Decision," *Texas Law Review* 67 (1989): 968 (Jefferson's bill "rested on explicitly religious premises").

76. *Report of the Revisors*, 58; *Papers of Thomas Jefferson* 2: 545. Jefferson's words "that free it shall remain" were deleted from the preamble by Senate amendment on 16 January 1786.

77. John Remington Graham has argued that "far from ordaining a separation of church and state, the Virginia Statute of Religious Freedom proclaimed a coopera-

tive friendship between the two: the existence of God who made the mind free was the statutory reason for governmental recognition of religious freedom." Graham, "A Restatement of the Intended Meaning of the Establishment Clause in Relation to Education and Religion," *Brigham Young Univ. Law Review* 1981 (1981): 348.

78. Thomas E. Buckley has contended that "the God described here is not deistical, remote from human beings or unconcerned with their affairs. Rather, Jefferson posited a creator who is personally involved and expects an individual response expressed in sincere belief." Buckley, "The Political Theology of Thomas Jefferson," in *Virginia Statute*, 87.

79. *Report of the Revisors*, 58; *Papers of Thomas Jefferson* 2: 545; Hening, *Statutes at Large* 12: 84.

80. One commentator has opined that the bill's prefatory language asserting that it was Almighty God's will that the human mind should remain free "might be offensive to some total separationists." Comment, "Jefferson and the Church-State Wall: A Historical Examination of the Man and the Metaphor," *Brigham Young Univ. Law Review* 1978 (1978): 665.

81. *American Jewish Congress* v. *City of Chicago*, 827 F.2d 120, 136 (7th Cir. 1987) (Easterbrook, C. J., dissenting).

82. *Report of the Revisors*, 59. The bill is reprinted in *Papers of Thomas Jefferson* 2: 553–54.

83. For a legislative history and analysis of a 1779 version of the bill, see Daniel Durham Rhodes, "The Struggle for Religious Liberty in Virginia, 1740–1802" (Ph.D. diss., Duke Univ., 1951), 129–32. Rhodes attributes authorship of this bill to George Mason. Regardless of who actually drafted the bill, Jefferson clearly endorsed it.

84. Randall, *The Life of Thomas Jefferson* 1: 221. Randall implies that Bill No. 83 was the product of Jefferson's pen (1: 219–21). Editors of the Jefferson papers attribute authorship of the bill to Jefferson. *Papers of Thomas Jefferson* 2: 320.

85. Randall, *The Life of Thomas Jefferson* 1: 221.

86. See "An act for exempting the different societies of Dissenters from contributing to the support and maintenance of the church as by law established, and its ministers, and for other purposes therein mentioned," in Hening, *Statutes at Large* 9: 164–67.

87. *Everson* v. *Board of Education*, 330 U.S. at 15.

88. *Report of the Revisors*, 59. The bill is reprinted in *Papers of Thomas Jefferson* 2: 555; Hening, *Statutes at Large* 12: 336–37.

89. Editors of the Jefferson papers attribute authorship of the bill to Jefferson. *Papers of Thomas Jefferson* 2: 318–20.

90. The Virginia code still contains a provision that exempts "ministers of the gospel" from arrest "while engaged in performing religious services . . . and while going to and returning from such" services. *Virginia Code, Annotated* (1984), sec. 8.01-327.2

91. *Report of the Revisors,* 59; *Papers of Thomas Jefferson* 2: 555; Hening, *Statutes at Large* 12: 337. This language from Bill No. 84 remained the law in Virginia without substantial amendment until 1960. See generally *Mandell* v. *Haddon,* 202 Va. 979, 121 S.E.2d 516 (1961) (legislative history of Sunday labor laws in Virginia). It is noteworthy that when the Virginia legislature enacted Bill No. 84, it apparently changed the fifth word of this paragraph from *Sunday* to *sabbath day.* See Hening, *Statutes at Large* 12: 337.

92. Robert M. Healey, *Jefferson on Religion in Public Education* (New Haven, Conn.: Yale Univ. Press, 1962), 140.

93. *Report of the Revisors,* 59; *Papers of Thomas Jefferson* 2: 555; Hening, *Statutes at Large* 12: 336–37.

94. Gen. 2: 2–3.

95. Exod. 20: 8–11; Exod. 31: 12–18.

96. Cf. *McGowan* v. *Maryland,* 366 U.S. 420 (1961) (Supreme Court upheld state Sunday closing law because the statute's present purpose and effect were not to aid religion by facilitating church attendance but to set aside a day for recreation and rest from secular employment).

97. Robert L. Cord, *Separation of Church and State: Historical Fact and Current Fiction* (New York: Lambeth Press, 1982), 219.

98. See William Gangi, review of *Separation of Church and State,* by Robert L. Cord, in *Harvard Journal of Law & Public Policy* 7 (1984): 600. One could argue that the word *Sabbath* was deliberately selected as an inclusive term that would enable various religious sects to observe the Sabbath on any day of the week designated by the sect. There is little, if any, historical evidence to support this interpretation.

99. *Report of the Revisors,* 59–60. The bill is reprinted in *Papers of Thomas Jefferson* 2: 556.

100. Although not explicitly attributing authorship of Bill No. 85 to Jefferson, the editors of his papers note that Jefferson apparently endorsed it. *Papers of Thomas Jefferson* 2: 556. Other scholars have described Jefferson as the author of this bill. See, e.g., Cord, *Separation of Church and State,* 220–21; Healey, *Jefferson on Religion in Public Education,* 135; Donald L. Drakeman, "Religion and the Republic: James Madison and the First Amendment," *Journal of Church and State* 25 (1983): 441; Comment, "Jefferson and the Church-State Wall," 657–66.

101. *Report of the Revisors,* 60; *Papers of Thomas Jefferson* 2: 556.

102. *Papers of Thomas Jefferson* 2: 556.

103. Indeed, the punitive provisions of Bill No. 85 are difficult to reconcile with that portion of Bill No. 82 declaring that "no man shall be compelled to frequent or support any religious worship, place, or ministry whatsoever." *Report of the Revisors,* 58; *Papers of Thomas Jefferson* 2: 546; Hening, *Statutes at Large* 12: 86.

It is similarly difficult to reconcile this bill with Justice Black's interpretation of the religion clauses in Everson: "The 'establishment of religion' clause of the

First Amendment means at least this: neither a state nor the Federal Government . . . can force nor influence a person to go to or to remain away from church against his will . . . No person can be punished . . . for church attendance or non-attendance." *Everson* v. *Board of Education,* 330 U.S. at 15–16. See also *Zorach* v. *Clauson,* 343 U.S. 306, 314 (1952) ("government . . . may not coerce anyone to attend church, to observe a religious holiday, or to take religious instruction").

104. Thomas Jefferson to Messrs. Nehemiah Dodge, Ephraim Robbins, and Stephen S. Nelson, A Committee of the Danbury Baptist Association In the State of Connecticut, 1 Jan. 1802, *Life and Selected Writings of Thomas Jefferson,* 332.

105. For an examination of the origin and application of Jefferson's wall, see Robert M. Healey, "Thomas Jefferson's 'Wall': Absolute or Serpentine?" *Journal of Church and State* 30 (1988): 441; Comment, "Jefferson and the Church-State Wall," 645.

106. *Everson* v. *Board of Education,* 330 U.S. at 16 ("In the words of Jefferson, the clause against establishment of religion by law was intended to erect 'a wall of separation between church and State.'").

107. Justice Rutledge, in dissent, offered a legislative history of the revisal. He acknowledged the contribution of Jefferson in drafting and Madison in sponsoring the revised code. *Everson* v. *Board of Education,* 330 U.S. at 35 n. 15 (Rutledge, J., dissenting). Thus, the Everson Court knew the legislative history of Bill No. 82 and should have known of companion Bills No. 83 to 86.

108. Many separationist commentators contend that throughout their public careers Jefferson and Madison were consistent advocates of absolute church-state separation. See, e.g., *Everson* v. *Board of Education,* 330 U.S. at 41 (Rutledge, J., dissenting) ("Madison and his coworkers made no exceptions or abridgments to the complete separation they created."). Leo Pfeffer similarly observed of Jefferson that "throughout his adult life Jefferson never swerved from his devotion to the principle of complete independence of religion and government." Pfeffer, *Church, State, and Freedom,* 94.

109. *Papers of Thomas Jefferson* 1: 105.

110. Jefferson, *Autobiography,* 8–9.

111. Martin E. Marty observed that this resolution "is hardly a noble charter, but it does show that Jefferson did, on occasion, allow for acts that clearly contradicted the bill of 1779 and the statute of 1786." Marty, "The Virginia Statute Two Hundred Years Later," in *Virginia Statute,* 9.

112. *Papers of Thomas Jefferson* 3: 177–79.

113. Rodney K. Smith, "Getting Off on the Wrong Foot and Back on Again: A Reexamination of the History of the Framing of the Religion Clauses of the First Amendment and a Critique of the *Reynolds* and *Everson* Decisions," *Wake Forest Law Review* 20 (1984): 622 n. 210.

114. Jefferson, Second Inaugural Address, 4 Mar. 1805, in *Life and Selected Writings of Thomas Jefferson*, 341.

115. In explaining why he chose not to follow his predecessors' example and proclaim national days of fasting and prayer, Jefferson stated: "I have ever believed that the example of state executives led to the assumption of that authority by the general [federal] government, without due examination, which would have discovered that what might be a right in a state government, was a violation of that right when assumed by another." Thomas Jefferson to the Reverend Samuel Miller, 23 Jan. 1808, in Dreisbach, *Real Threat and Mere Shadow*, 170–71.

116. Arthur Gilbert argues that Bills No. 84 and 85 are evidence that "both Madison and Jefferson lent their weight to legislation that provided state sanction for religious morality in general." Gilbert, "Religious Freedom and Social Change in a Pluralist Society: A Historical Review," in *Religion and the Public Order*, ed. Donald A. Giannella (Chicago: Univ. of Chicago Press, 1964), 101–2.

117. *Report of the Revisors*, 60. The bill is reprinted in *Papers of Thomas Jefferson* 2: 556–58.

118. *Report of the Revisors*, 60; *Papers of Thomas Jefferson* 2: 556–57.

119. There is less evidence establishing Jefferson's direct authorship of Bill No. 86 than the preceding four bills in the revisal. It is clear, however, that Jefferson authorized and endorsed the proposal given the dominant role he played in revising the laws of Virginia.

120. *Papers of Thomas Jefferson* 2: 558.

121. *Grand Rapids School District* v. *Ball*, 473 U.S. 373, 389–90 (1985).

122. For more on the Supreme Court's "symbolic union" analysis, see Theodore C. Hirt, "'Symbolic Union' of Church and State and the 'Endorsement' of Sectarian Activity: A Critique of Unwieldy Tools of Establishment Clause Jurisprudence," *Wake Forest Law Review* 24 (1989): 823; Note, "Symbolic Union and the Establishment Clause," *Missouri Law Review* 53 (1989): 139.

123. Even if it was established that Jefferson was not the actual draftsman of any one of Bills No. 83 to 86, the thesis of this article remains intact. Clearly, Jefferson was the chief architect of the revised code and was intimately involved in its preparation and presentation. It is widely acknowledged that virtually all the bills were framed by Wythe and Jefferson, and when the two men met in Williamsburg in February 1779 for a final revision of the bills, they examined the drafts "sentence by sentence . . . until [both men] had agreed on the whole." Jefferson, *Autobiography*, 46. There is little doubt that in this role Jefferson, at the very least, authorized and endorsed Bills No. 83 to 86 which, it is argued in this chapter, modify conventional interpretations of Bill No. 82.

124. *Everson* v. *Board of Education*, 330 U.S. at 35 n. 15 (Rutledge, J., dissenting).

125. Jefferson, *Autobiography*, 41.

126. Schachner, *Thomas Jefferson: A Biography* 1: 154. Lance Banning offers a similar observation of Madison: "As Madison went on, instead, to even larger deeds, his magnificent 'Memorial' assumed a rightful place beside his friend's great statute [for religious freedom] among the documentary foundations of the libertarian tradition." Banning, "James Madison, the Statute for Religious Freedom, and the Crisis of Republican Convictions," in *Virginia Statute*, 130.

127. Another explanation for the failure of virtually all biographers of Jefferson and students of church-state relations in revolutionary Virginia to recognize Jefferson's contributions to Bills No. 83 to 86 stems from an inordinate reliance on secondary sources. Most students of Jefferson have examined the religious freedom bill isolated from its legislative context or as interpreted by commentators. Few scholars, sadly, have returned to primary sources, such as the *Report of the Revisors*, to evaluate Bill No. 82 in its full legislative context. Extensive reliance on secondary source material has arguably detached the religious freedom bill from the historical, political, and ideological milieu in which it was written and promulgated the misunderstandings of Jefferson's church-state views examined in this chapter.

128. Healey, *Jefferson on Religion in Public Education*, 135.

129. James Lafayette Gurley, "Thomas Jefferson's Philosophy and Theology: As Related to His Political Principles, Including Separation of Church and State" (Ph.D. diss., Univ. of Michigan, 1975), 234–35.

130. Miller, *The First Liberty*, 49.

131. See, e.g., Thomas J. Curry, *The First Freedoms: Church and State in America to the Passage of the First Amendment* (New York: Oxford Univ. Press, 1986), 148 ("In the same sheaf of bills that contained the statute on religious freedom, Madison included [Bill No. 85]. . . . [T]here can be little doubt that Madison personally disapproved of it; but the fact that he included it in the collection was significant. Such incidents proceeded from the habits of mind and unchallenged assumptions about society of a people overwhelmingly Protestant Christian."); Robert D. McAninch, "James Madison on Church and State Relations" (M.A. thesis, West Virginia Univ., 1970), 53, 56 ("Madison did indeed introduce [Bill No. 84] into the Assembly, but it was buried in a package of one-hundred and seventeen other bills. . . . There is little evidence to demonstrate that Madison was in agreement with the substance of bill number 84, as it was simply part of the revised code. . . . Madison may have chosen to remain silent on bill number 84 so as to not weaken the tide of opposition that he had produced against the General Assessment.").

132. For a discussion on possible explanations for apparent inconsistencies in Jefferson's and Madison's church-state views, see Dreisbach, *Real Threat and Mere Shadow*, 107–11.

133. But cf. *Everson* v. *Board of Education*, 330 U.S. at 41 (Rutledge, J., dissenting)

("Madison and his coworkers made no exceptions or abridgments to the complete separation they created.").

134. Leonard W. Levy, for example, has asserted that "Jefferson's record on religious liberty was really quite exceptional—an almost consistent demonstration of devotion to principle." Levy, *Jefferson and Civil Liberties: The Darker Side* (Cambridge: Harvard Univ. Press, Belknap Press, 1963), 21.

In their declining years, upon mature reflection, both Jefferson and Madison acknowledged that on occasion in the heat of political battle they made critical compromises on church-state matters. See, e.g., Jefferson, *Autobiography*, 8–9, where Jefferson recounts that in May 1774, as a member of the House of Burgesses, he participated in drafting and enacting a "cooked up" resolution designating a "Day of Fasting, Humiliation, and Prayer" in order to excite public opposition to England. Likewise Madison, despite reservations about issuing religious day proclamations, acknowledged in his "Detached Memoranda" that during the 1812 war with England he succumbed to congressional pressure to designate a day of public humiliation and prayer. See Dreisbach, *Real Threat and Mere Shadow*, 188–89, 152–53. Significantly, neither Jefferson nor Madison gave any indication that their authorship and sponsorship, respectively, of Bills No. 83 to 86 were motivated, in whole or in part, by political considerations rather than principle. Moreover, the legislative compromises some commentators allege were made by Jefferson and Madison are antithetical to the underlying separationist position the two Virginians purportedly embraced. It is implausible that if Jefferson and Madison were ardent separationist they would have acceded to such accommodationist compromises. Arguably, the inconsistencies in Bills No. 82 to 86 only emerge when the measures are viewed from a twentieth century, secular separationist perspective.

135. See Gurley, "Thomas Jefferson's Philosophy and Theology," 227 (arguing that Jefferson "declared that the example of state executives in making religious pronouncements had influenced the presidents; however, he believed that what might be right for a state government would be wrong for the national government"); Adams and Emmerich, "A Heritage of Religious Liberty," 1586, 1607 (arguing Jefferson's disparate actions on the state and federal levels can, perhaps, be reconciled by reference to the principle of federalism because Jefferson believed state governments, not the federal government, exercised a degree of civil authority in religious matters).

136. The term *institutional separation* was deliberately chosen. It suggests that "the Founders conceived of separation in institutional rather than cultural terms. The principal evil they sought to avoid was an alliance of civil and ecclesiastical power that would threaten religious liberty; that religion and society should be separated was a notion that would have met with uniform disapproval." Adams and Emmerich, "A Heritage of Religious Liberty," 1615.

137. For an excellent study of the Jefferson image in American intellectual thought, see Merrill D. Peterson, *The Jefferson Image in the American Mind* (New York: Oxford Univ. Press, 1960).
138. The "law office historian," imbued with the adversary ethic, selectively recounts facts, emphasizing data that support the recorder's own prepossessions and minimizing significant facts that complicate or conflict with that bias.
139. Howe, *The Garden and the Wilderness*, 4.
140. See Healey, *Jefferson on Religion in Public Education*, 138–40, 250; Richard John Neuhaus, "Establishment Is Not the Issue," *The Religion and Society Report* 4, no. 6 (June 1987): 1–3.

REFERENCES

Adams, Arlin M., and Charles J. Emmerich. "A Heritage of Religious Liberty." *University of Pennsylvania Law Review* 137 (1989): 1559–1671.

Bowers, Claude G. *The Young Jefferson, 1743–1789*. Boston: Houghton Mifflin, 1945.

Boyd, Julian P., ed. *The Papers of Thomas Jefferson*. 25 vols. Princeton: Princeton Univ. Press, 1950–92.

Buckley, Thomas E. *Church and State in Revolutionary Virginia, 1776–1787*. Charlottesville: Univ. Press of Virginia, 1977.

Cord, Robert L. *Separation of Church and State: Historical Fact and Current Fiction*. New York: Lambeth Press, 1982.

Cunningham, Noble E., Jr. *In Pursuit of Reason: The Life of Thomas Jefferson*. Baton Rouge: Louisiana State Univ. Press, 1987.

Curry, Thomas J. *The First Freedoms: Church and State in America to the Passage of the First Amendment*. New York: Oxford Univ. Press, 1986.

Dumbauld, Edward. *Thomas Jefferson and the Law*. Norman: Univ. of Oklahoma Press, 1978.

Eckenrode, Hamilton James. *Separation of Church and State in Virginia: A Study in the Development of the Revolution*. Richmond: Davis Bottom, 1910.

Gurley, James Lafayette. "Thomas Jefferson's Philosophy and Theology: As Related to His Political Principles, Including Separation of Church and State." Ph.D. diss., Univ. of Michigan, 1975.

Healey, Robert M. *Jefferson on Religion in Public Education*. New Haven: Yale Univ. Press, 1962.

Hening, William Waller, ed. *The Statutes at Large; Being a Collection of all the Laws of Virginia, From the First Session of the Legislature, in the Year 1619*. 12 vols. Richmond: J. & G. Cochran, 1823.

Howard, A. E. Dick. *Commentaries on the Constitution of Virginia.* 2 vols. Charlottesville: Univ. Press of Virginia, 1974.

Howe, Mark DeWolfe. *The Garden and the Wilderness: Religion and Government in American Constitutional History.* Chicago: Univ. of Chicago Press, 1965.

"Jefferson and the Church-State Wall: A Historical Examination of the Man and the Metaphor." *Brigham Young University Law Review* (1978): 645–74.

Journal of the House of Delegates of the Commonwealth of Virginia. Richmond: Thomas W. White, 1828.

Journal of the House of Delegates of Virginia. Anno Domini, 1776. Richmond: Samuel Shepherd, 1828.

Journal of the Senate of the Commonwealth of Virginia. Richmond: Thomas W. White, 1827.

Koch, Adrienne, and William Peden, eds. *The Life and Selected Writings of Thomas Jefferson.* New York: Modern Library, Random House, 1944.

Levy, Leonard W. *The Establishment Clause: Religion and the First Amendment.* New York: Macmillan, 1986.

Lipscomb, Andrew A., and Albert Ellery Bergh, eds. *The Writings of Thomas Jefferson.* 20 vols. Washington, D.C.: Thomas Jefferson Memorial Association, 1905.

Malone, Dumas. *Jefferson the Virginian.* Boston: Little, Brown, 1948.

Miller, William Lee. *The First Liberty: Religion and the American Republic.* New York: Alfred A. Knopf, 1986.

Peterson, Merrill D. *Thomas Jefferson and the New Nation.* New York: Oxford Univ. Press, 1970.

Peterson, Merrill D., and Robert C. Vaughan, eds. *The Virginia Statute for Religious Freedom: Its Evolution and Consequences in American History.* New York: Cambridge Univ. Press, 1988.

Pfeffer, Leo. *Church, State, and Freedom.* Boston: Beacon Press, 1953.

Randall, Henry S. *The Life of Thomas Jefferson.* 3 vols. New York: Derby and Jackson, 1858.

Report of the Committee of Revisors Appointed by the General Assembly of Virginia in MDCCLXXVI. Richmond: Dixon & Holt, 1784.

Rutland, Robert A., and William M. E. Rachal, eds. *The Papers of James Madison.* 17 vols. Chicago: Univ. of Chicago Press, 1973–91.

Schachner, Nathan. *Thomas Jefferson: A Biography.* 2 vols. New York: Appleton-Century-Crofts, 1951.

Smith, Rodney K. "Getting Off on the Wrong Foot and Back on Again: A Reexamination of the History of the Framing of the Religion Clauses of the First Amendment and a Critique of the *Reynolds* and *Everson* Decisions." *Wake Forest Law Review* 20 (1984): 569–643.

Part III

Religion and the Law

5 ⦀ The Supreme Court, the Establishment Clause, and Incoherence

Frank Guliuzza

At a time when the judicial and scholarly interest in religion and politics is particularly keen, it is hard to imagine that as recently as the late 1970s constitutional scholars generally regarded the church-state controversy as a settled area of constitutional law. In their 1978 book on civil rights in the United States, Harriet Pollack and Alexander Smith asserted that "with the exception of the ongoing effort to obtain public support for parochial schools and the intermittent grumbling over prohibition of prayer in the public schools there are no religious issues in the public forum today."[1]

Of course, the situation today is very different. Not only has the Supreme Court decided cases whose reach extends beyond questions of government support for parochial schools and prayer in the public schools, but the Court's reconsideration of these traditional issues has intensified rather than settled the debate between those who oppose government support for religion and those who favor such support. Furthermore, one can now safely predict "a steady flow of establishment clause cases in the years ahead."[2]

It is worth noting that in the church-state debate the Court generates controversy as much from the inconsistency of its decisions as from their policy consequences. Mark Tushnet finds these decisions "incoherent."[3] Stephen Pepper argues that they are "in significant disarray."[4] Leonard Levy calls some decisions "disastrous."[5] Gerard Bradley says that "these counterintuitive judicial commandments are also historically counterfactual."[6] Francis Lee notes with respect to these cases that the "problems, rather than being resolved, seem to have been aggravated and inflamed by the Court's ministering."[7]

There are a variety of explanations for, and proposed solutions to, the Court's confusion. One line of thinking, offered both by strict separationists as well as those who support government accommodation of religion, seems to dominate the literature. It centers on the claim that the Court has departed from the framers' original understanding of the constitutional requirement that there be no "establishment" of religion in the United States. Separationists argue that the framers wanted so complete a division between church and state that any government accommodation would be unconstitutional.[8] Accommodationists, or nonpreferentialists, insist that the framers only intended to preclude the establishment of a national church, so the Court in the twentieth century has erred by seeking to erect a high wall of separation.[9]

The irony of this "quest for originalism" is that both sides are correct. The Court did deviate from the framers' intentions, and this explains its inconsistent rulings. The trouble with the historical approach is obvious. There are two distinct groups of jurists and scholars whose widely divergent interpretations of history cannot both be correct. A separationist interpretation of the historical data precludes an accommodationist interpretation, and vice versa. Unless the Court were suddenly to embrace one of the two historical interpretations and, more importantly, begin rendering decisions exclusively on the basis of that one historical interpretation, the "quest for originalism" is unlikely to prove a remedy for the Court's incoherence.

Perhaps there is a relatively more simple explanation for the Court's wandering establishment-clause jurisprudence. In fact, it might merely be a matter of definitional ambiguity. Could it be that the Court was doomed to incoherence from the outset due to a haphazard use of the terms *separation* and *neutrality?*

In this chapter, I will first look at three clusters of cases between the Court's two pivotal establishment-clause decisions: *Everson* v. *Board of Education*[10] (1947) and *Lemon* v. *Kurtzman*[11] (1971). In these early decisions, the Court offers two different definitions of separation, a strict definition and a softer one that is linked to the idea of neutrality. These key terms will be examined closely for clues as to the source of the Court's incoherence. Next, I will put forth three possible interpretations of the terms separation and neutrality and show that two of these are meaningless and the third, although coherent, was not embraced by the Court. Finally, I will point to the consequences of the Court's establishment-clause jurisprudence for religion and politics and individual religious liberty.

MESHING SEPARATION AND NEUTRALITY:
THE *EVERSON/LEMON* DOCTRINE

Cluster One: Everson, McCollum, *and* Zorach

The Court explicated its theory of establishment in the two seminal cases identified above. The *Everson* decision articulated the Court's requirement of "strict separation" between church and state. *Lemon* then clarified the Court's position by fully embracing the "neutrality" doctrine. A careful look at the three sets of cases from 1947 to 1971 reveals the progression from strict separation to neutrality and the implications of this transition.

The first cluster of cases was decided between 1947 and 1952, and the cases introduce and flesh out the separation doctrine. In *Everson* the majority does not equivocate on the issue of separation. The establishment clause, according to the majority opinion, prohibits the government from the following activities: setting up a church, passing laws that aid religion or prefer one religion over another, influencing a person to attend or not attend church, and punishing anyone for entertaining or professing a religious belief or disbelief. In addition, it requires that no tax can be levied by a state or the national government—no matter how large or small or no matter what the tax might be called—to support religious activities or instructions. Moreover, government cannot, openly or secretly, participate in the affairs of any religious organization. Black stated that the establishment clause "was intended to erect a 'wall of separation' between Church and State."[12]

There is a problem with the *Everson* decision, however. Justice Black's dicta arguably did not square with the results of the decision. A New Jersey school board was able to scale the wall of separation and reimburse parochial school students for riding on buses operated by the public transportation system. Defending the results of the case, Black conceded that the ordinance might make it easier and more attractive for parents to send their children to parochial schools. It provides an indirect benefit to the religious mission of the religious institution. For that matter, so do police and fire protection, sewage disposal, and sidewalks. Cutting off church schools from these essential services, services generally available to the community at large, argued Black, actually pits the state against the church as adversaries.

How does Black resolve the dilemma? He argues that it is obviously not the purpose of the First Amendment to promote hostility between church and state: "That Amendment requires the state to be neutral in its relations with groups of religious believers and non-believers; it does not require the state to be their adversary. State power is no more to be used so as to handicap religion than it is to favor them."[13]

Thus the majority upheld the school board's reimbursement plan. In order to square the dicta with the results of the decision, however, Black had to simultaneously define the establishment clause as erecting "a wall of separation between church and state" and requiring "the state to be neutral in its relations with groups of believers and non-believers."[14]

It is hard to follow the logic of Justice Black's argument. At first glance he appears to have meant for the establishment clause to require both "separation" and "neutrality." But a careful look at the opinion invites another interpretation. After rationalizing the decision to uphold New Jersey's program, over vigorous dissent,[15] Black once again returned to the separation theme. He argued, "The first amendment has erected a wall between church and state. That wall must be kept high and impregnable. We could not approve the slightest breach."[16] Because Black did not back away from his separationist argument but sandwiched his discussion of neutrality with two passionate statements supporting separation, the justice might well have interpreted neutrality and separation, in this context, as being synonymous. At the very least, he seems to view neutrality as a subcomponent of separation.

If there was any question that Black intended for the establishment clause to require strict separation, the justice settled the issue one year later in *McCollum* v. *Board of Education*.[17] Several statements affirm his commitment to separation. First, he argued that both the majority opinion and dissenting opinions in *Everson* "agreed that the first amendment's language, properly interpreted, had erected a wall of separation between church and state."[18] Second, he repudiated the traditional accommodationist, or nonpreferentialist, argument that "historically the first amendment was intended to forbid only government preference of one religion over another and not impartial governmental assistance of all religions."[19] Further, he distinguished separation, "a requirement to abstain from fusing functions of Government and of religious sects," from simply treating all religions equally.[20] Third, Black struck down the Champaign, Illinois, released time program, maintaining that the state cannot utilize its public school system to aid any or all religious faiths in the dissemination of their doctrines and ideals. Overturning the Illinois program did not constitute unlawful hostility toward religion.[21] He concluded by reiterating the separationist theme:

> For the first amendment rests upon the premise that both religion and government can best work to achieve their lofty aims if each is left free from the other within its respective sphere. Or, as we said in the Everson case, the first amendment has erected a wall of separation between Church and State which might be kept high and impregnable.[22]

The last decision in the Court's early trilogy of establishment clause cases, its decision to uphold New York's released time program in *Zorach* v. *Clauson*,[23] might be viewed as more of a reaction to the ensuing protest following *McCollum*.[24] It certainly is enigmatic in light of the *Everson* dicta and the unyielding support for strict separation in *McCollum*.

Justice Douglas distinguished New York's programs from its counterpart in Champaign, Illinois, and argued that rather than coercing students to get them to attend religious classes, as had the Illinois program, "the school authorities are neutral in this regard and do no more than release students whose parents so request."[25] The Court did not, he insisted, waver from its support for the separation doctrine. He noted that the church and state should be separated, that the separation must be complete and unequivocal, and that the first amendment permits no exception. "The prohibition," he said "is absolute."[26]

With that in mind, however, Justice Douglas's reasoning starts to look like Black's in *Everson*—only, unlike Black's opinion, it is almost impossible to outline any coherent argument. First, Douglas retreated from his commitment to strict separation. Early in the opinion he observed, "The first amendment, however, does not say that in every and all respects there shall be a separation of Church and State." Later he maintained, "The constitutional standard is the separation of Church and State. The problem, like many problems in constitutional law, is one of degree."[27] Surely, he argued, separation cannot be pushed to the degree that it would rob the church of police and fire protection, or disallow references to God in presidential addresses or prayers in our legislative halls. That scenario would leave the state and religion as aliens to each other—"hostile, suspicious, and even unfriendly." Next, he noted, "We are a religious people whose institutions presuppose a Supreme Being. . . . When the state encourages religious instructions or cooperates with religious authorities by adjusting the schedule of public events to sectarian needs, it follows the best of our traditions."[28] Therefore, in order to prevent hostility, he mandated that government be neutral, even accommodating, to the religious needs of the people.

Douglas uses three statements to support the shift from strict separation to neutrality and accommodation. He argued, first, that the state follows the best of our traditions when it cooperates with religion, "for then it respects the religious nature of our people and *accommodates* the public service to their spiritual needs."[29] Later, he insisted that "the government must be *neutral* when it comes to cooperation between sects."[30] Finally, he noted: "We follow the *McCollum* case. But we cannot expand it to cover the present released time program unless *separation* of Church and State means that public institutions can make no adjustments of their schedules to *accommodate* the religious needs of the people. We cannot read into the Bill of Rights such a philosophy of hostility toward religion."[31]

Douglas's opinion contains the following arguments: (1) *Everson* and *McCollum* were correctly decided—the establishment clause requires a strict separation of church and state, (2) the establishment clause cannot tolerate hostility, (3) government must therefore be neutral, or even accommodating, to circumvent hostility, and (4) neutrality is acceptable because strict separation does not mean strict separation. Thus the requirement of separation of church and state, in any given situation, becomes one of degree.

Justice Douglas's analysis follows Justice Black's reasoning in *Everson* with some notable exceptions. First, Douglas softened "strict separation." *Zorach* tells us "strict separation" is one of degree. Further, we discover in *Everson* and *Zorach* that the establishment clause will tolerate "less-than-strict separation," or what others might call neutrality, in the name of strict separation. This more flaccid definition of separation, Douglas's definition, will become important as the Court justifies its "benevolent neutrality" doctrine in future decisions. Ironically, Justice Douglas will be unable to accept some of the future excursions from strict separation that would emerge from his own softer definition.[32]

Second, Douglas, unlike any other separationist justice in the relatively brief history of the Court's interpretation of the establishment clause, appears to recognize that accommodation might be a legitimate subcomponent of neutrality. Thus he allowed for a more generous level of neutrality. He even spoke of government accommodation toward religion. Unfortunately, like Black in *Everson*, he wrapped the whole package—neutrality and accommodation—and placed it under the tree of separation. Although he recognized that neutrality and accommodation can fit together nicely, he failed to discern that neither accommodation nor neutrality squares with rigid separation. This analysis will become more critical below.

Third, and again rather profoundly, Douglas extended what it means to be hostile toward religion. He expanded the previous definition of hostility — denying religious groups essential government services—to one recognizing the possibility that government might actually prefer nonreligion to religion. This, noted Douglas, would cut against the grain of America's best traditions.

Thus, after analyzing the early establishment clause trilogy, the troubled marriage between separation and neutrality still holds up. Though the Court appears to clean up the inconsistencies evident in *Everson* by endorsing strict separation in *McCollum*, the justices revert to ambiguity in *Zorach*. The establishment clause requires separation. To avoid hostility, the establishment clause requires neutrality. Therefore, either separation is defined to equal neutrality or separation requires neutrality. As I shall indicate below, both conclusions are fatuous.

Cluster Two: Engel *and* Schempp

Ten years passed between the *Zorach* and the Bible reading and prayer decisions, *Engel* v. *Vitale*[33] and *School District* v. *Schempp*.[34] *Engel* reads very much like *McCollum*—a strident affirmation of the separation doctrine. The Court overturned the New York State Board of Regent's prayer, composed by state officials, and said daily in public schools. Writing for the majority, Justice Black said, first, that the prayer was an unconstitutional violation of the separation doctrine:

> The State's use of the Regent's prayer in its public school system breaches the constitutional wall of separation between Church and State. We agree with that contention since we think that the constitutional prohibition against laws respecting an establishment of religion must at least mean that in this country it is no part of the business of government to compose official prayers for any group of the American people to recite as a part of a religious program carried on by government.[35]

Further, Justice Black strongly dismissed the charge that prohibiting religious services in the public schools is to "indicate a hostility toward religion or toward prayer":

> Nothing, of course, could be more wrong. . . . It is neither sacrilegious nor antireli-

gious to say that each separate government in this country should stay out of the business of writing or sanctioning official prayers and leave that purely religious function to the people themselves and to those the people choose to look to for religious guidance.[36]

Although *Engel* speaks of strict separation, *Schempp* is couched almost exclusively in terms of neutrality. In his majority opinion, which struck down Bible reading and recitation of the Lord's Prayer in Pennsylvania and Maryland, Justice Clark described the "wholesome neutrality" between government and religion. To test if a statute violates the wholesome neutrality, thereby threatening a fusion of governmental and religious functions, Clark proposed to look at the purpose and primary effect of the enactment. To "withstand the strictures of the establishment clause," he argued, "there must be a secular legislative purpose and a primary effect that neither advances or inhibits religion."[37] The decision, noted Clark, does not disallow classroom Bible study for its literary or historic qualities, or forbid a general study of religion, when presented as part of a secular program of education. But, he observed, the exercises in question do not fall into those categories:

> They are religious exercises, required by the States in violation of the command of the first amendment that the Government maintain *strict neutrality*, neither aiding nor opposing religion. Finally, we cannot accept that the concept of *neutrality*, which does not permit a State to require a religious exercise even with the consent of the majority of those affected, collides with the majority's right to free exercise of religion.[38]

Justice Brennan's concurring opinion supported Clark's plea for neutrality. Brennan noted, "I think a brief survey of certain of these forms of accommodation will reveal that the first amendment commands not official hostility toward religion, but only strict neutrality in matters of religion."[39] Further, Brennan carefully distinguished between the restrictions placed on governmental involvement with religion in order to satisfy the first amendment's neutrality requirement and "hostility":

> The State must be steadfastly neutral in all matters of faith, and never favor nor inhibit religion. In my view government cannot sponsor religious exercises in the public schools without jeopardizing that neutrality. On the other hand, hostility, not neutrality, would characterize the refusal to provide chaplains and places of

worship for prisoners and soldiers cut off by the State from all civilian opportunities for public communion, the withholding of draft exemptions for ministers and conscientious objectors, or the denial of the temporary use of an empty public building to a congregation whose place of worship has been destroyed by fire or flood. I do not say that government must provide chaplains or draft exemptions, or that the courts should intercede if it fails to do so.[40]

One might make the case that *Schempp* actually represents a shift in the Court's approach from strict separation to "strict neutrality."[41] That conclusion is erroneous for several reasons. First, it ignores the impact and reasoning of *Engel*. It would be one thing if the Court maintained a consistent separationist position in the first cluster of cases and then, ten years later, undercut the separation doctrine in favor of "neutrality." *Engel*, however, was decided just one year before *Schempp;* it deals with roughly the same constitutional questions and the outcome was the same. It simply makes better sense to treat the two cases as one grouping and look for them to form one coherent position, than to insist they are distinct and that the Court's doctrine evolved sharply in twelve months.

Second, even though the Court speaks of neutrality in *Schempp*, and not strict separation, one must note how Justice Clark defined neutrality: "As we have indicated, the establishment clause has been directly considered by this Court eight times in the past score of years and, with only one Justice dissenting on the point, it has been consistently upheld that the clause withdrew *all* legislative power respecting religious belief or the expression thereof."[42] By withdrawing all legislative power respecting religious belief or the expression thereof, Clark, like Black and Douglas before him, meshed separation and neutrality and makes them one doctrine.

Third, Justice Brennan, whose concurring opinion in *Schempp* was so influential, did not forsake the separation doctrine in favor of strict neutrality. More than twenty years later, in *Grand Rapids School District* v. *Ball*,[43] Brennan reiterated Justice Black's separationist argument in order to strike down a remedial and enhancement program operated by the Grand Rapids, Michigan, public school district.

Cluster Three: Allen, Walz, *and* Lemon

A third cluster of cases was decided between 1963 and 1971. In *Board of Education* v. *Allen*,[44] the Court applied the *Schempp* test to a program of lending state-approved textbooks free of charge to all secondary school students, including those

in private schools, and found that there was indeed a "secular purpose" and that
"the primary effect" of the program neither advanced nor inhibited religion. Speaking for the Court, Justice White insisted that the "constitutional standard" is the
separation of church and state. He conceded, however, that "the line between state
neutrality to religion and state support of religion is not easy to locate." Separation of
church and state, observed White, like most constitutional problems, is one of
degree.[45] Justice White almost used separation and neutrality interchangeably as
the Court started to fashion a new meaning for the separation doctrine.

In *Walz* v. *Tax Commission,* Chief Justice Burger's majority opinion upholding
tax exemptions for religious property expanded upon the shifting definition of
separation articulated in *Allen.* Burger cited the opinion in *Zorach* to argue that the
first amendment does not say that "in every and all respects there shall be a separation of Church and State."[46] There are some general principles, Burger said,
deducible from the first amendment, over which there is no debate:

> We will not tolerate either governmentally established religion or governmental
> interference with religion. Short of those expressly proscribed governmental acts
> there is room for play in the joints productive of a benevolent neutrality which will
> permit religious exercise to exist without sponsorship and without interference.[47]

Burger argued further that "no perfect or absolute separation is really possible; the
very existence of the Religion Clauses is an involvement of sorts—one that seeks
to make boundaries to avoid excessive entanglement."[48]

Like *Allen,* the majority in *Walz* attempted to limit the separation doctrine and
square it with an acceptable standard of neutrality. In *Lemon,* the Court finished
administering its deathblow to strict separation. Chief Justice Burger distinguished
parochial school aid programs in Pennsylvania and Rhode Island from *Walz:* the
former is unconstitutional aid, the latter is not. The objective of the establishment
clause, noted Burger, is to prevent the intrusion of either church or state into the
precincts of the other and not to construct walls of separation:

> Our prior holdings do call for total separation between church and state; total
> separation is not possible in an absolute sense. Some relationship between govern-
> ment and religious organizations is inevitable. Fire inspections, building and zon-
> ing regulations, and state requirements under compulsory school attendance laws
> are examples of necessary and permissible contacts. Indeed, under the statutory

exemption before us in *Walz,* the State had a continuing burden to ascertain that the exempt property was in fact being used for religious worship. Judicial caveats against entanglement must recognize that the line of separation, far from being a "wall," is a blurred, indistinct, and variable barrier depending on all the circumstances of a particular relationship.[49]

There can be little doubt that the last cluster of cases radically changed the Court's approach to the establishment clause. By the *Lemon* decision, strict separation was out of the picture. The scope of strict separation is obvious. Strict separation will tolerate no accommodation. Government, arguably, could not provide police and fire protection to church buildings—maybe not even to parsonages. Even if unequivocal separation did not require a fireman to look askance at a blazing church building, the implications of strict separation are ominous. The government could not distribute hot lunches, provide educational equipment, medical or psychological treatment, or even diagnostic testing, to thousands of children attending parochial schools. Government could not provide funding for church hospitals or child-care facilities. Military academies could not fund chaplains. Soldiers could not be afforded religious comfort on the battlefield. Congress and the Supreme Court could not open sessions with reference to God—-whose name, no longer the source of our trust, would be unceremoniously (since any ceremony would smack of a government approved religious service) stricken from our money.

Despite the severity of their language in the majority opinion in *McCollum* and the dissenting opinion in *Zorach,* the separationists on the Court do not push *Everson* to its logical extreme. They support *Everson*'s rhetoric and historical analysis but refuse to wash neutrality out of the equation in favor of unbridled separation. In fact, the Court further extricated itself from strict separation by declaring that Americans are a religious people whose institutions presuppose a Supreme Being, by noting that government cannot be hostile toward religion, and by taking steps to identify programs that are neutral. Thus, despite the fact that enforcing strict separation would provide the Court with coherence, strict separation is not a desirable option. It never could be—neither in the 1780s nor two centuries later.

The shift did not mean, however, that the separation doctrine had been abolished. Just as Justice Douglas had done in *Zorach,* in *Lemon* the Court only softened the separation doctrine; they did not eliminate it. Not unlike Plato's Socrates in "The Statesman,"[50] who, though not a major actor in the dialogue, remains in the background as an ever-present and dominant figure, the "wall of separation" affects every establishment clause decision.

In the three clusters of cases between *Everson* and *Lemon,* the Court actually fashioned two competing views of separation: "strict" separation, evidenced in Black's dicta in *Everson* and the majority opinions in *McCollum* and *Engel;* and "softer" separation, evidenced in Douglas's opinion in *Zorach* and the majority opinions in *Schempp* and *Lemon.* The essential difference is that after *Lemon,* the separation doctrine has a dual nature. When the Court speaks of separation, and means strict separation, it says *separation.* When the Court speaks of separation, and the justices mean the softer—or partial—separation, it says *neutrality.*

Justice Powell's opinion in *Committee for Public Education* v. *Nyquist* illustrates the dual nature of separation.[51] He starts his analysis by noting Madison's commitment, shared by Jefferson and others, to strict separation. Madison was so jealous for religious freedoms, Powell said, that he hoped they would never become entangled in precedents. Powell noted, however, that despite Madison's admonishment and the "sweep of the absolute prohibitions" of the clauses, this nation is not, nor ever has been, "one of entirely sanitized separation between Church and State."[52] Total separation has never been thought either possible or desirable. As a result, he observed, the church-state cases have "presented some of the most perplexing questions to come before the Court. Those cases have occupied the concern and thoughtful scholarship of some of the Court's most respected former Justices."[53] Consequently, Powell argued, the Court no longer meanders all over the map when adjudicating church-state cases. The constitutional standards are well defined:

> As a result of these decisions and opinions, it may no longer be said that the Religion Clauses are free of "entangling" precedents. Neither, however, may it be said that Jefferson's metaphoric "wall of separation" between Church and State has become "as winding as the famous serpentine wall" he designed for the University of Virginia. Indeed, the controlling constitutional standards have become firmly rooted and the broad contours of our inquiry are now well defined.[54]

In his introductory argument, Powell never spoke of neutrality. The context of his argument deals with separation. Yet Powell applies *Lemon*'s test for neutrality to evaluate New York's aid package thereby putting neutrality into the context of his modified view of separation. He neatly bridges the gap between separation and neutrality.

The only substantial difference between Powell's "contemporary" approach, illustrated by his opinion in *Nyquist,* and Justice Black's original separationist argument in *Everson* is what each justice meant by *separation.* Black spoke of strict separation. Powell referred to a less rigid type of separation. One might even argue that because Black spoke of separation and neutrality simultaneously, and authored the majority opinion in a case that upheld governmental aid to parochial schools, there is really very little difference between the *Everson* approach and the *Lemon* approach. Both are rooted in separation but end up defining the separation doctrine to require neutrality. As it turns out, cases like *McCollum* and *Engel,* because of their doctrinal purity, do not fit the pattern. The intensity with which they push the separation doctrine sets them apart from the general level of definitional ambiguity demonstrated by the Court.

SEPARATION, NEUTRALITY, AND DOCTRINAL INTEGRITY: THREE OPTIONS

The Supreme Court has defined the establishment clause to require separation of church and state (*Everson, McCollum, Engel*). The Court has also defined the establishment clause to require neutrality (*Everson, Schempp, Lemon*). In the more than forty years since *Everson,* the Court has softened and yet perpetuated the doctrine of separation, embraced and elaborated on its understanding of neutrality, and, as a result, has created a theory of church-state relations that brings the two concepts together in one of three ways: (1) the Court has defined separation as neutrality, so that they are synonyms and the terms can be used interchangeably; (2) the Court has isolated neutrality as a subcomponent of separation; and (3) the Court has interpreted the establishment clause to require both separation and neutrality between church and state with neutrality subsequent to separation. Of the three options, the final option is the only one that is acceptable. The others do not make sense. Yet the final interpretation arguably has never been applied by the Court to the establishment clause.

Synonyms: Separation and Neutrality?

One way to summarize the Court's treatment of separation and neutrality is to argue they have been interpreted synonymously. Justice Black, in *Everson,* intended to use the two words interchangeably in order to both create the separation doctrine and safeguard against hostility toward religion. If we were to outline the *Everson* decision it might look something like this:

> 1. The establishment clause means strict separation between government and religion; thus the establishment clause is synonymous with separation.
>
> 2. Strict separation, however, often engenders hostility between government and religion.
>
> 3. Therefore, the establishment clause also means there must be neutrality between government and religion and nonreligion; thus the establishment clause is synonymous with neutrality.
>
> 4. As a result, strict separation means, or is synonymous with, neutrality.

This is a formula designed to produce chaos. It is unlikely, however, that either Justice Black or the Court intended to proffer this interpretation. Put very simply, it is absurd. Separation does not mean neutrality. Separation and neutrality cannot be used interchangeably.

There is something very intriguing about these two concepts. Separation implies the breakup of two or more who are in a relationship. Separation must come from those within a closed set such as a marriage, a covenant relationship, a club, or a political organization. Their separation might be very bitter. It might be amiable. For obvious reasons it cannot be "neutral."

Conceptually, neutrality need not be severed completely from separation. Neutrality, however, is but one possible relationship those previously outside the set might have with those who, from within the set, have separated. Those outside the set might be neutral to both parties. They might favor one party over the other. They might even merge with one of the parties who have separated and form a new set. To be neutral requires one to be a third party to a relationship. Neutrality refers to someone outside of the closed set.

Separation of church and state implies that these two institutions, which had previously shared a relationship, have, in effect, divorced; they have ceased sharing their previous commitment. Neutrality toward church and state, therefore, requires that there be a third party who does not align with church or state. By definition, one cannot be both separate and neutral.

Neutrality: A Subset of Separation?

Although one might embrace such an interpretation, it is unlikely the Court intended to define "separation of church and state" to mean neutrality. Perhaps, however, one can rescue the Court from its lack of clarity. Suppose the Court in *Everson* had defined separation to require neutrality. The logic of the argument would be as follows. The establishment clause requires separation of church and state. If anything can be used synonymously, the justices could reason, it is *establishment clause* and *separation*. Because of the potential of hostility to religion, however, neutrality is a necessary subcomponent of separation. Again, if we were to outline the argument it might look something like this:

1. The establishment clause means strict separation between government and religion; thus the establishment clause is synonymous with separation (*Everson*).

2. Strict separation, however, often engenders hostility between government and religion.

3. Therefore, the establishment clause requires neutrality between government and religion and nonreligion.

4. As a result, strict separation requires neutrality.

It is easy, however, to demonstrate that this explanation, too, is seriously flawed. Separation cannot coexist conceptually with neutrality with separation as the dominant concept. To suggest otherwise engenders the same problems discussed above, either definitional ambiguity or failure to recognize the special nature of neutrality.

The Court cannot, logically, expect the government to be neutral in its own relationship with religious institutions. That would require government to be both a participant in a relationship and a third party to the same relationship simultaneously. Each of the following statements describes a logically acceptable connection between government and religion: government must be separate from religion, government must be hostile toward religion, and government must be benevolent toward religion. The following statement, however, describes a relationship that makes no sense: government must be neutral toward religion. The statement is incomplete. It demands we identify another party to whom government must be neutral—a party contending with religion. The following statements do make sense: government must be neutral toward church *and those outside of church*, government must be neutral toward religion *and nonreligion*, and government must be neutral toward believers *and unbelievers*.

The Court can dictate that government be neutral in its relationships with competing churches or in its relationship between religion and nonreligion. However, consistent with this analysis, the requirement of neutrality is not a subcomponent of separation. To require separation directly affects government in its own relationship with religion. Separation might be friendly or strict but, to be true to our definition, no neutral relationship can exist between church and state. However, separation, like accommodation, can be an acceptable subcomponent of neutrality. Separation can coexist with neutrality but only if neutrality is the principal concept.

The Establishment Clause: Both Separation and Neutrality?

At first glance, the first and second options do seem to place the Court in a position of defending a logical inconsistency. The Court cannot require government to be both separate from the church and neutral toward the church simultaneously. Why not? Neutrality requires a third party, outside of the closed set of those in the original relationship, to deal with the separating parties. The problem with evaluating the first and second interpretations, however, is the assumption that the Court's approach to the establishment clause is a one-step process. Such an interpretation places the Court in an impossible position. It is a root cause of the Court's incoherence.

If, however, one recognizes the Court's interpretation of the establishment clause as a two-step process, the reasoning makes much more sense. The establishment clause requires both separation and neutrality—with neutrality emerging from a condition of separation. The Court, not unlike a local judge in a divorce decree, declares a divorce, a separation, between the state and church. The church loses its preferred position with the state, and the state becomes free to be neutral toward those outside of church. To guard against potential hostility toward church, the Court declares that government must be neutral toward the contending parties.

In this illustration of the Court's treatment of the establishment clause, neutrality emerges from separation. By severing a preferred relationship, the government is free to elevate a party, previously in a subordinate position, to an equal status. For example, when a nation ends the practice of racial apartheid, and repudiates a doctrine of white supremacy, it is free to be neutral to all races by lifting up those previously at odds with the government into a position of equality with those previously favored.

This final interpretation explains how the Court might mix separation and neutrality so freely in its establishment clause jurisprudence. Keeping the interpretation in mind, one can go back through the Court's establishment clause cases and find that they might make some sense. It does not, however, explain why, in some instances, the Court will uphold government aid to religion and, in other instances, will disallow support.

Yet although the Court must embrace this third interpretation if its reasoning in the early establishment clause cases discussed above is to make sense, there is little evidence that suggests it has actually done so. First, in defending this interpretation, the Court has to prove that the church was ever in a preferred relationship with the national or state governments. That means, among other things, the Court must identify, specifically, the "church" that enjoyed such a preferred relationship. If there was no government preference shown toward the church, then the establishment clause requires the state to separate itself from an institution from which it was already separated. It would require there be a divorce when, in fact, there had never been a marriage. A separation doctrine would, therefore, be redundant. There would be no need for government to be separate from the church—only to be neutral toward the church and those outside the church.

Second, if the Court intended to proffer this interpretation, why has it softened its definition of separation? The reason undoubtedly is that the justices recognized the unacceptable policy implications inherent in a position of strict separation and, therefore, have backed away from complete separation (*McCollum* or *Engel* separation), substituting in its place *Lemon* separation. However, the level of separation required by *Lemon* is unacceptable. Strict separation between church and state would be necessary for the Court to be coherent. The Court could have required complete separation of church and state and still have avoided the policy implications of strict separation by allowing for benevolent neutrality, even accommodation, between religion and state. The Court cannot equivocate regarding "separation," however. The preferred relationship must be terminated in order for there to be genuine neutrality.

Therefore, an evident source of the Court's incoherent approach to the religion clauses is its substitution of "separation" for "no law respecting an establishment." To avoid the policy implications of strict separation the Court has defined the establishment clause to require both separation and neutrality. As a result, it has created a theory of church-state relations that brings the two concepts together in one of three ways. Two interpretations are so illogical that it is impossible to believe the Court could have seriously entertained them. The third interpretation makes better sense, but the Court seriously damages the interpretation's applicability by softening the requirement of strict separation. Substituting separation for no law respecting an establishment doomed the Court to incoherence.

THE CONSEQUENCES OF INCOHERENCE

Apart from the sustained scolding the justices have received, are there any specific consequences attributable to the Court's establishment-clause jurisprudence? The Court's haphazard approach to the religion clauses indeed has had more substantial repercussions. The jurisprudence has not been without important policy consequence. First, there is the troubling lack of consistency in adjudicating the Constitution's religion clauses, a fact that is well documented in most textbooks in American constitutional Law. In one decision, religious institutions will receive governmental aid; in another, apparently similar to the first, religious institutions are denied support.[55] One decision might exalt the religious freedom of an individual or group; other decisions have placed what seemed to be unnecessary restrictions on the free exercise of religion.[56] Moreover, when one looks at the establishment clause more carefully, one discovers that the analysis behind the decisions is suspect. Often the justices' reasoning has been so counterintuitive that inconsistent results were inevitable.[57]

Perhaps more important, the Court's jurisprudence has created a mind-set that the establishment clause requires strict separation of church and state. Although in practice the Court has retreated from the strict separation doctrine, it is hard to overestimate the impact Justice Black's argument in *Everson* has had upon the thinking of the American public. M. Glenn Abernathy notes that "the 'establishment' clause of the first amendment has long since been rephrased in the general literature and the popular mind to become simply a guarantee of 'separation of church and state.'"[58] As Gerard Bradley has observed, "'Separation of church and state' is right up there with Mom, apple pie, and baseball in American iconography." Bradley indicates that the public must be assured that "of course, God and Caesar remain securely in their respective domains."[59]

This misperception about the requirements of the establishment clause fosters two particular sets of unacceptable results that have a most direct impact upon political life and the education of children. First, the misperception has obscured the vital role religion plays in American public life, thus tending to "secularize" the public square. Already in 1958, Loren Beth warned of the consequences that would follow should religion be banished from the public arena. Religion, noted Beth, offers the national moral foundation that claims to be higher than that of the state. Without competing standards for morality the state must articulate and enforce a moral position that most do not believe to be absolute and that could not be judged by reference to any other standard. Whether seen as offering an absolute an absolute standard of morality, or merely a relative moral position that competes with the state, religion, argued Beth, occupies a crucial position in the society:

> If it represents absolute morality, and infallibility, it provides a definite standard by which to judge the morality of the state and the actions of the state; if it represents merely *another* standard of mortality, it still provides a necessary alternative to the state's course of action. Democracy depends greatly on the existence of such an alternative and on the maintenance of the freedom of the citizenry to choose this alternative in preference to that of the state.[60]

However, largely because of a failure by the courts to articulate clear-cut standards, one observes an erosion of the impact religion is permitted to have in the public square. One look at the contemporary literature confirms the relevancy of the argument that Beth expressed thirty-five years ago. A wide range of scholars, including Mark Tushnet,[61] Harold Berman,[62] Robert Bellah,[63] Richard J. Neuhaus,[64] Michael Perry,[65] A. James Reichley,[66] and Paul Vitz[67] vindicate Beth's thesis.[68] They have discovered that there is an effort to silence religion from the public area—often in the name of pluralism and toleration.

Tushnet has identified two principles that explain much of what the Supreme Court has done to emasculate religion: the reduction principle and the marginality principle. The reduction principle strips from religious belief anything that would distinguish it from other types of belief. The rituals of religious belief are treated like symbolic speech and tested by the standards developed in symbolic speech cases. Further, the reduction principle applies similar rules to actions motivated by religious belief that govern in cases in which speech is suppressed because of its affect on governmental interests.[69] The marginality principle holds that the law need only recognize religion to the degree that religion has no socially significant consequence; it will not do so if religion is socially significant. This principle requires the state to balance the interests of religion against its own regulatory interests.[70] The result has been the curtailment of religion's role in the public arena:

> Religion . . . has no distinctive role to play in the shaping of public policy. Indeed, by treating individual preferences as outside the scope of political analysis, the liberal tradition excludes religion from public life. It then seeks a theoretical expression for what it has done. The reduction and marginality principles together provide that expression: religion is still largely private, and its intrusion into the public sphere is small and unimportant.[71]

One identifiable impact of the confused case law is the unfortunate "secularization" of public school education. In his study conducted for the Department of Education, Paul Vitz examined sixty social studies textbooks used by more than 85 percent of America's grade school children. Vitz looked for "primary" references to religious activity, such as prayer, church attendance, or participation in religious ceremonies, and "secondary" references, such as citing the date when a church was built. Vitz found a "total absence of any primary religious reference about typical contemporary American religious life." He also discovered very few secondary references. Even when it is necessary to refer to religion in order to present an accurate view of remote points in history, textbooks and educators will go out of their way to "separate" religion from a given historical narrative.[72]

The second unacceptable result is that, in the name of safeguarding individual liberties, the misperception has cut deeply into the religious rights of many American citizens. Beth has argued that total separation is only a theoretical idea; in practice, it is impossible to avoid all conflict between church and state. The model simply assumes that religion is pietistic and privatized, yet, with the exception of some of the German Pietistic sects, and, on occasion, the Quakers, religion in Western civilization does not fit the model. Christianity, for instance, seeks to guide the believer's actions as well as his spirit and soul. But unless religion is restricted "to so small an area of human activity that it would cease to be a real force in human society," it must inevitably come into conflict with the state.[73]

One might argue that the single-minded pursuit of total separation has not only succeeded in making the separation doctrine look rigid and ridiculous,[74] but that it threatens religious liberty just as seriously as would unrestrained government accommodation. The application of an extreme separation doctrine has generated often disastrous results. One example is found in those decisions that prevent parochial school students—who are required by state law to attend school six to eight hours a day and whose parents must pay to support remedial and extracurricular programs in the public schools—from receiving benefits that their state and national policy makers felt should be available to all students, even if provided by the community after school or on Saturdays.[75] Furthermore, the perception that the establishment clause erects a wall of separation can cut deeply into the rights of those who, though required by law to attend school, wish to exercise their religious beliefs in ways that, perhaps unlike public prayer or Bible reading, do not foster coercion or oppression. One such example is the fight by some school boards and principals to keep religious groups or clubs off campus—even though Congress passed legislation in 1984 allowing equal access for such groups in a limited public forum.[76] One principal in Nebraska held that, should he lose in court, he would close down all after-school extracurricular activities in order to prevent a prayer and Bible club from meeting on campus.[77]

Moreover, there are myriad examples of religious discrimination that are not argued before the Supreme Court. In fact, they may never come to trial. These less notorious cases reveal very real examples of religious discrimination, of students and teachers who are told they are "breaking the law" when they exercise their religious beliefs. A public school student was told by his teacher not only that he could not read his Bible in class during free time, despite the fact that other students could read materials of their own choosing, but that he could not even bring it onto the school grounds.[78] A public school math teacher was prohibited from reading her Bible while performing her duties as lunch-room monitor, though teachers frequently would read material of their choice while on monitor duty. One school district proposed a policy that would effectively forbid teachers from having any conversation or discussion dealing with religious topics—even among themselves. A high school principal prohibited the class valedictorian from mentioning Jesus

Christ in her valedictory address.[79] Patricia Lines reveals that in some school districts student distribution of Bibles has been prohibited. She notes that in Florida one girl who gave a report to her class on the New Testament and distributed copies to her friends was taken to the principal's office. The principal confiscated all copies of the New Testament, including her personal copy, and told her that she could not quote the Bible in her book report. According to Lines, one Oklahoma child "caught bowing his head to pray before taking the math section of a standardized test was taken to the principal's office and ordered to write 'I will not pray in class' 500 times."[80]

It is difficult to blame educators, who have been led to believe the Constitution demands absolute separation of church and state, when they forbid students to exercise their religious liberties. They merely reflect the reasoning of those scholars and jurists who believe that separation is an all or nothing proposition and who, therefore, will accept nothing less than total separation. Just as it is unreasonable, however, to believe that uncontrolled accommodation between church and state will have no negative impact on churches and individuals, it is likewise unrealistic to believe that total separation has not fostered religious discrimination.

SUMMARY

The historical debate that is prominently featured in the literature cannot provide an immediate or satisfying resolution to the church-state controversy. It is possible, however, apart from the "quest for originalism," to identify the origins of the Court's incoherence. It lies in the Court's unorthodox treatment of the concepts separation and neutrality in its establishment-clause jurisprudence.

As we have seen, by interpreting the establishment clause to require both separation and neutrality, the Court in *Everson* put itself in a tough spot. Either it meant to define the two terms synonymously, to require neutrality to serve as a subcomponent of separation, or to read the establishment clause as requiring a two-stage process, with neutrality following separation. Only the final interpretation rescues the Court from incoherence. The Court has not, however, embraced this third interpretation.

The impact of the Court's incoherence is profoundly troubling. First, at a tangible level, there is the obvious lack of consistency in adjudicating the

Constitution's religion clauses. Second, the Court's jurisprudence has created a mind-set that the establishment clause requires strict separation of church and state. This has served to markedly diminish the impact of religion in the public arena and has cut deeply into the religious rights of many American citizens.

NOTES

1. Harriet Pollack and Alexander Smith, *Civil Liberties and Civil Rights in the United States* (St. Paul: West Publishing, 1978), 91.

2. See Norman Redlich, "Separation of Church and State: The Burger Court's Torturous Journey," *Notre Dame Law Review* 60 (1985): 1–94.

3. Mark Tushnet, "The Constitution of Religion," *Red, White, & Blue* (Cambridge: Harvard Univ. Press, 1988), 247.

4. Stephen Pepper, "The Conundrum of the Free Exercise Clause—Some Reflections on Recent Cases," *Northern Kentucky Law Review* 9 (1982): 303.

5. Leonard Levy, *The Establishment Clause* (New York: Macmillan, 1986), 140.

6. Gerard Bradley, *Church-State Relationships in America* (New York: Greenwood Press, 1987), xiii.

7. Francis Lee, *Wall of Controversy* (Malabar, Fla.: Robert E. Krieger, 1986), 6.

8. Although there are substantial differences between them, the following scholars offer an historical argument for a separation of church and state: Levy, *The Establishment Clause;* Thomas Curry, *The First Freedoms* (New York: Oxford Univ. Press, 1986); Douglas Laycock, "'Nonpreferential' Aid to Religion: A False Claim About Original Intent," *William & Mary Law Review* 27 (1986): 875–923; Dallin Oaks, "Separation, Accommodation, and the Future of Church and State," *De Paul Law Review* 35 (1985): 1–22; James Wood, "'No Religious Test Shall Ever Be Required,' Reflections on the Bicentennial of the United States Constitution," *Journal of Church and State* 29 (1987): 199–208; Leo Pfeffer, *God, Caesar, and the Constitution* (Boston: Beacon Press, 1975); Pfeffer, *Religion, State, and the Burger Court* (Buffalo: Prometheus, 1985); Steve Gey, "Rebuilding the Wall: The Case for a Return to the Strict Interpretation of the Establishment Clause," *Columbia Law Review* 81 (1981): 1463–90; Richard Hoskins, "The Original Separation of Church and State in America," *Journal of Law and Religion* 2 (1984): 221–39; Robert Alley, "Introduction," *James Madison on Religious Liberty* (Buffalo: Prometheus, 1985); Mark Howe, *The Garden and the Wilderness* (Chicago: Univ. of Chicago Press, 1965); and Derek Davis, *Original Intent* (Buffalo: Prometheus, 1991).

9. Several other works also take the Court to task for its usage of history. They, however, reject the wall of separation erected by the Court in *Everson* v. *Board,* 330
   U.S. 1 (1947). See, for example, Edward Corwin, "The Supreme Court as National School Board," *Law and Contemporary Problems* 14 (1948): 3–22; John
   Courtney Murray, "Law or Prepossessions," *Law and Contemporary Problems* 14
   (1948): 23–43; Chester Antieau et al., *Freedom From Federal Establishment* (Milwaukee: Bruce Publishing, 1964); Michael Malbin, *Religion & Politics* (Washing-
   ton, D.C.: American Enterprise Institute, 1978); Walter Berns, *The First Amend-
   ment and the Future of Democracy* (New York: Basic Books, 1976); Robert Cord,
   Separation of Church and State (New York: Lambeth Press, 1982); Robert Cord,
   "Church-State Separation: Restoring the 'No Preference' Doctrine of the First
   Amendment," *Harvard Journal of Law and Public Policy* 9 (1986): 129–72; Harold
   Berman, "Religion and the Law: The First Amendment in Historical Perspective,"
   Emory Law Review 35 (1986): 777–93; Gary D. Glenn, "Forgotten Purposes of
   the First Amendment Religious Clauses," *Review of Politics* 49 (1987): 340–67;
   Bradley, *Church-State Relationships in America;* Gerard Bradley, "No Religious Test
   Clause and the Constitution of Religious Liberty," *Case Western Reserve Law Review* 37 (1987): 674–749; Daniel Dreisbach, *Real Threat and Mere Shadow*
   (Westchester, Ill.: Crossway Books, 1987); and Rodney Smith, "Establishment
   Clause Analysis: A Liberty Maximizing Proposal," *Notre Dame Journal of Law,
   Ethics, and Public Policy* 4 (1990): 463–511.
10. 330 U.S., 1 (1947).
11. 403 U.S. 602 (1971).
12. *Everson* v. *Board of Education,* 18.
13. Ibid.
14. Ibid.
15. *Everson* was a five-to-four decision. Justice Rutledge authored a dissenting opinion
    that is far less ambiguous. Rutledge argues for a very consistent separationist posi-
    tion. He did not view the New Jersey program as part of the general government
    services to be afforded to religious groups. Rather, he felt New Jersey used its tax-
    ing power to furnish support for religion. And, he held, this sort of taxing power
    was a threat to strict separation: "Hence today, apart from efforts to inject religious
    training or exercise and sectarian issues into the public schools, the only serious
    surviving threat to maintaining that complete and permanent separation of religion
    and civil power which the first amendment commands is through the use of taxing
    power to support religion, religious establishments, or establishments having a reli-
    gious foundation whatever their form or special religious function."
16. *Everson* v. *Board of Education,* 18.
17. 333 U.S. 203 (1948).

18. Ibid., 211.

19. Ibid.

20. Ibid.

21. Ibid. He does not explain why it is not "hostility." Rather, he almost waves off the charge by, in effect, saying "Hostility would be wrong. Therefore, it's not hostility." Black notes, "A manifestation of such hostility would be at war with our national tradition as embodied in the first amendment's guarantee of the free exercise of religion."

22. 333 U.S. 203 (1948), 212. Justice Frankfurter, in his concurring opinion at 232, agreed with Black's separationist argument: "We renew our conviction that 'we have staked the very existence of our country on the faith that complete separation between the state and religion is best for the state and best for religion.' *Everson* v. *Board of Education.* If nowhere else, in the relation between Church and State, good fences make good neighbors."

23. 343 U.S. 306 (1952).

24. See, for example, Corwin, "The Supreme Court as National School Board," and Murray, "Law or Prepossessions."

25. *Zorach* v. *Clauson,* 311. Note that in *McCollum* v. *Board of Education,* the Court held neutrality of this type was not sufficient to satisfy the separation requirement.

26. Ibid., 312.

27. Ibid., 314.

28. Ibid., 313–14. See Frank Guliuzza, "Beyond Incoherence: Making Sense of the Church-State Debate" (Ph.D. diss., Univ. of Notre Dame, 1990).

29. Zorach, 315 (emphasis added).

30. Ibid. (emphasis added).

31. Ibid. (emphasis added).

32. See Justice Douglas's dissent in *Walz* v. *Tax Commission,* 397 U.S. 664 (1970), 700.

33. 370 U.S. 421 (1962).

34. 374 U.S. 203 (1963).

35. *Engel* v. *Vitale,* 425.

36. Ibid., 434–35.

37. *School District* v. *Schempp,* 222.

38. Ibid., 225–26 (emphasis added).

39. Ibid., 295.

40. Ibid., 299. Some of Justice Brennan's argument illustrates the reasoning discussed in the introduction. Why is providing a public building to a congregation for worship services not an unconstitutional advance of religion? Why can government pay for religious services for soldiers and prisoners and not for students who are com-

pelled, by law, to attend school five days a week? If government is not required to
provide chaplains or draft exemptions—in other words it can refuse to do so—why
is that not "official hostility" toward religion by Brennan's own definition? It seems
that several of the justices are unwilling to address these potential inconsistencies.
See Guliuzza, "Beyond Incoherence," chap. 2, for a general discussion of the
Court's inconsistent reasoning.

41. See A. E. Dick Howard, who identifies a transition in the Court's establishment
     clause requirements from separation to accommodation, in "The Supreme Court
     and the Establishment of Religion," *James Madison on Religious Liberty,* ed. Robert
     Alley (Buffalo: Prometheus, 1985). David Leitch, "The Myth of Religious Neu-
     trality by Separation in Education," *Virginia Law Review* 71 (1985): 127–72, offers
     three distinct phases of establishment clause interpretation by the Court: separation
     (Everson), accommodation (Lemon), and pluralistic integration (*Widmar* v.
     Vincent, 450 U.S. 909 [1981]). David Felsen, in "Developments in Approaches to
     Establishment Clause Analysis: Consistency for the Future," *American University
     Law Review* 38 (1989): 395–428, lists three doctrinal positions—strict separation,
     accommodation, and pluralism "which encourages government's equal treatment of
     all religions." These are all approaches, he argues, aimed at producing "neutrality."
     Laycock also reads the Court's decisions as requiring, and flushing out the defini-
     tion of, "neutrality"; see "Formal, Substantive, and Disaggregated Neutrality To-
     ward Religion," *DePaul Law Review* 39 (1990): 993–1078, and "'Neocoercive' Sup-
     port for Religion," *Valparaiso Law Review* 26 (1991): 37–69.

42. *School District* v. *Schemmp,* 222.

43. 473 U.S. 373 (1985). One can argue convincingly that although "strict separation"
     can never be a reality, the doctrine is operative nearly ten years later—even after
     Justice Brennan left the Court. Consider the Court's favorable treatment of the
     Everson v. *Board of Education* decision and the concept of separation in *Lee* v.
     Weisman, 112 S. Ct. 2649 (1992); in particular, see Justice Blackmun's concurring
     opinion. Compare this decision with the Court's recent ruling to uphold the Fifth
     Circuit in *Jones* v. *Clear Creek,* 977 F2d, 963, 5th Cir (1992).

44. 392 U.S. 236 (1968)

45. Ibid., 242.

46. *Walz* v. *Tax Commission,* 669.

47. Ibid.

48. Ibid., 670. He went on to say, "Separation in this context cannot mean absence of
     all contact, the complexities of modern life inevitably produce some contact and
     the fire and police protection received by houses of worship are within a State's
     boundaries, along with many other exempt organizations."

49. *Lemon* v. *Kurtzman,* 614.

50. See Plato's "Statesman," in *The Collected Dialogues of Plato,* trans. J. B. Skemp and ed. Edith Hamilton and Huntington Cairns (Princeton, N.J.: Princeton Univ. Press, 1971), 1018.

51. 413 U.S. 756 (1973).

52. Ibid., 760.

53. Ibid., 760–61.

54. Ibid., 761.

55. State aid to sectarian schools in the form of textbooks is acceptable; supplies and services are not. Compare *Board of Education* v. *Allen,* 292 U.S. 236 (1968) with *Meek* v. *Pittenger,* 421 U.S. 349 (1975). Salary supplements to parochial school teachers are not acceptable but property tax exemptions to all religious institutions are permitted. Compare *Lemon* v. *Kurtzman* with *Walz* v. *Tax Commission.* In many cases the Court determined that government support for institutions, individuals, or religious activities is unacceptable. See *Nyquist; Grand Rapids School District* v. *Ball,* 473 U.S. 373 (1985); *Aguilar* v. *Felton,* 473 U.S. 402 (1985); *McCollum* v. *Board of Education; Engel* v. *Vitale; School District* v. *Schempp; Stone* v. *Graham,* 449 U.S. 39 (1980); and *County of Allegheny* v. *ACLU,* 109 S.Ct. 3086 (1989). In other cases the Court upheld government support. See *Tilton* v. *Richardson,* 403 U.S. 672 (1971); *Wolman* v. *Walter,* 433 U.S. 229 (1977); *Bowen* v. *Kendricks,* 108 S. Ct. 2562 (1988); *Mueller* v. *Allen,* 463 U.S. 388 (1983); *Witters* v. *Washington,* 474 U.S. 481 (1986); *Everson* v. *Board of Education; Zorach* v. *Clauson; Marsh* v. *Chambers,* 463 U.S. 783 (1983); *Lynch* v. *Donnelly,* 465 U.S. 668 (1984); and *Board of Education* v. *Mergens,* 496 U.S. 226 (1990).

56. Why, for example, is the government required to compensate Sabbatarians who refuse to work on Saturdays (*Sherbert* v. *Verner,* 374 U.S. 398 [1963]) but not required to accommodate those who can demonstrate dire financial consequences from Sunday closing laws (*Braunfeld* v. *Brown,* 366 U.S. 420 [1961])? Why does the free exercise clause protect a young man from military combat during wartime (*United States* v. *Seeger,* 374 U.S. 398 [1965]) but not safeguard an officer who wishes to wear his yarmulke with his uniform (*Goldman* v. *Weinberger Social,* 475 U.S. 503 [1986])? Compare the recent decision, *Employment Division* v. *Smith,* 494 U.S. 872 (1990), which held that a compelling interest test would not apply to free exercise claims seeking exemption from what otherwise neutral laws of general applicability, with *Wisconsin* v. *Yoder,* 406 U.S. 205 (1972). The Court's treatment of the free exercise clause has produced a debate in the literature regarding the constitutional validity of religion-based exemptions. See William Marshall, "The Case Against the Constitutionality of Compelled Free Exercise Exemptions," *Case Western Reserve Law Review* 40 (1990): 357–412; Ellis West, "The Case Against a Right to Religion-Based Exemptions," *Notre Dame Journal of Law, Ethics, and Pub-*

lic Policy 4 (1990): 591–688; and Michael McConnell, "The Origins and Historical Understanding of Free Exercise of Religion," *Harvard Law Review* 103 (1990): 1409–1517.

57. Redlich, "Separation of Church and State," and Guliuzza, "Beyond Incoherence."

58. M. Glenn Abernathy, *Civil Liberties under the Constitution* (New York: Dodd, Mead, 1968), 249.

59. Gerard Bradley, "Church Autonomy in the Constitutional Order: The End of Church and State," *Louisiana Law Review* 49 (1989): 1057. Bradley, 1057, reprints the quotation offered by Vice-President Bush when he was a candidate for the presidency in 1988. Recounting how he felt when, as a young pilot in World War II, he was shot down, Bush noted: "Was I scared floating around in a little yellow raft off the coast of an enemy-held island, setting a world record for paddling? Of course I was. What sustains you in times like that? Well, you go back to funda- mental values. I thought about Mother and Dad and the strength I got from them—about God and faith and the separation of Church and State."

60. Loren Beth, *The American Theory of Church and State* (Gainesville, Fla.: Univ. of Florida Press, 1958), 143.

61. Tushnet, "The Constitution of Religion."

62. Berman, "Religion and the Law."

63. See Robert Bellah, "Cultural Pluralism and Religious Particularism" in *Freedom of Religion in America,* ed. Henry Clark (Los Angeles: Center of the American Expe- rience, 1982).

64. Richard J. Neuhaus, *The Naked Public Square* (Grand Rapids, Mich.: Eerdmans, 1984).

65. Michael Perry, *Love and Power* (New York: Oxford Univ. Press, 1991).

66. A. James Reichley, *Religion in American Public Life* (Washington, D.C.: Brookings Institution, 1985).

67. Paul Vitz, *Censorship: Evidence of Bias in Our Children's Textbooks* (Ann Arbor, Mich.: Servant Books, 1986).

68. Also see the collection of essays *Articles of Faith, Articles of Peace: The Religious Lib- erty Clauses and the American Public Philosophy,* ed. James Davison Hunter and Os Guinness (Washington, D.C.: Brookings Institution, 1990). Further, Frederick Gedicks, "Some Political Implications of Religious Belief," *Notre Dame Journal of Law, Ethics, and Public Policy* 4 (1990): 419, indicates the importance of "religion" entering into the political arena as a competing interest group and laments the per- ception that American political culture seeks to exclude religion. John Robinson, "Foreword: Religious Discourse and the Reinvigoration of American Political Life," *Notre Dame Journal of Law, Ethics, and Public Policy* 4 (1990): 385, identifies the importance of "full/authentic" religious discourse.

69. Tushnet, "The Constitution of Religion," 257–64.

70. Ibid., 264.

71. Ibid., 272.

72. Vitz, *Censorship*, 15–16. For a summary of Vitz's study, see Vitz, "A Study of Religion and Traditional Values in Public School Textbooks," in *Democracy and the Renewal of Public Education*, ed. Richard J. Neuhaus (Grand Rapids, Mich.: Eerdmans, 1987), 116–40. Patricia Lines, "Three Criteria for Constitutional Interpretation: Predictability, Flexibility, and Intelligibility," *Notre Dame Journal of Law and Public Policy* 4 (1990): 549, 553–54, provides many examples that support Vitz.

73. Beth, *The American Theory of Church and State*, 126.

74. See Levy, *The Establishment Clause*, 177.

75. See *Grand Rapids* v. *Ball* and *Aguilar* v. *Felton*, discussed above.

76. See *Board of Education* v. *Mergens* and Nat Hentoff, "A Bible Study in a Public School?" *Washington Post*, 14 Mar. 1989, p. A-27.

77. *Mergens* v. *Westside Community Schools*, CV 85-0-426, slip op. (D. Neb. Feb. 2, 1988) at 13.

78. See Nat Hentoff, "James Gierke's Right to Read His Bible," *Washington Post*, 10 June 1989, p. A-19.

79. "Defending and Restoring Religious Freedom Nationwide," an information handout provided by the National Legal Foundation, Virginia Beach, Virginia. See *The National Legal Foundation Minuteman* 1 (Winter 1987–88): 1; and Robert DuPuy, "Religion, Graduation, and the First Amendment: A Threat or a Shadow?" *Drake Law Review* 35 (1985–86): 323, for other examples.

80. Lines, "Three Criteria for Constitutional Interpretation," 553–54. Of course one can cite several instances of coercion and oppression by those in the "majority" who wished to impose their religious beliefs on others. These cases certainly remind us why the establishment clause was drafted and ratified, and they indicate why the courts must be ever vigilant in defending the First Amendment. They do not, however, justify an interpretation of the establishment clause that serves to validate the results discussed above.

REFERENCES

Abernathy, M. Glenn. *Civil Liberties under the Constitution*. New York: Dodd, Mead, 1968.

Beth, Loren. *The American Theory of Church and State*. Gainesville: Univ. of Florida Press, 1958.

Berman, Harold. "Religion and the Law: The First Amendment in Historical Perspective." *Emory Law Review* 35 (1986): 777–93.

Bradley, Gerard. "Church Autonomy in the Constitutional Order: The End of Church and State." *Louisiana Law Review* 49 (1989): 1057–87.

———. *Church-State Relationships in America.* New York: Greenwood Press, 1987.

Felsen, David. "Developments in Approaches to Establishment Clause Analysis: Consistency for the Future." *American University Law Review* 38 (1989): 395–428.

Guliuzza, Frank. "Beyond Incoherence: Making Sense of the Church-State Debate." Ph.D. diss., Univ. of Notre Dame, 1990.

Howard, A. E. Dick. "The Supreme Court and the Establishment of Religion." In *James Madison on Religious Liberty,* ed. Robert Alley. Buffalo: Prometheus Books, 1985.

Hentoff, Nat. "James Gierke's Right to Read His Bible." *Washington Post,* 10 June 1989, p. A-19.

Hunter, James Davison, and Os Guinness, eds. *Articles of Faith, Articles of Peace: The Religious Liberty Clauses and the American Public Philosophy.* Washington, D.C.: Brookings Institution, 1990.

Laycock, Douglas. "'Neocoercive' Support for Religion." *Valparaiso Law Review* 26 (1991): 37–69.

Lee, Francis. *Wall of Controversy.* Malabar, Fla.: Robert E. Krieger, 1986.

Leitch, David. "The Myth of Religious Neutrality by Separation in Education." *Virginia Law Review* 71 (1985): 127–72.

Levy, Leonard. *The Establishment Clause.* New York: Macmillan, 1986.

Neuhaus, Richard J. *The Naked Public Square.* Grand Rapids, Mich.: Eerdmans, 1984.

Pepper, Stephen. "The Conundrum of the Free Exercise Clause—Some Reflections on Recent Cases." *Northern Kentucky Law Review* 9 (1982): 265–303.

Perry, Michael. *Love and Power.* New York: Oxford Univ. Press, 1991.

Pollack, Harriet, and Alexander Smith. *Civil Liberties and Civil Rights in the United States.* St. Paul: West Publishing, 1978.

Redlich, Norman. "Separation of Church and State: The Burger Court's Torturous Journey." *Notre Dame Law Review* 60 (1985): 1–94.

Reichley, James. *Religion in American Public Life.* Washington, D.C.: Brookings Institution, 1985.

Tushnet, Mark. "The Constitution of Religion." In *Red, White, and Blue: A Critical Analysis of Constitutional Law.* Cambridge: Harvard Univ. Press, 1988.

Vitz, Paul. *Censorship: Evidence of Bias in Our Children's Textbooks.* Ann Arbor, Mich.: Servant Books, 1986.

6

‖ The Courts' Definition of Religious Activity:
Protection of Diversity
or Imposition of a Majority View?

Julia K. Stronks

Religion in the United States is an emotion-packed topic. It affects public policy matters from public schools to medical research to taxes. Recent analyses indicate that American churches are experiencing a "return to religion" in record numbers, and the growth of New Age spirituality indicates that Americans are seeking something that addresses fundamental questions in life. In addition, the year 1991 marked the bicentennial of the United States Bill of Rights. It is fitting, therefore, to consider the American approach to religious us freedom as articulated in the First Amendment.

The First Amendment to the United States Constitution provides in part that "Congress shall make no law respecting an establishment of religion, or prohibiting the free exercise thereof."[1] On its face this means that Americans are allowed to practice "freedom of religion" unburdened by state interference and unencumbered by government discrimination. But what does it mean to freely practice a religion? What is religion under American law? And what part have the courts played in defining what is and what is not religious activity?

Many Americans today have accepted a broad "anthropological" definition of religion, wherein faith, once seen as Protestant, Christian, Judeo-Christian, or theistic, can be said to include many world views and perspectives.[2] But it is not clear from U.S. public law that the First Amendment encompasses a similar anthropological definition of religion.

Despite two hundred years of First Amendment jurisprudence, many groups still claim to be discriminated against on the basis of their religion. Although the Supreme Court has made numerous decisions concerning the implication and applications of the First Amendment, these decisions have been of little help in answering the question, What is religious activity, and how far will we as a nation go to protect it? The Supreme Court has not been able to resolve these issues because it makes its decisions in the context of dilemmas and ambiguities which it does not see. It is true that defining religious freedom is a difficult task, and the justices of the Supreme Court are not philosophers, historians, or theologians. However, with respect to the basic protections articulated in the Bill of Rights, American citizens as well as state and lower federal courts have the right to expect two things from the nation's highest court: guidance in protecting the minority from majoritarian interests and guidance in defining constitutional concerns so that Americans in all jurisdictions enjoy the same liberties. In this task the Court has failed.

This chapter makes the argument that by accepting certain definitions of "religion" to the exclusion of others, and by fashioning Constitutional "tests" that give little guidance to state or lower federal courts, the Supreme Court has politicized the First Amendment in a way that results in discrimination against particular groups of people. Similar concerns were expressed in a May 1991 Philadelphia conference on Religion and Public Life. The conference drew together almost three hundred lawyers and political scholars concerned with the development of religious freedom in this country. Supreme Court Justice Sandra Day O'Connor addressed the group, saying that she believed freedom of religious expression was in danger. Her concern stemmed from the recent Supreme Court decision *Employment Division* v. *Smith*. This case effected a change in First Amendment jurisprudence, and, in the words of law professor Douglas Laycock, has created the "legal framework for persecution of religion in America."[3]

This chapter examines judicial decisions that have defined the way religious activity is to be protected in the United States. The first section illustrates how the definition of religion has developed. The second section examines the changes in the way the Supreme Court has balanced people's right to practice a religion with the government's interest in limiting their activity.

A HISTORICAL CONTEXT

Americans believe that we tolerate great religious diversity. We boast of religious pluralism and can point to the more than twelve hundred different religious bodies that coexist in the United States.[4] Moreover, we also allow religious "individualism"—activity or belief apart from membership in formal groups—to flourish.[5] We hold the concepts of freedom of religion, governmental neutrality toward religion, and the separation of church and state as examples for the world to follow.[6]

However, despite Americans' belief that tolerance and government neutrality toward religions dominate the political arena, First Amendment jurisprudence is in flux and is constantly under attack. Constitutional scholars decry the inconsistency and instability of First Amendment theory.[7] And religious groups claim that the courts' interpretation of the First Amendment discriminates against specific religions as well as religion in general.

This scholarly and popular ferment raises a crucial question: What is "religion" to the American court and which religions are protected? The judicial system's role in defining "protected religious activity" has developed in two phases. Some courts attempt to determine what is and what is not "religion." Other courts skirt this issue and assume what a litigant asserts as a legitimate First Amendment issue. They then focus on whether the state interest standing in the way of the religious expression is sufficient to override the constitutional protection. This chapter examines the courts' approaches to religion in both of these phases.

To understand the state and federal courts' definition of religion, the historical context in which the definition developed must first be examined. By the end of the nineteenth century, the United States had a public commitment to the separation of church and state. This commitment included a consensus that religion was related to churches and to personal, private faith. Religious freedom was freedom of "personal conviction" and freedom of "ecclesiastical association."[8] Churches and private beliefs were not to be limited or encouraged by government; the government was "neutral" toward religion. The role of the government was to serve the "secular interest" as defined by a neutral, majoritarian consensus. This consensus included a particular perspective of what "religion" is—a perspective that is evident in decisions of justices of both the Supreme Court and lower federal courts. It is this public/private split, the idea that what is public is "nonreligious" or neutral, that is at the foundation of American courts' confusion in addressing the question of what is religion.

One problem is that acceptance of the phrase *government neutrality* detracts attention from the ways in which the state and other public entities reflect a particular religious outlook. Government institutions offer public acknowledgment of the importance of religion in presidential inaugurations and speeches, courtroom proceedings, and legislative sessions. Prayers, blessings, or oaths invoking God's name are common in each branch of government. This, along with the belief that what is "religious" is private but what is public may be controlled by the majority, has led some to conclude that a "religiosity," a civil religion, defines the nation's public life.[9]

Civil religion is a "shared public statement of beliefs and symbols" that indicate an "accepted religious legitimation of political authority."[10] As historian Sidney Mead states, American culture exhibits "the religion of the democratic society and nation. This was rooted in the rationalism of the Enlightenment . . . and was articulated in terms of the destiny of America, under God, to be fulfilled by perfecting the democratic way of life for the example and betterment of all mankind."[11] This civil religion results in unexamined assumptions about legitimate state interests and appropriate behavior on the part of individuals. It is a societal consensus that can lead to discrimination against other religious groups. Judges come to their cases with this cultural or majoritarian consensus, a fact which is evident in their approach to what is and what is not religious activity.

A second problem is that judicial beliefs that religion can be and must be excluded from the public sphere ignore the all-encompassing nature of religion. Many faiths articulate a world view in which religion has a necessary impact on the public arena—including schooling of children, employment decisions, and the use of money such as tax funds. This approach highlights the relationship between the free exercise clause and the establishment clause in that sometimes when people are prohibited by government from exercising their religion they are coerced into participating in what they view as an established government religion. For example, when an employer believes that religion prohibits him from hiring people from outside his or her faith, the government's insistence on nondiscrimination becomes a religious statement for that employer. Critics of this argument will say that government endorsement of nondiscrimination in employment is "neutral" toward religion, but if a person believes that all of life is religious, can the government endorsement really be neutral?

These two problems have existed throughout American history, but the growth of the regulatory state during the early twentieth century has increased people's dependence on government. As the state has increased its role in distributing resources and defining social relationships, articulating and implementing consistent First Amendment theory has become nearly impossible.[12] If America continues to take seriously the ideas of toleration and the nondiscriminatory treatment of religion, courts must become more sensitive to the assumptions that underlie their decisions.

DEFINING RELIGION

Over the course of free exercise jurisprudence, the Supreme Court claims to have recognized that people's ability to act in accordance with their belief underlies the fundamental right of religious freedom. The Court's decisions have acknowledged that the right to free exercise extends to conduct. But it is the legal definition of religion that first determines when the First Amendment is invoked, what activity it will limit and what it will protect.[13]

To assist them in defining religion some courts have made use of the distinction between *substantive* and *functional* definitions.[14] Substantive definitions define people as religious or nonreligious on the basis of their belief in a specific doctrine or a particular Being. Unfortunately, this results in disputes about "truth" that cannot be settled by a court. Because content-based definitions exclude beliefs that are unfamiliar, they not only exclude certain faiths but allow judges to second-guess the centrality or particular tenets of a faith. As a consequence, nonmainstream religions will suffer discrimination because of their unorthodoxy. Moreover, adherents to mainstream religions that interpret sections of the Bible or the Talmud differently than do the judges will also be left out.

Functional definitions limit inquiry into the content of belief but declare people religious or nonreligious based on how their beliefs function in their life. Has a person built a life around a belief that incorporates "ultimate values"? However, such an all-encompassing definition has problems of its own. As the following cases illustrate, if religion is that which deals with fundamental questions, all perspectives are arguably religious.

During the first 150 years of First Amendment jurisprudence, the Supreme Court defined religion substantively. In the 1890 case *Davis* v. *Beason*, the Court declared that religion involved belief in and worship of a deity (133 U.S. 333 [1890]):

> The term "religion" has reference to one's views of his relations to his Creator, and to the obligations they impose of reverence for his being and character, and of obedience to this will. . . . The first amendment . . . was intended to allow every one under the jurisdiction of the United States to entertain such notions respecting his relations to his Maker. (*Davis*, 342)

Thus the Court's traditional definition of religion involved a belief in a Maker, or a relationship with God.

However, over time the federal courts began to develop the definition of religion so that the focus was no longer on the substance of belief but rather on the life of the believer. How did the belief define the life led by the believer? In the 1961 case *Torcaso* v. *Watkins,* for example, the Court invalidated a provision of the Maryland Declaration of Rights that required public officials to declare a belief in God (367 U.S. 488 [1961]). The Court spoke of religion based on other than a belief in God, holding that

> neither a State nor the Federal Government can constitutionally force a person "to profess a belief or disbelief in any religion." Neither can constitutionally pass laws or impose requirements which aid all religions as against non-believers, and neither can aid those religions based on a belief in the existence of God as against those religions founded on different beliefs. (*Torcaso,* 495)

In a footnote, the Court added that among "religions" that do not teach what would generally be considered a belief in God were Buddhism, Taoism, Ethical Culture, and Secular Humanism. Implied is a comprehensive view of religion. The groundwork is laid for the view that religion is a commitment to a particular definition of reality, the nature of humanity and people's place in the world. The distinction between secular and religious begins to blur.

By 1965 the Court seemed to reject the substantive approach to defining religion and to advocate a functional approach. In *United States* v. *Seeger,* the Court criticized the congressional exemptions set forth in the Universal Military Training and Service Act (380 U.S. 163 [1965]). The act called for belief in "a Supreme Being" as a prerequisite to conscientious objector status. According to the Court, the only legitimate issue to be considered was "whether the beliefs professed by a registrant are sincerely held and whether they are, in his own scheme of things, religious." In addressing the issue of a Supreme Being, the Court said that some people believe in a purely personal God, some in a supernatural deity, others think of religion as a way of life envisioning as its ultimate goal the day when all men can live together in perfect understanding. All these approaches were to be considered religious. The courts were not allowed to determine the validity of a claimant's vision of truth or to question the existence of his or her "Supreme Being."

At the same time, however, the Court said that those beliefs that were based on a "merely personal moral code" were not allowed exemption from the draft. The only definition of "moral code" the Court gave was that which was not related to a Supreme Being. The Court then further confused the issue by citing approvingly Paul Tillich's assertion that if the word *God* has no meaning for an individual, *God* could be the same as that belief that an individual had regarding the "source of your being, of your ultimate concern, of what you take seriously without any reservation." The difference between this and a moral, personal code was never made clear. Five years later, though, in *Welsh* v. *United States*, the Court affirmed the functional approach by citing the *Seeger* test:

> The reference to the registrant's own scheme of things was intended to indicate that the central consideration in determining whether the registrant's beliefs are religious is whether these beliefs play the role of a religion and function as a religion in the registrant's life. (398 U.S. 333, 339 [1970])

In both *Welsh* and *Seeger*, the Court allowed legislators to exempt conscientious objectors from the draft only after the Court determined that the claimants' beliefs were "religious." The Court did this even though the litigants claimed that their objections were not, to them, religiously based. Then, in 1971, the Court sustained a congressional military service exemption that favored pacifistic religions over those that distinguished between wars. In *Gillette* v. *United States* the Court upheld that part of the Universal Military Training and Service Act that exempted those who opposed all wars from military service (401 U.S. 437 [1971]). It denied the exemption to those who opposed only unjust wars or those who analyzed individual conflicts case by case determining the morality of each.

The Supreme Court cases that have developed the definition of religion raise difficult issues. It may well be true that allowing people exemptions from laws that conflict with their moral outlook, personal code, philosophy of life, and religion would wreak havoc on the military and other aspects of society, but does the First Amendment allow legislators to differentiate between religious and nonreligious persons?[15] What is a "nonreligious" person? May lawmakers create laws that distinguish between different religions? And what of those laws that appear to apply to all persons equally but have a disparate effect on persons of a particular religion?

Immediately problems emerge. Despite the broad definition of religion in

Seeger, the Court's insistence on the possibility of nonreligion, and the distinction between morals and religion, forces it to draw arbitrary lines in constitutional jurisprudence. Which types of beliefs will the First Amendment protect? Perhaps sensing this dilemma, the Supreme Court has not specifically advanced any approach to defining religion since deciding the military conscientious objector cases.

The problem is that lower courts do not have the luxury of declining to rule on these issues. The following five cases illustrate the lower courts' predicament. In two of the cases the federal courts have relied on the *Seeger* definition but declared the claimants' perspective on life to be nonreligious. In the next two cases, the court admitted that the claimants were religious, but declared that their particular activity was not an important part of their religion. In the last case, the court assumed the neutrality of the public school system and refused to deal with the claimant's argument that the activity of the government was religious in character.

MOVE

In 1981, in the case *Africa* v. *Pennsylvania,* the Third Circuit Court of Appeals tried to implement the functionalist approach of the *Seeger* Court but failed (662 F.2d 1025 [3d Cir. 1981]). Frank Africa was a "Naturalist Minister" of a group named MOVE. At the time of the suit, he was a prisoner who claimed that the state violated his right to freedom because it refused to provide him with the special diet of raw food required by his religion. The district court and the court of appeals both held that MOVE was not a religion and, therefore, Africa was not entitled to any First Amendment consideration for his claim. The courts relied on the broad, subjective approach to defining religion set forth in *Seeger,* but the judges' bias and preconceptions about religion are revealed in their application of *Seeger* standards.[16]

The MOVE religion was characterized by Africa and other witnesses as involving the following: (1) its goals were to bring about absolute peace, to stop violence and all that is corrupt; (2) there was no governing hierarchy because all members were equal; (3) adherents were committed to a natural, moving, generating way of life, and thus to eat anything other than raw food would be in violation of the religion (the power that commands the flow of life would bring more force to members if they ate raw food—this diet of raw food was provided by God); and (4) there were no distinct ceremonies or rituals, because every act of life was invested with religious meaning or significance; every time a MOVE person opened his or her mouth, church was held.

The court determined that it had to find three conditions for a religion to exist.

The beliefs would be religious in nature if they addressed "fundamental and ulti-mate" questions having to do with "deep and imponderable matters." Second, a religion is comprehensive in nature; it consists of a "belief-system" as opposed to an "isolated teaching." And third, a religion could be recognized by external signs.

These three conditions reflect a particular cultural approach that defines re-ligion as that which contains elements found in mainstream American religions. Moreover, in finding that MOVE did not meet the three conditions, the court gave little credence to testimony that addressed these issues in concepts unfamiliar to the justices.[17] For example, the court first ruled that MOVE did not address deep and imponderable matters despite the uncontradicted claim that the perspective gave the adherents a system by which to determine right from wrong and good from evil:

> MOVE is absolutely opposed to all that is wrong . . . we believe in using things
> [but] not misusing things . . . the air is first, but pollution is second. Water is first,
> but poison is second. The food is first, but the chemicals that hurt the food are
> second. . . . We believe in the first education, the first government, the first law.
> (*Africa,* 1025)

The court also said that MOVE was not a belief system in that it was not com-prehensive. It ignored testimony that the MOVE religion is "total"; it encompassed every aspect of MOVE members' lives; there was "nothing that is left out." In the court's opinion this was not sufficiently life encompassing. Finally, the court listed signs that could identify a group's belief as a religion: services, ceremonies, clergy, proselytizing, and observance of holidays. Even though the court's description of MOVE included the group's perspective of its holidays, ceremonies, and hierar-chical structure, and the group testified that one goal was to revolutionize the world to its view, the court held that none of the five signs existed. The court emphasized MOVE's lack of specific holidays or scriptures. These factors exclude new or developing religions, which is troublesome because it means that the ability of future religions to emerge "hinges on the breadth of judicial imagination."[18]

In sum, the court's finding that MOVE was not a religion hinged on factors indicating that MOVE was unlike mainstream American religions.[19] The fact that any definition of religion involves the bias of those creating the definition is clearly illustrated in *Africa.* The following case illustrates the problem further.

Cat Food

The plaintiff, Stanley Oscar Brown, brought a suit against the director of the Equal Employment Opportunity Commission (EEOC) when the director dismissed without hearing his claim that he had been discriminated against in his employment for exercising his religion (*Brown* v. *Pena*, 441 F Supp 1382 [S.D. Florida 1977]). Brown asserted that his "personal religious creed" required that he eat a particular brand of cat food; this consumption would contribute to his state of well being and to his overall work performance by increasing his energy. The EEOC dismissed the case because Brown failed to establish a religious belief "generally accepted" as a religion.

When the case was brought to the federal court, the judges cited approvingly the approach taken by the Supreme Court in *Seeger*, emphasizing the fact that there was a difference between a "moral code" and a religion which included a place for a Supreme Being. The court found it significant that throughout case law unique personal moral preferences were excluded from the characterization of religious beliefs. The only finding of fact that the court made or referred to was that "Plaintiff's personal religious creed concerning Kozy Kitten Cat Food can only be described as . . . *a mere personal preference,* therefore, it is beyond the parameters of the concept of religion as protected by the constitution" (*Brown*, 1385 [emphasis added]).

There was no discussion, no hearing, no testimony. There was no evidence to dispute the "religious" base of Brown's claim other than the justices' own beliefs. The court simply relied on its own perspective and on the conclusions of the EEOC director—conclusions also reached without a hearing on the merits of the claim.

The problem with this case is not so much that Stanley Brown was unsuccessful in seeking protection of his religion. Without knowing the circumstances of his employment or termination it is impossible to determine whether injustice was done. However, the fact that the court assumed that the difference between a religion and a moral code is self-explanatory is problematic. To the extent that a court assumes there is universal agreement on the definition of these terms, this case illustrates that what we think of as "neutral" judicial reasoning will often disguise a judge's own bias or perspective.

Mixing Races

The effect that Civil Rights statutes have on sectarian schools is an area of the law that is in flux. One federal court has held that 42 U.S.C. sec 1981 prohibits private schools from excluding children because of their race. In *Brown* v. *Dade Christian*

School, Inc., parents brought suit under section 1981 against a church operated school after being informed that their children were refused admission because they were black (556 F2d 310 [5th Cir 1977]). The Fifth Circuit Court of Appeals was faced with a free exercise claim when the school asserted that intermingling of races was in violation of its religious tenets.

The court considered whether the school's defense was actually based on a religious belief and concluded that free exercise was not an issue because the religion did not really include separating the races as an element. This conclusion was based on the court's perception that the school as an institution and the church it was affiliated with did not have a clearly articulated policy of segregation. The court focused on the adherents' inability to clearly articulate their beliefs even though the principal and pastor had testified both that enrolling blacks would constitute disobedience to the Bible and that integration of races was against biblical authority as set forth in the stories of the Tower of Babel, the confusion of tongues in Acts, and God's dealing with the nation of Israel. Despite this, the court found that segregation was not religious belief and refused to allow even a hearing on the First Amendment issue. In the court's opinion, the belief was one of social policy or philosophy, not religion.

One of the concurring judges, Justice Goldberg, wrote a separate opinion cautioning the court against judicial policy that discriminates against small groups that have yet to articulate their beliefs fully. He said that the plurality opinion of the court illustrated how "findings of fact" on religious issues may mask a value-laden assumption about what religion really is. However, although Judge Goldberg believed that the discriminatory admissions policy was based on religious conviction, he went on to state that this particular tenet of the faith was "not central to their faith." Integration of the races, "although constituting disobedience to God, would not endanger salvation" (321), and thus was a minor element. On that basis he concurred with the court's decision that the school should be enjoined from barring other races.

When courts assess the sincerity of a claimant's religious belief the inquiries can become a tool to impose a majoritarian view of what a religious practice is or should be. The case that follows further illustrates this point.

Chapel Attendance

In *EEOC* v. *Townley Engineering* the Ninth Circuit Court of Appeals issued an injunction prohibiting an employer from requiring that all employees attend a devotional service during the work week (859 F 2d 610 [9th Cir 1988]). Although the Townley Engineering Company paid the employees for their attendance, and made it clear to the employees before hiring them that attendance would be mandatory, the court found that the practice violated Title VII of the Civil Rights Act of 1964, which prohibits employers from religious discrimination.

In making its determination, the court conceded several facts. Jack and Helen Townley, in founding their company, made a covenant with God that their business would be a "Christian, faith-operated business." They were "born again believers in the Lord Jesus Christ" who were "unable to separate God from any portion of their daily lives, including their activities at the Townley company" (612). The company reflected this commitment by enclosing a gospel tract in all outgoing mail, printing biblical verses on all company invoices and other documents, giving financial support to churches and missionaries, and holding devotional services once a week during office hours.

The court said that civil rights statutes required corporate owners to excuse employees with religious objections from attending devotional services at work, and the court held that this did not unduly burden the owners' free exercise rights. The corporation was "secular" in that it was not affiliated with a church and therefore was not "religious." Moreover, Townley's accommodation of employees who objected to the services would not cause undue hardship to the company because in the court's opinion, spiritual hardship did not have an adverse impact on the conduct of the business. Townley argued that releasing employees from devotions would have a chilling effect on his mandate to share with all of his employees the spiritual aspects of the company. Yet this argument failed because to the court, "chilling" was irrelevant if it had no effect on the company's "economic well-being" (616). Finally, the court concluded that even if ending mandatory attendance at devotional services would have an impact on the Townleys' religious practice, it would not be an unreasonable or extreme impact.

In the last paragraph of the decision, the court confused the issue by amending the decision of the lower district court. The lower court had enjoined mandatory services for all employees, whether or not the objections to the services were "religious" in nature. The appellate court said that the goal of the civil rights statutes was to end religious discrimination; therefore, the Townleys had only to excuse those employees who raised religious objections to the services. As in the cases *Brown, Dade Schools,* and *Africa,* the court failed to explain how litigants were to distinguish between religious objections and those objections based merely on conscience or moral codes.

The problem here is that the court's attempt to distinguish between religious and nonreligious practice is untenable to people who perceive life as an integral whole. The Townleys viewed all of life in religious terms, rather than divided into areas clearly religious or nonreligious. The dissenting judge, Justice Noonan, recognized this when he stated the following:

> The . . . Court appear[s] to assume that there must be a sharp division between secular activity and religious activity. Such a sharp division . . . such a dichotomy, is a species of theology. The theological position is that human beings should worship God on Sundays or some other chosen day and go about their business without reference to God the rest of the time. Such a split is attractive to some religious persons. It is repudiated by many, especially those who seek to integrate their lives and to integrate their activities. Among those who repudiate this theology is the Townley Manufacturing Company. (*Townley*, 625)

Creation-Science

In 1982 an Arkansas "equal-time" statute mandated that "public schools within this State shall give balanced treatment to creation-science and to evolution-science." In *McLean* v. *Arkansas Board of Education*, the constitutionality of the statute was successfully challenged on the theory that by teaching creation-science the law established a religion in the school (529 F Supp 1255 [E.D. Arkansas 1982]). The federal district court hearing the case in Arkansas focused its analysis on the allegation that creation science is a religious belief.

Although *McLean* is perceived to be an establishment-clause case, the argument of the statute's supporters is relevant to a free exercise analysis. Proponents of the equal time statute argued that two positions exist that attempt to explain the origins and development of the earth and life: creationism and evolution. Evolutionary theory is, like scientific creationism, an explanation of the origin of humanity. It is based on presupposed naturalistic processes, such as mutation and natural selection. Both scientific creationism and evolutionary theories can be considered "scientific" in that they explore natural phenomena. But both also can be called "religious" because they entail a foundational or pretheoretical commitment—a commitment without the benefit of conclusive scientific evidence—to assumptions concerning the development of life.[20] Because evolution expressed a religious perspective, excluding creation science from the classroom violated both the establishment clause and the free exercise rights of those who rejected evolution.

Whether the equal time statute violated the establishment clause is one issue. But the court's refusal to consider the religious aspect of evolution reflects again a majoritarian consensus that asserts religion as a private belief; public institutions, however, can be "neutral." The court dismissed the argument that evolution is a religion in one paragraph, concluding that the argument had no legal merit: "It is clearly established in the case law, *and perhaps also in common sense,* that evolution is not a religion and that teaching evolution does not violate the Establishment Clause" (*McLean,* 1274 [emphasis added]).

Is there a religious aspect not only to evolutionary theory but to any scientific theory? In one analysis of the *McLean* case, political theorist David Caudill explains that philosophers of science recognize that natural science is founded on an "aspect of faith or a belief in certain presuppositions"—belief in the scientific enterprise itself.[21] He cites Michael Polanyi, who in *Science, Faith and Society,* stated:

The premises of science on which all scientific teaching and research rests are the beliefs held by scientists on the general nature of things.

The influence of these premises on the pursuit of discovery is great and indispensable. They indicate to scientists the kind of questions which seem reasonable and interesting to explore, and the kind of conceptions and relations that should be upheld as possible, even when some evidence seems to contradict them, or that, on the contrary, should be rejected as unlikely, even though there was evidence which would favour them.

The premises of science are subject to continuous modifications. . . . Every established proposition of science enters into the current premises of science and affects the scientist's decision to accept an observation as a fact or to disregard it as probably unfounded. [The history of Physics] refutes the widely-held view that scientists necessarily abandon a scientific proposition if a new observation conflicts with it.

. . . Stephen Toulmin has shown systematically that the framework of *scientific theory contains general suppositions which cannot be put directly to an experimental test of truth or falsity.*[22]

As Caudill points out, it is this pretheoretical commitment among scientists to a framework or paradigm that led Thomas Kuhn to speak of the "faith" aspect of science. Although a commitment among scientists to the Christian scriptures does not exist, other presuppositional frameworks do guide the work of contemporary scientists. In Caudill's words, "to the extent that a set of unproved assumptions provides unity and guidance to a scientific discipline, one may speak of the religious or ideological character of science."[23] Evolutionary theory does present a religious perspective equal to that of creationism.

Caudill explains that the court's decision in this case was determined at the beginning by the presumption that creationism was religious and that evolution was not. The court emphasized the creationists' belief in supernatural intervention and their reliance on a spiritual, biblical account of the history of the world and man. By contrast, the court characterized evolutionary science's emphasis on natural law as an empirical, falsifiable explanation. However, creation scientists affirm natural laws, and they do empirical, falsifiable research.[24] Moreover, both perspectives have foundational questions that they hope to verify. The court emphasized those of the creation scientists' biblical account but was unable to recognize the equally religious approach of evolution. In support of this position, Caudill refers to Carl Sagan's television series "Cosmos." In this program, scientists with an evolutionary outlook say that the "cosmos is all that is or ever will be," and it "is the universe that made us." The program is often shown in public schools where the students also learn that it is science that gives "reliable knowledge," whereas religion is associated with "narrowness of mind and bigotry."[25]

This identification of foundational beliefs as "religious" parallels the subjective, functionalist view of religion articulated in *Seeger*, but the court ignored it, failing even to address the issue. Moreover, the justices refused to consider the possibility that what to them was clearly a nonreligious, neutral teaching, to others could be a government establishment of religion. For the justices to dismiss this possibility as flying in the face of "common sense" shows only their insensitivity to the difficulties inherent in First Amendment jurisprudence.

These five cases indicate that there are two major problems in articulating a definition of religion. First, in distinguishing the religious from the nonreligious those who most need protection, like Brown or Africa, will be left out because their views are not understood. Judges' own perspectives concerning religion affect their decisions to the detriment of certain groups. In *Dade Schools, McLean,* and *Townley* the court was dealing with a mainstream faith, Christianity, but believed that it knew better than the claimants what constituted the important elements of that faith.

Secondly, the courts continue to insist on the possibility of neutrality by the judiciary. But, if one assumes the impossibility of nonreligion, as in the *McLean* and *Townley* cases, then neutrality is not really viable. The definition of religion or faith is not a clear, factual issue, so a court's case law can do little more than show one perspective of what religion is. Defining faith or religion is an extremely difficult task. Even if the legal definitions are rejected as faulty, it is difficult to criticize judges for failing to develop an adequate approach to concepts such as science and religion, which are the domain of extralegal disciplines. Any discussion of religion is necessarily interdisciplinary. But this is exactly what makes courts particularly ill-suited to make this definition. Is it then necessary for religion to be judically defined, or is there an alternative?

Since the mid-1960's the Supreme Court has declined to expand on the *Seeger* definition of religion. In the free exercise cases that have come before the Court since then, the emphasis has been on the tension between an admittedly religious practice and a competing regulatory interest of the state, such as the health or safety of citizens. If a court simply assumes an asserted religious practice to be religious, when do governmental interests override an individual's right to practice his or her religion?

The problem is that a judge's approach to what religion is will affect his or her approach to when religious activity is to be protected. The assumption that private religion can be separated from the public domain and that it is different from personal morality leads the Court into a tangled thicket when it tries to decide when state interest should override religious expression. The fact is that issues relating to religious expression unavoidably involve the public domain. Rearing and schooling of children, for example, relates to family and education laws, and ingestion of any substance during a sacrament involves Food and Drug Administration regulations. If we do not encourage judges to acknowledge and focus on the relationship between the public and the private spheres, we cannot hope for coherence in their decisions.

BIAS AND CONFUSION IN THE
COMPELLING INTEREST STANDARD

In 1878 a man named George Reynolds was convicted of polygamy in a case that is widely recognized as the beginning of free exercise jurisprudence (*Reynolds* v. *United States*, 98 U.S. 145 [1878]). As a Mormon, Reynolds argued that his act was based on a religious doctrine, and to convict him amounted to a violation of the free exercise clause. The Court, however, assumed that it was possible to separate religion and action. It concluded that even though polygamy may be based in religion, it was belief not behavior that was protected by the First Amendment. By prohibiting polygamy, Congress was protecting a "valid" societal interest.

The importance of this decision is two-fold. First, it reveals the Court's understanding of religion as a matter of "private belief." When a person acts on his or her belief in a way that does not conform to the will of the public, the public interest may control individuals' behavior by legally prohibiting it.[26] Actions are under the authority of the government, even if they are required by a belief system.

Second, the *Reynolds* case is the first of a line of cases in which the Supreme Court has tried to determine the difference between religious activity in general and protected religious activity. It is the beginning of what Douglas Laycock has called "conscientious objector" law. Given the political process in this country, it often happens that "neutral" legislation, that is, legislation that does not specify any particular religion, still has the effect of limiting people's expression of religion. For example, prohibiting the sale or consumption of alcohol in the 1920s affected Catholic and other groups' participation in Communion; criminalizing drug use affects the Native American groups that ingest the cactus peyote in their sacraments; requiring autopsies affects groups that believe the body must be buried in a particular fashion after death; child labor laws affect children's participation in some groups' proselytizing requirements.

In certain cases, the state or federal legislators exercise sensitivity to religious groups and create exemptions from the law which accommodate their beliefs. For instance, communion services were exempt from the Prohibition laws of the early twentieth century, and some states exempt peyote use from illegal drug prosecutions. However, when the legislators refuse to accommodate religious beliefs, and individuals "conscientiously object" to the law, the courts step in to determine whether or not the state has the Constitutional obligation to exempt the religious objector from the law.

In making this decision, the Supreme Court has fashioned a series of balancing tests. Today, whenever a state infringes on an individual's activity, the legislation is subject to either the rational relationship test (often referred to as a "reasonableness" standard) or the strict scrutiny test (referred to as the "compelling interest" standard).[27] If a right asserted by an individual is clearly protected in the Bill of Rights, such as free speech or equal protection, the Court subjects the legislation to strict scrutiny: Is the state interest a "compelling" interest, and is the legislation the "least restrictive alternative" to achieve that interest? In other circumstances, the Court defers to the legislators, asking only if the legislation has a "legitimate" state interest and if the legislation is "rationally or reasonably related" to achieving the state's goal.

These tests may appear straightforward, but in theory as well as in practice, their development has been fraught with confusion. Although the Supreme Court's free exercise decisions have increasingly recognized that constitutional analysis must be controlled by the effect of a religion in a person's life, traditionally the Court deferred to the legislature in free exercise challenges. Much later, the Court applied strict scrutiny, but only when the challenged regulation interfered directly with religious practices by criminalizing them. Then the Court applied strict scrutiny to regulations that indirectly burdened religious practices—although the activities were not criminalized it was more difficult or expensive for litigants to practice their religion. This increased the scope of free exercise protection. However, beginning in 1980 and culminating with the 1990 *Smith* case, the Court has come full circle in its jurisprudence, returning to legislative deference.

In the *Reynolds* polygamy case, the Court began its First Amendment analysis by balancing individual and state interests with one eye toward the will of the majority, not protection of minority rights. "Congress was deprived of all legislative power over mere opinion, but was left free to reach actions which were in violation of social duties or subversive of good order" (*Reynolds*, 164). The test was deferential—judges looked only to their view or the majority's view of the good social order to determine whether or not legislation was "valid". The primary concern was that to do otherwise, to protect religious practices contrary to those recognized by the majority, would be to "make . . . professed doctrines of religious beliefs superior to the law of the land, and in effect to permit every citizen to become *a law unto himself*. Government could exist only in name under such circumstances" (*Reynolds*,

167 [emphasis added]). This language is important because it surfaces over and over as the Court applies its tests and as the tests change.

In *Cantwell* v. *Connecticut* (310 U.S. 296 [1940]), the Court developed a balancing test with regard to First Amendment claims. Cantwell, a Jehovah's Witness, was charged with violating a statute prohibiting the solicitation of money for religious ends without approval from the secretary of Public Welfare. The Court pointed out that the First Amendment involved both the freedom to believe and the freedom to act. But, although the first concept was absolute, the second was protected only under certain circumstances. Freedom to act was subject to a two-part test: does the government action in question limit religious belief or activity, and if so, is the government action *necessary* to protect the peace, good order and comfort of the community. The assumption in *Reynolds* that the will of the majority created a valid state interest is no longer sufficient. Although the public order and comfort of the community as a whole still takes precedence over the individual's expression of religion, the test requires that the legislation be necessary, not just desirable, to the protection of the community.

In 1963, the Court appeared to reject the distinction between private belief and action, and it changed the test once more employing the "strict scrutiny standard" (*Sherbert* v. *Verner*, 374 U.S. 398 [1963]). Sherbert was a Seventh-day Adventist working a five-day week in a textile mill. However, when the mill changed its schedule to a six-day work week, which conflicted with her worship on Saturdays, Sherbert refused to work on Saturdays and was fired. When she applied for unemployment compensation, she was denied benefits. The Supreme Court ruled that Sherbert was entitled to unemployment compensation because her right to the free exercise of her religion could not be infringed by the government agency. It was true that the government agency had not tried to criminalize her religious expression, but when government policy made her religious expression more difficult it violated the free exercise clause.

In *Sherbert*, Justice Brennan's analysis specifically shifted the burden of proof from the religious objector to the state. After an initial showing by the objector that a religious interest was impaired, the state must assert a "compelling government interest" and show that there was no "less restrictive" means to further this interest. "It is basic that no showing merely of a rational relationship to some colorable state interest would suffice; in this highly sensitive constitutional area '[o]nly the gravest abuses, endangering paramount interest, give occasion for permissible limitation'" (*Sherbert*, 406, citing *Thomas* v. *Collins*, 323 U.S. 516, 530 [1949]).

The state asserted as its interest the fact that to allow a claim to receive unemployment insurance under these circumstances would give rise to an unmanageable number of lawless people fraudulently claiming that they quit their jobs because of religious reasons. This concern parallels the Court's concern in *Reynolds,* that to allow one exemption would permit citizens to become laws unto themselves. Although this possibility was determinative in *Reynolds,* it failed in *Sherbert.* The Supreme Court easily dismissed the state's concern by saying that there was no specific evidence that this lawlessness would happen.

The compelling interest test was developed further in *Wisconsin* v. *Yoder* (406 U.S. 205 [1972]). In this case the Amish fought a Wisconsin law requiring school attendance for all children. In holding that the regulation burdened the free exercise of religion, the Court carefully examined the interests of both the Amish and the state. It analyzed the arguments set forth by each side, and it articulated the strengths and weaknesses of each. The Court concluded that the state interest in preparing children to be independent in the world could be met with alternatives other than compulsory education by state-certified schools. Thus, the "less restrictive alternative" arm of the strict scrutiny test was not met.

But though the interests of the Amish were protected in this case, *Yoder* is not an example of unambiguous constitutional analysis. Chief Justice Burger tried to eliminate the belief/action dichotomy by arguing that the failure of Amish parents to send their children to public high school was not simply an "action" subject to the criminal law. The action was an expression of faith. In this case "belief and action cannot be neatly confined in logic-tight compartments" (*Yoder,* 220).

However, Burger also stated that the Amish could be protected only because they adhered to a truly "religious" belief. "A way of life, however, virtuous and admirable, may not be interposed as a barrier to reasonable state regulation of education if it is based on purely secular considerations; to have the protection of the Religion Clauses, the claims must be rooted in religious belief" (*Yoder,* 215). Burger's assumptions reveal his bias about religion, and they lead to confusion about the purpose and breadth of protection that the First Amendment entails. First, he believes it is possible to distinguish those people whose lives are determined by religion from those who are guided by secular considerations.[28] The weakness of this assumption is illustrated by the cases in which federal courts have tried to make the distinction. Religion cannot be clearly distinguished from secularity or irreligion.

Burger also assumes that the First Amendment defines religion in a way that unambiguously excludes irreligious or nonreligious persons.[29] And, he believes that it is legitimate for these irreligious people to be subject to the majoritarian educational requirements or state laws that are imposed on citizens.[30] As in the cases of military conscientious objectors and *Africa, Brown,* and *Townley,* those people who assert a world view that is a "moral code" rather than a "religion" do not escape the requirement of the law. Although this may be discrimination, it is not "religious" discrimination.

An analysis of Burger's next statement shows how false the above distinction really is. Burger argued that the concept of ordered liberty

> precludes allowing every person to make his own standards on matters of conduct in which society as a whole has important interests. Thus, if the Amish asserted their claims because of their subjective evaluation and rejection of the contemporary secular values accepted by the majority, much as Thoreau rejected the social values of his time and isolated himself at Walden Pond, their claims would not rest on a religious basis. Thoreau's choice was philosophical and personal rather than religious, and such belief does not rise to the demands of the Religion Clauses. (*Yoder,* 216)

When Burger says that the "secular values of the majority" have moral authority over "society as a whole," he expresses his own philosophy. Only if people can appeal to the religion clauses with a private religion, recognizable as religion by Burger, may they be exempt from the rules of the majority.[31] What Burger has failed to do is to demonstrate why the Amish way of life is religious and his own perspective is not religious. Moreover, he gives no explanation as to why Thoreau's beliefs are nonreligious when in fact Thoreau may well have believed that his life was a religious commitment.[32]

Over the next ten years, the Court continued to protect religious interests but was not able to clear up the confusion about religious versus moral or philosophical beliefs. For example, in *Thomas* v. *Indiana Employment Security Division,* the Supreme Court, citing *Yoder* and *Sherbert,* reversed a lower court ruling that denied a Jehovah's Witness unemployment compensation after he had refused to work for religious reasons (450 U.S. 707 [1981]). Thomas had objected to a transfer within his steel processing plant that would have involved him more directly in the production of munitions. Other Jehovah's Witness adherents did work in the plant, and this led the lower court to determine that it was Thomas's personal philosophy, not religion, that kept him from his work. The Supreme Court rejected the lower court's determination that Thomas had made a personal philosophical choice rather than a religious one:

> Although the claimant's reasons for quitting were described as religious, it was un-clear what his belief was, and what the religious basis of his belief was. In that court's view, Thomas had made a merely "personal philosophical choice rather than a religious choice." (*Thomas*, 713, citing 391 NE2d at 1131) As in *Sherbert*, even though Thomas's religious activity was not criminalized by the government activity, the government had made his religious expression more difficult with its policy. This violated the First Amendment.

Unfortunately, although the Court did protect Thomas's religious expression, it still failed to show how religious claims ought to be examined. Even though Thomas's religion was recognized by the Court, the opinion stated:

> Intrafaith differences of [this] kind are not uncommon among followers of a particular creed, and the judical process is singularly ill equipped to resolve such differences in relation to the Religion Clauses. *One can, of course, imagine an asserted claim so bizarre, so clearly non religious* in motivation, as not to be entitled to protection under the Free Exercise Clause. (*Thomas*, 717 [emphasis added])

However, as the *Africa* and *Brown* cases illustrate, what is bizarre to a court may well be religious to a litigant.

The dissent in *Thomas* was written by William Rehnquist, who is today the chief justice of the Supreme Court. The dissent is important because Rehnquist's concerns foreshadow a major change in First Amendment protection. Rehnquist states: "Where, as here, a State has enacted a general statute, the purpose and effect of which is to advance the State's secular goals, the Free Exercise Clause does not in my view require the State to conform that statute to the dictates of religious conscience of any group" (*Thomas*, 721).

Rehnquist's assumption is that government interests are obviously different from religious interests in that they are "secular." But he makes this statement without clearly articulating what he means by religion. Although Rehnquist claims that he is moving the Court away from the problems experienced when it tries to define religion, his own assumption reflects a particular cultural bias about the ability of a government to be truly neutral toward "religious" interests. He further confuses the issue by stating that this case is distinguishable from *Sherbert* because Thomas left his job for purely personal reasons, whereas Sherbert left for religious reasons.

Beginning in the 1980s, the Supreme Court developed Rehnquist's dissent in *Thomas* and began to deny claims by religious objectors seeking relief from regulations that appeared to be neutral but, in fact, limited their religious expression. In *United States* v. *Lee*, the Court rejected an Amish farmer's request to be exempt from social security taxes. (455 U.S. 252 [1982]). The Court recognized the sincerity of Lee's religious objection to mandatory social security payments but said that the government interest in collecting taxes was compelling. The Court did not explain why the federal interest in collecting taxes was more compelling than a state interest in educating children (*Yoder*) or the federal interest in regulating unemployment (*Sherbert* and *Thomas*). This case and those following can be explained by a change in the political persuasion of the Court, but they also indicate that the Supreme Court's approach to religious protection is both flexible and confused. The various tests and the varied ways in which they are applied allow the Court to justify any result it wishes. Moreover, they illustrate the Court's inability to develop a comprehensive theory about religious protection, an inability that stems in part from the confusion about what religion is and what it is not.

In *Bowen* v. *Roy*, the Court faced a free exercise challenge brought on behalf of a Native American child. The argument was that statutory requirements conditioning welfare benefits on parents' willingness to use the Social Security number of their child violated the family's religious freedom (476 U.S. 693 [1986]). The parents' objection was that the use of the number would rob the child of her spirit. A plurality of the Court denied Roy's claim. The judges distinguished between those claims that involved the mere denial of a government benefit and those that imposed criminal sanctions on conduct that had religious implications. This distinction was what *Sherbert* and *Thomas*, both government benefits cases, had denied.

Another significant aspect of this case is that three concurring members of the Court advocated a lower standard of review than the strict scrutiny test. Applying this lower standard, these justices determined that the Social Security number requirement was a "reasonable" means of promoting the "legitimate" public interest to prevent proliferation of fraud. Because a lower test was used, this interest outweighed the parents' free exercise interest. The previous cases which claimed clear evidence had to exist that fraud actually would occur were not controlling because they were determined with a more strict test. Although a decision by three members of the Court does not by itself change precedent, the case lay the ground work for future decisions.

During the same period that *Lee* and *Roy* were decided, the Court decided three free exercise cases in which the majority of the justices applied the lower "reasonableness" test rather than the strict scrutiny test. In each case the Court articulated why the particular facts warranted an exception to the strict scrutiny standard, but by 1990 it became clear that these cases were the beginning of a new First Amendment era. In *Goldman* v. *Weinberger,* the Court upheld an Air Force regulation prohibiting indoor headgear (475 U.S. 503 [1986]). Goldman, a captain in the Air Force, wore a yarmulke. When he refused to remove it during a court proceeding, he was told that it violated military regulations. He sued, claiming infringement of his First Amendment rights. In analyzing the case, the Supreme Court emphasized the need for deference to military authority and declined to apply the standard of strict scrutiny developed in *Sherbert.* The Court required only that the regulation advance "legitimate" military ends.

A second exception to the rule of strict scrutiny was set forth in *Lyng* v. *Northwest Indian Cemetery Protection Assn.* (485 U.S. 439 [1988]). In this case Native Americans objected to the government's plan to build a highway on government land that ran through sacred ground. The ground was used by the group in religious ceremonies, and the road would preclude the worship because no other land had the same religious significance. The Court held that the government was not barred from constructing a road. It stated that the free exercise clause does not give individuals the right to dictate to the government how to conduct its internal affairs or how to use its own land. The government was not required to show a compelling justification for its actions when the burden on a claimant was simply the "incidental effect" of a government program. In the Court's opinion, the government's program may have rendered the religious activity more difficult, but it did not force the Native Americans to act in ways contrary to their beliefs. In this case the Court in essence concluded that it knew better than Native Americans which elements of the faith were significant and which were "incidental." The fact that Indian ceremony relates to sacred, site-specific land was not recognized.

In the third case the free exercise rights of prisoners were addressed (*O'Lone* v. *Estate of Shabazz,* 482 U.S. 342 [1987]). Muslim prisoners' worship at Friday prayer services was denied because prison regulations required those who worked outside the prison to return at specific hours. The Court held that because of the special situation of prisons, the regulations that burdened constitutional rights were to be judged by a "reasonableness" test rather than the strict scrutiny test. Although there may be legitimate reasons for prison officials to limit religious expression by inmates, the Court's deference to administrative decisions, its refusal to question legislative authority, and its willingness to lower the balancing test in all three of these cases is significant.

In 1990, when the Supreme Court handed down *Smith*, constitutional scholars across the nation decried the case as a disaster in First Amendment jurisprudence.[33] Justice Scalia wrote the opinion, which held that the right of free exercise does not relieve an individual of the obligation to comply with a valid and neutral law of general applicability just because the law constricts activity that he or she thinks a religion requires.

In *Smith*, two Native American men claimed that an EEOC decision denying their plea for unemployment insurance discriminated against them on the basis of their religion (*Employment Division Dept.* v. *Smith*, 110 S Ct 1595 [1990]). The EEOC denied the claim because the men were fired from their jobs for ingesting peyote, a hallucinogenic cactus, during religious ceremonies. The men were fired from their jobs for participating in wrongful conduct. This precluded them from collecting unemployment insurance.

The facts and result in *Smith* are relatively insignificant in terms of free exercise claims. Over the years in cases like *Roy*, many litigants have been denied governmental benefits because the state interest was compelling and outweighed their right to religious expression. The importance of *Smith* lies in the Court's specific rejection of the compelling interest test.[34] A plurality of the Court, four justices, said that an individual's religious beliefs do not excuse him from compliance with an otherwise "valid" law. In determining whether or not the legislation was "valid," the Court asked if it was "reasonable."

Furthermore, the Court acknowledged that leaving accommodation of religious expression to the legislative, political process could place minority religions at a disadvantage. Calling this the unavoidable consequence of democratic government, the Court stated that it was preferred to a system in which each conscience is a law unto itself. The similarity of this case to the 1878 *Reynolds* polygamy case should be noted. A state statute must be "valid," and it is assumed that when the majority agrees on a statute, validity occurs. And, the primary reason given for refusing exemption for those claimants who say the law violates their religious freedom is that to do otherwise would bring on a lawless society. In the span of 120 years, the Supreme Court has come full circle in applying its First Amendment test.

The impact of *Smith* has yet to be seen. On one hand it can be anticipated that the case will have little more than symbolic meaning. Although religious interests have been protected at certain times during American political history, protection has had less to do with the test applied than with the personal appreciation or perspective that individual justices bring to a particular situation.

An important part of *Smith,* however, is that the Court simply dismissed the interests of the Native American Church rather than dealing with the strengths and weaknesses of either the Indian or the state arguments. This is important because such a dismissal injects confusion and uncertainty into all free exercise balancing. It is possible to argue that there are a variety of reasons why the Supreme Court would want to avoid a clear definition of religion—majority interests do, after all, play a role in democratic politics—but this misses the point. The point is that if the Court does not force itself to actually weigh competing interests it creates room for the unexamined biases of legislators and other judges. This sends a dangerous message to state and lower federal courts, and it is here that the impact of *Smith* could be significant. Moreover, when the Supreme Court steps away from a conflict, or sends the message that the political process should receive deference even in the area of fundamental civil rights, it invites inconsistency in the state legislatures and in the lower courts. For example, even after *Smith,* individuals in Minnesota who assert religious interests fare well, as the following two cases illustrate.

In *State of Minnesota* v. *French,* a landlord claimed to exercise his religious beliefs by refusing to rent to an unmarried cohabiting couple (460 NW 2d 2 [1990]). The lower courts found that this constituted "marital status" discrimination, which was against Minnesota law. In refusing to allow the First Amendment argument, the lower court said that the state interest in eradicating discrimination was compelling. When the case was appealed to the Minnesota Supreme Court, at the same time that *Smith* was being decided in Washington, D.C., the Minnesota court denied that the state could have a compelling interest in protecting activity that violated its fornication statutes. When asked how the *Smith* decision would effect its ruling, the Court said, "In light of the unforeseeable changes in established first amendment law set forth in recent decisions of the United States Supreme Court ...justice demands that we analyze the present case in light of the protections found in the Minnesota Constitution."[35]

The Minnesota Constitution protects religious liberty with the following language: "The right of every man to worship God according to the dictates of his own conscience shall never be infringed . . . nor shall control of or interference with the right of conscience be permitted" (Minnesota Constitution, Art. 1, sec. 16). This language saved the religious interests of the landlord in *French*, and it protected the interests of the Amish in *State* v. *Hershberger* (462 NW 2d 393 [1990]). *Hershberger* was a case that had been brought to the United States Supreme Court by Amish who claimed that the Minnesota regulation requiring a Slow Moving Vehicle emblem on their buggies violated their exercise of religion. The large sign and the bright colors were antithetical to Amish belief. The Amish had offered to use a silver reflective tape on the buggy, which could be a less restrictive alternative to achieve the state interest of public safety.

The U.S. Supreme Court sent the case back down to the Minnesota court after *Smith* had been decided. It said that the state court had to make a determination with regard to the effect *Smith* had on the *Hershberger* argument. If the compelling interest test was removed, the less restrictive alternative argument the Amish made would carry no weight. The Minnesota court avoided the opportunity to develop the Supreme Court approach, "declined" to use the *Smith* analysis, and decided the case under the state constitution instead. The Amish beliefs were thus ensured protection.

But individuals in other states are subjected to a more haphazard approach. Nowhere is this more clear than in the health and welfare arena. When children are involved the tension between parental religious beliefs and the state interest in protecting children is extremely difficult to resolve. The courts have done nothing to assist government institutions or families in dealing with this issue. After *Smith* was decided, South Dakota revoked its statutory exemptions that previously had allowed families of certain faiths to use treatments other than conventional medical treatment for sick children. Moreover, the state provided that courts could order medical treatment for children or disabled adults who were solely under treatment by spiritual means.[36]

In Florida, the Court of Appeals affirmed the conviction of Christian Scientist parents for felony murder when lack of medical treatment resulted in the death of their daughter (see *Hermanson* v. *Florida*, 570 So 2d 322 [1990]). The parents had claimed that the medical intervention conflicted with their faith. However, in the California Superior Court, a jury was allowed to award half a million dollars in damages against a hospital and medical staff, finding that it had violated fiduciary duties when blood transfusion was performed for the child of Jehovah's Witness parents (see *Lunsford* v. *Regents of the University of California,* No. 837936, Sup Ct Cal [1990]).

The extent to which "religious freedom" is to be protected seems now to be a function of the legislatures. The effect of the First Amendment on those legislatures is less clear now than it was two hundred years ago.

CONCLUSION

The dilemma the American courts face in protecting religious interests is, in part, the result of unquestioned assumptions. But recognizing this dilemma is only one aspect of the problem. The fact is that no matter how religion is defined, in some cases the public authorities will be required to limit the individual's expression of religion. If a religion's precepts hurt children or prevent citizens from participating in the defense of a country or deceive the public or discriminate against women, how is the state to balance the importance of freedom of religion?

However we choose to make this balance, it is important to recognize one thing. If we define religion in a way that excludes some groups, or if we define religion in a way that does not acknowledge the presuppositions of those who are making decisions, we fail to maintain the "wall of separation," and we fail to treat groups equally. This may be the choice we make—but it must be acknowledged, not hidden under a rubric of constitutional "neutrality."

The issues are important because more and more groups that feel discriminated against are looking to the courts for political and legal redress. Unless the courts come up with a way to protect "religion" in a way that treats all groups alike, adversaries will continue to use the legal system in an attempt to shift the legislative balance of power in their favor.[37] Whether or not political use of the Court is desirable or unavoidable is another question, but it cannot be denied that litigation of this type uses vast amounts of resources.

Moreover, the lack of insight on the part of the Supreme Court with respect to its narrow interpretation of religion, the inconsistency of its definitions and tests, and its inability to recognize its own fundamental beliefs and assumptions have serious implications. When the state as an institution refuses to acknowledge its own basic commitments and insists on the possibility of religious neutrality, injustice results to particular groups in society. This undermines confidence in the Supreme Court and weakens its function in society.

NOTES

1. The two sections of this provision are referred to as the Free Exercise Clause and the Establishment Clause. Although the clauses affect each other, case law has developed each concept separately.

2. This observation is made by Martin Marty in the forward to Rockne McCarthy, James W. Skillen, and William A. Harper, *Disestablishment a Second Time: Genuine Pluralism for American Schools* (Grand Rapids, Mich.: Christian Univ. Press, 1982), xiv; see also, David Caudill, "Law and Worldview: Problems in the Creation-Science Controversy," *Journal of Law and Religion* 3 (1985): 1–46.

3. The papers presented at this conference have been compiled in *The George Washington Law Review* 60 (1992): 599–856. The summary of the conference and the statements by Laycock and O'Connor appear as reported in *Public Justice Report* 14, no. 9 (1991): 1.

4. See J. Gordon Melton and James Geisendorfer, *A Directory of Religious Bodies in the United States* (1977), as cited in Note, "Developments—Religion and the State," *Harvard Law Review* 100 (1987): 1606–1781 (hereafter referred to as "Developments").

5. Ibid., 1613.

6. The American excitement over the 1990 Freedom of Conscience laws of Central and Eastern Europe illustrates this point.

7. Works by the following scholars, among others, illustrate this point best: Michael McConnell, Douglas Laycock, Mark Tushnet, Philip Kurland, William Marshall, and Robert Clinton.

8. This paragraph is a summary of the argument presented in McCarthy et al., *Disestablishment a Second Time*, 76.

9. See McCarthy et al., *Disestablishment a Second Time*; and "Developments," citing Robert Bellah, *Beyond Belief: Essays on Religion in a Post-Traditional World*, (New York: Harper & Row, 1970).

10. "Developments," 1620.

11. Sidney Mead, *The Lively Experiment* (New York: Harper & Row, 1963), 135.

12. "Developments," 1609, 1707.

13. Ibid., 1609

14. Use of the terms *substantive* and *functional* are not unique to this paper, nor is the application of the terms to the cases *Davis* v. *Beason, Torcaso* v. *Watkins, United States* v. *Seeger, Welsh* v. *United States,* and *Gillette* v. *United States.* These definitions are cited in most literature dealing with legal definition of religion; "Developments," 1621, provides one of the best definitions. This discussion draws from that application.

15. See "Developments," 1717.

16. The *Africa* v. *Pennsylvania* case is often cited as an example of a court's refusal to acknowledge a religion. See "Developments," 1625–31, for the most thorough explication of this case, including a discussion of how American courts reflect a Western perspective of what religion is. The argument from "Developments" is presented here.

17. The three examples that follow provide the foundation for most scholarly criticism of this case. They appear first in "Developments," 1627–28.

18. "Developments," 1631.

19. Ibid., 1630.

20. Caudill, "Law and Worldview," 8.

21. Ibid., 17.

22. Michael Polanyi, *Science, Faith and Society* (Chicago: Univ. of Chicago Press, 1946), 11–12 (emphasis added).

23. Caudill, "Law and Worldview," 34.

24. Ibid., 40.

25. Ibid., 42, citing the work of Richard Baer, "They are Teaching Religion in the Public Schools," *Christianity Today,* Feb. 17, 1984, p. 12.

26. This understanding of the belief/action dichotomy is articulated in McCarthy et al., *Disestablishment a Second Time,* 94.

27. This is a somewhat simplistic presentation of balancing tests. Constitutional analyses often use tests that fall somewhere between these two.

28. For this argument, see McCarthy et al., *Disestablishment a Second Time,* 86.

29. Ibid.

30. Ibid., 87.

31. Ibid.

32. Ibid.

33. The petition for rehearing of the *Employment Division* v. *Smith* case included a coalition of more than one hundred constitutional law scholars as well as a broad spectrum of interest groups. The petition was denied in June of 1990.

34. In rejecting the test for this particular case, the Court went to great lengths to distinguish *Smith* from *Sherbert* v. *Verner*. It said that the Sherbert case was a "hybrid" involving First Amendment issues in addition to the religion clauses. For an excellent discussion of the weakness of the decision in its entirety, see Michael McConnell, "Free Exercise Revisionism: The Smith Decision," *University of Chicago Law Review* 57 (1990): 1109–54.

35. Phillip H. Harris, "Leaping Headfirst Into the *Smith* Trap," *First Things* 10 (1991): 37–39.

36. This information is as reported in *Religious Freedom Reporter* 10 (1990): 77.

37. For a discussion of the creation-science advocates' attempt to use the courts to influence public policy decisions in their favor, see Wayne McIntosh, "Litigating Scientific Creationism, or "Scopes" II, III, . . . ," *Law and Policy* 7, no. 3 (July 1985): 375–94.

REFERENCES

Caudill, David. "Law and Worldview: Problems in the Creation-Science Controversy." *Journal of Law and Religion* 3 (1985): 1–46.

"Developments—Religion and the State." *Harvard Law Review* 100 (1987): 1606–1781.

Harris, Phillip H. "Leaping Headfirst Into the *Smith* Trap." *First Things* 10 (1991): 37–40.

McCarthy, Rockne, James W. Skillen, and William A. Harper. *Disestablishment a Second Time: Genuine Pluralism for American Schools.* Grand Rapids, Mich.: Christian Univ. Press, 1982.

Mead, Sidney. *The Lively Experiment.* New York: Harper & Row, 1963.

Polanyi, Michael. *Science, Faith and Society.* Chicago: Univ. of Chicago Press, 1946.

Religious Freedom Reporter 10 (1990): 77.

7

║ "The Three Uses of Law":
Towards a Protestant Theory of Criminal Law

John Witte, Jr.

Recent writings have uncovered a robust interaction between the spheres of law and religion. Law and religion are conceptually related. They embrace closely analogous concepts of sin and crime, covenant and contract, righteousness and justice. Law and religion are formally related. They both have liturgy and ritual, concepts of tradition and precedent, sources of authority and power. Law and religion are methodologically related. They maintain analogous hermeneutical methods of interpreting texts, casuistic and rhetorical methods of argument and instruction, systematic methods of organizing their doctrines. Law and religion are professionally related. They both have officials charged with the formulation, implementation, and demonstration of the norms and habits of their respective fields. Law and religion are institutionally related, through the multiple relations between political and ecclesiastical officials and institutions.[1] Through these and other channels of interaction, law and religion exert a formative influence on public life and public morality.

This chapter focuses on the collaboration of Protestant theology and criminal law in shaping American public life and public morality. I argue (1) that the Protestant theological doctrine of the uses of moral law has helped to shape our modern views of the purposes of criminal law and punishment, and (2) that this theological doctrine provides important signposts to the development of a more integrated moral theory of criminal law and punishment. Part 1 of this chapter briefly sets out the theological doctrine of the "civil," "theological," and "educational" uses of the moral law, as articulated by sixteenth-century Lutherans and Calvinists. Part 2 analyzes the analogous "deterrent," "retributive," and "rehabilitative" purposes of criminal law, as articulated by early modern Anglo-American jurists and moralists,

I would like to thank my students Bruce P. Frohnen and M. Christian Green for their able and ample research assistance, and my colleagues Frank S. Alexander, Harold J. Berman, and Donald W. Fyr for their helpful comments on an earlier draft of this article.

and explores the historical cross-fertilization between these theological and legal doctrines. Part 3 explores contemporary American criminal law developments in light of this three-uses doctrine.

This inquiry illustrates various modes of interaction between law and religion. Jurists and theologians, statesmen and churchmen collaborated closely in the for mulation of modern Anglo-American theories of crime and punishment. The concepts of crime and criminal law they developed drew upon analogous concepts of sin and natural law. The measures and purposes of criminal punishment that they chose drew on parallel models of divine punishment and ecclesiastical discipline.

THE THEOLOGICAL DOCTRINE
OF THE USES OF MORAL LAW

The theological doctrine of the uses of law was forged in the Protestant Reforma-tion.[2] It was a popular doctrine, particularly among Lutheran and Calvinist reform-ers. Martin Luther, Philip Melanchthon, John Calvin, and a host of other Refor-mation theologians gave the doctrine a considerable place in their writings.[3] It was also a pivotal doctrine, for it provided the reformers with something of a middle way between Catholic legalism on the one hand and Anabaptist antinomianism on the other. It allowed them to reject the claims of certain Catholics that salvation can be achieved by works of the law as well as the claims of certain Anabaptists that those who are saved have no further need of the law.

The reformers focused their uses doctrine primarily on the natural or moral law—that compendium of moral rights and duties that transcend the positive laws of the state.[4] God, they believed, has written a moral law on the hearts of all persons, rewritten it in the pages of Scripture, and summarized it in the Ten Command-ments. Though a person can be saved if he obeys the moral law perfectly, his sinful nature renders him incapable of such perfect obedience. Nonetheless, the moral law still has important uses or functions in a person's life. The reformers distinguished three such uses, which they variously called (1) a civil or political use, (2) a theo-logical or spiritual use, and (3) an educational or didactic use.[5]

First, the moral law has a civil use to restrain persons from sinful conduct by threat of divine punishment. "The law is like a halter," Calvin wrote, "to check the raging and otherwise limitlessly ranging lusts of the flesh. . . . Hindered by fright or shame, [persons] dare neither execute what they have conceived in their minds, nor openly breathe forth the rage of their lust."[6] The law thus imposes on saints and sinners alike what Calvin called a "constrained and forced righteousness" or what Melanchthon called "an external or public morality."[7] Threatened by divine sanctions, they obey the basic commandments of the moral law—to obey authorities, to respect their neighbor's person and property, to honor their marital vows, and to testify truthfully. Such "public morality," Melanchthon wrote, "does not merit forgiveness of sin, [yet] it is pleasing to God." For it ensures some peace and stability in the world. It enables persons who later become Christians to know at least the rudiments of Christian morality and to fulfill the vocations to which God has called them. It allows "God continually to gather to himself a church among men."[8]

Second, the moral law has a theological use to condemn sinful persons for their violations of the law. Such condemnation ensures both the integrity of the law and the humility of the sinner. On the one hand, the violation of the law is avenged, and the integrity, the balance of the law is restored. On the other hand, the violator of the law is appropriately chastened. In Luther's hard words, the law serves as a mirror "to reveal to man his sin, blindness, misery, wickedness, ignorance, hate, contempt of God. . . . When the law is being used correctly, it does nothing but reveal sin, work wrath, accuse, terrify, and reduce consciences to the point of despair."[9] Such despair, the reformers believed, was a necessary precondition for the sinner both to seek God's help and to have faith in God's grace.

Third, the moral law has an educational use of teaching those who have already been justified "the works that please God."[10] Even the most devout saints, Calvin wrote, still need the law "to learn more thoroughly . . . the Lord's will [and] to be aroused to obedience."[11] The law teaches them not only the "public" or "external" morality that is common to all persons but the "private" or "internal" morality that is becoming only of Christians. As a teacher, the law not only coerces them against violence and violation but cultivates in them charity and love. It not only punishes harmful acts of murder, theft, and fornication but prohibits evil thoughts of hatred, covetousness, and lust.[12]

This theological doctrine of the three uses of the moral law was rooted in the early Protestant theology of salvation. Following St. Paul, the reformers recognized an inevitable process and progress of salvation—from predestination to justification to sanctification.[13] The moral law, they believed, plays a part in all three steps of the soteriological process. It coerces sinners so that they can be preserved. It condemns them so that they can be justified. And it counsels them so that they can be sanctified. The doctrine was also rooted in the reformed theology of the person. Following Luther, the reformers emphasized that a person is *simul iustus et peccatur*, at once saint and sinner, spirit and flesh. The moral law serves both the spiritual and the carnal dimensions of his or her character. The person of the flesh is coerced to develop at least a minimal public or external morality; the person of the spirit is counseled to develop a more holistic private or internal morality.

The theological doctrine of the three uses of moral law has remained a staple of Protestant dogma to this day. A steady stream of sermons and writings on the doctrine can be found among European and American ecclesiastics and theologians from the seventeenth to the twentieth centuries. The great Protestant masters of the twentieth century—Bonhoeffer, Barth, Brunner, among many others—have all included the doctrine in their theological systems.[14]

THE LEGAL DOCTRINE OF THE USES OF CRIMINAL LAW

The uses doctrine was not just a theological doctrine of the uses of moral law in the lives of saints and sinners. It also became a legal doctrine of the uses or purposes of criminal law in the lives of criminals and communities. The sixteenth-century Protestant theologians adumbrated this legal doctrine in their discussions of ecclesiastical law[15] and their asides on criminal law.[16] Several early Protestant jurists, notably Johann Oldendorp,[17] Nicolaus Hemming,[18] Benedict Wincler,[19] and Johannes Althusius,[20] elaborated this legal doctrine under the direct inspiration of the early Protestant theologians. A long tradition of Anglo-American jurists and moralists, from the seventeenth to the nineteenth centuries, perpetuated this legal doctrine in an array of treatises,[21] pamphlets,[22] and sermons.[23]

The legal doctrine of the purposes of criminal law and punishment was similar in formulation but different in focus than its theological analog. Like the theologians, the jurists argued that God has created a moral law, that He has vested in this moral law three distinctive uses, and that He imposes divine punishments to ensure that each use is fulfilled. The jurists argued further that state officials must represent and reflect God's authority on earth, that the criminal laws which they promulgate must encapsulate and elaborate the principles of God's moral law,[24] and that the criminal punishments they inflict must confirm and complement the uses of God's moral law.[25] As Blackstone put it, "The state's criminal law must play the same role in man's civil life that God's moral law plays in man's spiritual life."[26]

From these premises, the jurists argued that criminal law and punishment serve three uses or purposes in the lives of the criminal and the community. These they variously called: (1) deterrence or prevention, (2) retribution or restitution, and (3) rehabilitation or reformation—the classic purposes of criminal law and punishment that every law student learns still today. The precise definition of these purposes, and the relative priority and propriety of them, were subjects of endless debate among jurists and judges. Individual jurists, particularly those inspired by Enlightenment and utilitarian sentiments, championed deterrence theories alone.[27] But all three purposes were accepted at English and American criminal law until the end of the nineteenth century. The jurists' definitions of the deterrent, retributive, and rehabilitative purposes of criminal law bear a striking resemblance to the theologians' definitions of the civil, theological, and educational uses of the moral law.

First, the jurists believed, criminal law and punishment have a deterrent function. The criminal law prohibits a variety of harmful and immoral acts—murder, rape, battery, and other violations of the person; arson, theft, burglary, and other violations of property; riot, tumult, nuisance, and other violations of public peace and order. A person who violates these prohibitions must be punished.

Criminal punishment is designed to deter both the individual defendant (special deterrence) and other members of the community (general deterrence) from committing such violations. The punishment imposed must be sufficiently onerous and automatic to deter the individual defendant from repeating the violation. It must also be sufficiently grave and public so that others will see the defendant's plight and be deterred from similar conduct.[28] This was part of the reason for the traditional publicity of the criminal justice system—with its public trials, public confessions, public pillories, public brandings, and public executions. Criminal punishments, Samuel Johnson quipped, "are intended to draw spectators; if they do not, they don't answer their purpose."[29] Most jurists and moralists had little compunction about using the punishment of one individual to serve the ends of both the criminal and the community.[30] "When a man has been proved to have committed a crime," the American moralist Sydney Smith put it, "it is expedient that society should make use of that man for the diminution of crime; he belongs to them for that purpose."[31]

Through these prohibitions and punishments, the jurists believed, the criminal law coerces persons to adopt what they called an external, public, or civic morality—the very same terms the theologians had used. This, to be sure, is only what Justice Joseph Story called a "minimal morality." It consists only of "thou shalt not" commands, not "thou shouldst do" commands. It defines only the outer boundaries of propriety and civility. It provides only the barest modicum of civil order and stability. Yet the jurists believed that, given the inherent depravity of all persons and given the inevitable presence of some persons who yield to their depravity, such a deterrent function of criminal law is indispensable.

There are close parallels between the deterrent function of criminal law and the civil use of the moral law. The theologians stressed the "wrath of God against all unrighteousness" to coerce persons against following their natural inclination to sin, and adduced ample biblical examples of the ill plight of the sinner to bring home their point.[32] The jurists stressed the "severity of the magistrate against all uncivil conduct" and used examples of the law's harsh public sanctions against law breakers to deter persons from all such "uncivil" conduct.[33]

Second, many jurists believed, the criminal law has a retributive function.[34] Retribution, like deterrence, has both a communal and an individual dimension. On the one hand, the criminal law provides a formal procedure for the community to avenge a defendant's violation of both its morality and its security. Criminal conduct, Henry Fielding put it, "tears both the moral fiber and the social fabric of the community; criminal punishment serves to mend that tear."[35] If punishment is not imposed, both the moral fiber and the social fabric of the community will eventually unravel—and, in the view of some early moralists, God's vengeance will be visited on the whole community.[36] This is a second reason for the publicity of the prosecution and punishment of criminals—not only so that others may be deterred from crime but so that the community can avenge the violation of itself and its law. In James Fitzjames Stephen's famous words,

> The sentence of the law is to the moral sentiment of the public in relation to any offence what a seal is to hot wax. It converts into a permanent final judgment what might otherwise be a transient sentiment. . . . The infliction of punishment by law gives definite expression and a solemn ratification and justification of the hatred which is excited by the commission of the offence, and which constitutes the moral

or popular as distinguished from the conscientious sanction of that part of morality which is also sanctioned by the criminal law.[37]

On the other hand, criminal punishment induces the individual criminal to reconcile himself to God. Though the state itself cannot forgive the sinner, it can induce the sinner to repent from his evil, confess his sin, and seek God's forgiveness.[38] This was one of the principal early rationales for the establishment of penitentiaries in England and America—to give prisoners the solitude and serenity necessary to reflect on their crime and seek forgiveness for it.[39] This was one of the principal rationales for infliction of hard labor and harsh suffering on criminals in workhouses and labor gangs—"to soften the hardened soul the way fire softens hardened steel."[40] This was one of the principal rationales for delaying the execution of a criminal for a time after he is convicted for a capital crime, and furnishing him with chaplain services and execution sermons—to give him opportunity to reconcile himself to God before he meets his end.[41]

There are close parallels between this retributive function of the criminal law and the theological use of the moral law, though the emphases are different. The theologians emphasized the need to avenge violations of the moral law and to impel a sinner to seek grace. The jurists emphasized the need for the community to participate in such avenging of its law and emphasized the responsibility of the state to induce the sinner to seek God's gracious forgiveness. Even the hardiest moralists, however, recognized the inherent limitations of the criminal law. Only God's grace could forgive the sinner. The state and its criminal law could merely initiate and facilitate the sinner's supplication.

Third, criminal law and criminal punishment have the function of rehabilitation or reformation. This function, like retribution and deterrence, has both a communal and an individual dimension. On the one hand, criminal law serves to restore in the community a knowledge and respect for the requirements of moral law. In the view of many jurists, the criminal law must not only teach citizens a minimal "public" morality of avoiding harm and threats to others. It must also teach them a more expansive "private" morality of avoiding fault and evil. Thus, historically, the criminal law established one Christian religion and punished heresy, blasphemy, idolatry, false swearing, and violations of the Sabbath. It prescribed various acts of charity and good samaritanism and punished shrewd dealing, unfair bargaining, and ignorance of the poor and needy. It prescribed sexual propriety and restraint and punished sodomy, homosexuality, bestiality, buggery, pornography, prostitution, masturbation, concubinage, and other types of sexual misconduct.[42]

On the other hand, the criminal law serves to reform and reeducate criminals who have violated the moral law. Criminals are punished not only to induce them to seek God's grace but to instruct them on godly virtue. This was the second principal rationale for the penitentiary and the workhouse. They served, in the words of an early English statute on penitentiaries, "by sobriety . . . solitary confinement, . . . labour, [and] due religious instruction . . . to accustom [prisoners] to serious reflection and to teach them both the principles and practices of every Christian and moral duty."[43]

There are striking analogies between this rehabilitative function of criminal law and the educational use of moral law, though here, too, the emphases are different. The theologians emphasized the moral reeducation of justified sinners alone; the jurists emphasized the moral reeducation of all persons, including convicted criminals. The theologians recognized that the moral education and rehabilitation, even of Christians, would remain incomplete until the life hereafter. The jurists recognized that the criminal law was inherently limited in its ability to educate and rehabilitate morally the recalcitrant. In Alexis de Tocqueville's words:

> The moral reformation of . . . a depraved person is only an accidental instead of being a natural consequence of the penitentiary system[;] it is nevertheless true that there is another kind of reformation, less thorough than the former, but yet useful for society, and which the system we treat of seems to produce in a natural way. We have no doubt, but that the habits of order to which the prisoner is subjected for several years, influence very considerably his moral conduct after his return to society. The necessity of labor which overcomes his disposition to idleness; the obligation of silence which makes him reflect; the isolation which places him alone in presence of his crime and suffering; the religious instruction which enlightens and comforts him. . . . Without loving virtue, he may detest the crime of which he has suffered the cruel consequences; and if he is not more virtuous he has become at least more judicious; his morality is not honour, but interest. His religious faith is perhaps neither lively nor deep; but even supposing that religion has not touched his heart, his mind has contracted habits of order, and he possesses rules for his conduct in life; without having a powerful religious conviction, he has acquired a taste for moral principles which religion affords.[44]

The theological doctrine of the uses of moral law and the legal doctrine of the purposes of criminal punishment are analogous not only in their formulation but also in their foundation. Like the theologians, the jurists believed that persons and societies are at once sinful and saintly. They thus tailored the criminal law as a whole to both types of persons and the criminal punishment of any individual to both dimensions of his or her character. Also like the theologians, the jurists subsumed and integrated their "uses" doctrine in a more general theory. The theologians subsumed their uses doctrine in a more general theology of salvation. For them, the moral law played an indispensable role in the process from predestination to justification to sanctification. The jurists subsumed their uses doctrine in a moral theory of government. For them, the criminal law played an indispensable role in discharging the divinely ordained tasks of the state to coerce, discipline, and nurture its citizens.

It would, of course, be too strong to say that the Protestant theological doctrine of the three uses of moral law was the source of the modern Anglo-American doctrine of the purposes of criminal law and punishment. Western writers since Plato have reflected on the purposes of criminal law,[45] and the early modern Anglo-American jurists drew on these writings as much as those of Protestant theology. Yet the Protestant theological "uses" doctrine provided an important source of integration and instruction for the jurists. Several early Protestant jurists explicitly linked the theological and legal "uses" doctrines. Jurists and theologians thereafter regularly collaborated in formulating theories of crime and punishment. The close analogies between the structure and content of the theological and legal uses doctrines amply demonstrate the cross-fertilization between them.

THE USES DOCTRINE IN
CONTEMPORARY CRIMINAL LAW

Even in late twentieth-century America, vestiges of this traditional understanding of criminal law and punishment remain evident. Consistent with traditional formulations, modern American criminal law still includes deterrence, retribution, and rehabilitation among the principal purposes of punishment. Late nineteenth and early twentieth century experiments at reducing the purposes of criminal punishment to deterrence or rehabilitation alone have proved to be unpersuasive in theory and unworkable in practice.[46] The 1984 Federal Sentencing Act, for example, now indicates that criminal punishments must be imposed on criminals "(A) to reflect the seriousness of the offense, to promote respect for the law, and to provide just punishment for the offense; (B) to afford adequate deterrence to criminal conduct; (C) to protect the public from further crimes of the defendant; and (D) to provide the defendant with needed educational or vocational training, medical care, or other correctional treatment in the most effective manner."[47] A few contemporary jurists, such as Johannes Andenaes, Lon Fuller, and Joel Feinberg, retain a rather traditional Protestant tone and terminology in describing these functions, arguing that criminal law and punishment must induce respect for formal law and social norms, confirm moral inhibitions and habits of citizens, and "shape the framework of moral education."[48] Most contemporary jurists, however, define these three purposes in less moralistic, and more mechanistic, terms. They define deterrence as making the crime too costly to risk, retribution as paying the criminal what he or she owes, rehabilitation as returning the criminal to an acceptable level of social conformity and functionality.[49]

Also consistent with traditional formulations, contemporary criminal law continues to inculcate various "levels of morality" in its citizens.[50] The criminal law still proscribes conduct that harms others. Homicide, rape, battery, and other personal offenses; arson, theft, burglary, and other property offenses; tumult, riot, nuisance, and other public offenses are still prohibited and punished. Through such prohibitions and punishments, the criminal law supports a basic "public" or "civic" morality. The criminal law also continues to punish attempts, polygamy, obscenity, sodomy, and similar actions that, though not directly harmful to other persons, are nonetheless considered morally and socially unacceptable. Through such punishment, the criminal law supports at least a "quasi-private" form of morality. Certain specialized bodies of criminal law, like juvenile law, go even further to inculcate in juveniles charity, piety, sobriety, and other purely private virtues. Whether accidental or deliberate, modern criminal law still defines and enforces distinctive moral values in American society.

Most contemporary jurists, however, have abandoned the three cardinal premises upon which the traditional doctrine of the purposes of criminal law and punishment was founded. They have thus lost the point of unity and integration inherent in the traditional doctrine.

First, most contemporary jurists have abandoned the theory of natural law, which inspired both the form and the content of early Anglo-American criminal law. Arguments from moral relativism, cultural pluralism, separation of church and

state, and the rights of privacy have all contributed to this erosion. The Supreme
Court has reified this erosion through it broad interpretation of constitutional
freedoms. Traditional criminal laws against blasphemy or false swearing, for example, though once widely enforced, have today been eclipsed by the expansion
of free speech protections of the First Amendment. Traditional laws against Sab-
bath-breaking, heresy, idolatry, or nonconformity have been eclipsed by the expansion of the free exercise and establishment clause protections of the First Amendment. Traditional laws against various forms of sexual license and deviance have
been eclipsed by a new privacy right imputed to the due process clause of the
Fourteenth Amendment and similar state constitutional provisions. Second, most
contemporary writers have abandoned the traditional anthropological assumption
that human beings and human communities are at once saintly and sinful, *simul
iustus et peccatur.* Some stress the inherent goodness of the person and consider
crime as aberrational and correctable. They have, accordingly, emphasized the
rehabilitative purpose of criminal law and have deprecated particularly its retributive purpose. Others stress the inherent depravity of the person and consider crime
inevitable. They have, accordingly, stressed the deterrent and retributive functions
of criminal law and have deprecated the rehabilitative purpose.

Third, most contemporary writers have abandoned the traditional moral theory
of government which helped to integrate the three purposes of criminal law and
punishment. The state is seen as a representative of the people, not a vice-regent
of God. Its laws must effectuate the will of the majority, not appropriate the will
of God. The notion that the three functions of criminal law can thus be integrated
into the divinely ordained tasks of the state to coerce, discipline, and nurture its
citizens is foreign to our modern understanding.

Without these three cardinal premises, modern American criminal law has lost
its traditional moorings. Jurists oscillate among positivist, utilitarian, sociological,
and numerous other theories of crime and punishment. Judges play retribution,
deterrence, and rehabilitation against each other, rather than directing these values
to common moral and social goals. Accordingly, a number of writers have called
for a reintegration of morality and criminal law, and a reintegration of the three
functions of criminal law and punishment—thus far, with only a modest response.[51]

To bring to light a Protestant source of our modern theories of criminal law
and punishment is not to offer a panacea. One cannot readily transpose the moral
concepts and criminal law institutions of the sixteenth century into our culture. But
the Protestant tradition offers important insights for our day. Protestant writers

recognized that a system of criminal law depends upon a transcendent moral source for its contents and its structure, that any measure of criminal punishment must balance the values of deterrence, retribution, and rehabilitation, and that through punishment the state serves at once as disciplinarian, counselor, and teacher of its citizens. Protestant writers also recognized that the state and its criminal law are themselves fallen and therefore inherently limited in their capacities and incapable of operating alone. Other social institutions alongside the state, such as the family, the school, the church, and other voluntary associations, must play complementary roles. Each of these social institutions, too, bears the responsibility of encapsulating and elaborating moral principles. Each of these social institutions, too, must participate in the deterrence and retribution of crime, and the rehabilitation and reformation of the community. These time-tested insights provide important signposts along the way to the development of a new integrative theory of criminal law and punishment for contemporary America.

NOTES

1. See particularly Harold J. Berman, *Faith and Order: The Reconciliation of Law and Religion* (Atlanta: Scholars Press, 1993) and John Witte, Jr., and Frank S. Alexander, eds., *The Weightier Matters of the Law: Essays on Law and Religion* (Atlanta: Scholars Press, 1988). For an introduction to the literature, see Howard J. Vogel, "A Survey and Commentary on the New Literature in Law and Religion," *Journal of Law and Religion* 1 (1983): 79–169.

2. For discussions of this Protestant doctrine, and its biblical and theological antecedents, see, e.g., Frank S. Alexander, "Validity and Function of Law: The Reformation Doctrine of *Usus Legis*," *Mercer Law Review* 31 (1980): 509–29; Ragnar Bring, *Gesetz und Evangelium und der dritte Gebrauch des Gesetzes in der lutherischen Theologie* (Abo: Abo Akademie, 1943); Werner Elert, "Eine theologische Fälschung zur Lehre vom tertius usus legis," *Zeitschrift für Religions- und Geistesgeschichte* 1 (1948): 168–70; Josef Bohatec, *Calvin und das Recht* (Graz: H. Boeklaus, 1934); Lauri Haikola, *Usus Legis* (Uppsala: Lundequistska Bokhandeln, 1958); Harold J. Berman and John Witte, Jr., "The Transformation of Western Legal Philosophy in Lutheran Germany," *Southern California Law Review* 62 (1989): 1573, 1608 ff., 1622 ff.

3. See *D. Martin Luthers Werke, Kritische Gesamtausgabe* (Weimar: Hermann Bohlau, 1883–1979), 10: 454 ff., 16: 363 ff., 40: 481 ff. (hereafter cited as *Luther, WA*); Philip Melanchthon, *Werke*, rpt. in *Corpus Reformatorum*, ed. G. Bretschneider, 88 vols. (Leipzig: N. Henschius Nachfolger, 1834–60), 1: 706 ff., 11: 66 ff., 21: 405 ff.,

716 ff., 22: 248 ff. (hereafter cited as *Melanchthon, CR*); John Calvin, *Institutes of the Christian Religion,* 2 vols. (1559), trans. Ford Lewis Battles and ed. John T. McNeill (Philadelphia: Westminster Press, 1960), bk. 2, chap. 7. See also the summaries of these and other early Protestant writings on the uses of law in Friedrich Gentzken, *Dissertatio de jure divino circa poenis* (Leipzig, 1714); Andreas Gronwall, *Dissertatio gradualis de poena vitiorum naturali* (Uppsala, 1730); Christoph Matthaus Pfaff, *Dissertatio theologica de poenis divinis ob aliena peccata inflictis* (Tübingen, 1747).

4.   On Protestant theories of natural and moral law, see, e.g., Berman and Witte, "The Transformation"; Bohatec, *Calvin und das Recht;* Otto Krause, *Naturrechtsler sechszehnten Jahrhunderts* (München, 1982); August Lang, "The Reformation and Natural Law," in *Calvin and the Reformation* (New York: Fleming H. Revell, 1959), 56–98; Hans Liermann, "Zur Geschichte des Naturrechts in der evangelischen Kirche: Eine rechts- und geistesgeschichtliche Studie," in *Festschrift für Alfred Bartholet zum 80. Geburtstag* (Berlin, 1950), 294–324; John T. McNeill, "Natural Law in the Teaching of the Reformers," *Journal of Religion* 26 (1946): 168–82; Erik Wolf, *Rechtstheologische Studien* (Frankfurt am Main: Vitoria Klostermann, 1972), 3–23.

5.   Lutherans tended to emphasize the theological use of the moral law, and Calvinists tended to emphasize the educational use. See, e.g., *Luther, WA* 10: 454, 40: 486 (calling the theological use "the true office and the chief and proper use of the law"); Calvin, *Institutes,* bk. 2, section 7.12 (calling the educational use the "third and principal use"). See also Werner Elert, *Law and Gospel,* trans. Edward H. Schroeder (Philadelphia: Fortress Press, 1967), 38 ff.; Wilfred Joest, *Gesetz und Freiheit: Das Problem des Tertius Usus Legis bei Luther und die neutestamentliche Parainese* (Göttingen: Vandenhoek and Ruprecht, 1961), 48 ff., on the controversy over the educational use in later Lutheran theology.
The differences between the Lutheran and Calvinist formulations, however, should not be exaggerated. The influential Lutheran writer Philip Melanchthon stressed the educational use of the law from 1535 onward, and his formulations appear in several authoritative Lutheran confessions and theological tracts of the sixteenth and seventeenth centuries. See *Melanchthon, CR* 21: 406. See also the summary of the Lutheran position in the *Formula of Concord* (1577), pt. 6, rpt. in *Triglott Concordia: The Symbolic Books of the Ev. Lutheran Church* (St. Louis: Concordia Publishing House, 1921), at 805: "The law was given to men for three reasons: first, that thereby outward discipline might be maintained and wild and intractable men may be coerced by certain rules; second, that men thereby may be led to the knowledge of their sins; third, that men who have already been reborn . . . may on account of this have a fixed rule according to which they can and ought to form their whole life."

6. Calvin, *Institutes*, bk. 2, section 7.10.

7. Calvin, *Institutes*, bk. 2, section 7.10; bk. 4, section 20.3.; *Melanchthon, CR* 1: 706–8.

8. *Melanchton, CR* 22: 151, 250. See also Calvin, *Institutes*, bk. 2, chaps. 7.10–11, 8.11, 51.

9. *Luther, WA* 40: 481–86. See also Calvin, *Institutes*, bk. 3, chap. 4.

10. *Melanchthon, CR* 21: 406.

11. Calvin, *Institutes*, bk. 2, section 7.12.

12. See Calvin, *Institutes*, bk. 2, section 8.6, where he contrasts "outward honesty and legality" with "inward and spiritual righteousness." God, he writes, "is concerned not so much with the outward appearance as with purity of heart, [and thus] under the prohibition of fornication, murder, and theft, forbids lust, anger, hatred, coveting a neighbor's possessions, deceit, and the like. For because he is a spiritual lawgiver, he speaks no less to the soul than to the body. But murder that is of the soul consists in anger and hatred; theft, in evil covetousness and avarice; fornication, in lust." See also *Melanchthon, CR* 1: 706–8; Martin Bucer, *Deutschen Schriften*, ed. R. Stupperich, 16 vols. (Halle: Güterslohrer Verlagshaus Mohn, 1960), 1: 36 ff., and discussion in Karl Köhler, *Luther und die Juristen. Zur Frage nach den gegenseitigen Verhältnis des Rechts und der Sittlichkeit* (Gotha: Verlag von Rud. Besser, 1873), 104 ff.; Berman and Witte, "The Transformation," 1588–95, 1623–35.

13. See Romans 5–6, 8: 28–30. See also, Calvin, *Institutes*, bk. 3, chap. 14.

14. See, e.g., Dietrich Bonhoeffer, *Ethics*, trans. Neville H. Smith and ed. Eberhard Bethge (New York: Macmillan, 1955, 1965), 303 ff.; Emil Brunner, *Dogmatik*, 3 vols. (Zurich: Zwingli-Verlag, 1960), 2: 131 ff., 3: 306 ff.; Emil Brunner, *The Mediator: A Study of the Central Doctrine of the Christian Faith*, trans. O. Wyon (London: Lutterworth Press, 1934), 441 ff.; Karl Barth, *Ethics*, trans. R. Dietrich Braun (Seabury, N.Y.: Seabury Press, 1981), 58 ff. For other modern accounts, see, e.g., Gerhard Ebeling, *Word and Faith*, trans. J. W. Leitch (Philadelphia: Fortress Press, 1963), 74 ff.; Alec R. Vidler, *Christ's Strange Work: An Exposition of the Three Uses of God's Law*, rev. ed. (London: SCM Press, 1963), and sources cited therein.

15. On early Lutheran theories, see W. Maurer, *Die Kirche und ihr Recht. Gesammelte Aufsaetze zum evangelischen Kirchenrecht* (Tübingen: Mohr, 1976); Hans Liermann, *Deutsches evangelischen Kirchenrecht* (Stuttgart: F. Enke, 1933). On early Calvinist theories, see Josef Bohatec, *Calvins Lehre von Staat und Kirche* (Aalen: Scientia, 1961). These reformers' sentiments on the purposes of ecclesiastical discipline were woven into the church orders and creeds of later Protestant denominations. See, e.g., the Waldegrave Liturgy (c. 1567), section on "The Order of the Ecclesiastical Discipline": "As the word of God is the life and soul of the Church, so this godly order and discipline is, as it were, sinews in the body, which knit and join the

members together with decent order and comeliness. It is a bridle to stay the
wicked from their mischiefs; it is a spur to prick forward such as be slow and neg-
ligent: yea, and for all men it is the Father's rod, ever in a readiness to chastise
gently the faults committed, and to cause them afterward to live in more godly fear
and reverence." Qtd. by Horton Davies, *The Worship of the English Puritans* (London: Dacre Press, 1948), 232–33. For discussion of other Protestant formulations
on ecclesiastical discipline, see David H. Flaherty, *Privacy in Colonial New England*
(Charlottesville: Univ. Press of Virginia, 1974), 151–63; and John Witte, Jr., "The
Plight of Canon Law in the Early Dutch Republic," in *Canon Law in Protestant
Lands,* ed. R. H. Helmholz (Berlin: Duncker and Humblot, 1992), 77, 84 ff., and
sources cited therein.

16. See, e.g., *Luther, WA* 6: 267 ff., 19: 626 ff., 32: 394 ff.; *Melanchthon, CR* 22: 224
ff., 615 ff., with discussion in H. Mayer, "Die Strafrechtstheorie bei Luther und
Melanchthon," in *Festgabe für Binder* (Berlin: Dunker, 1930), 77–110; Wolfgang
Naucke, "Christliche, aufklarerische, und wissenschaftstheoretische Begrundung
des Strafrechts (Luther-Beccaria-Kant)," in *Christentum, Säkularisation und
modernes Recht,* ed. Luigi L. Vallauri and Gerhard Dilcher, 2 vols. (Baden-Baden:
Nomos Verlagsgesellschaft, 1981), 2: 1201. See Calvin, *Institutes,* bk. 4, sections
12.4–6 and 20.3, and discussion in E. William Monter, "Crime and Punishment
in Calvin's Geneva, 1562," *Archiv für Reformationsgeschichte* 64 (1973): 281–87;
Herbert Foster, "Calvin's Programme for a Puritan State in Geneva," *Harvard
Theological Review* 1 (1908): 391–424; J. Baur, "Gott, Recht und weltliches
Regiment im Werke Calvins," in *Schriften zur Rechtslehre und Politik* (Bonn, 1965),
44–69.

Among the early Protestant reformers, Melanchthon offered the fullest statements
on the uses of the criminal law and punishment. See, e.g., *Melanchthon, CR* 22:
152: "All punishments by the state and others should remind us of God's wrath
against our sin, and should warn us to reform and better ourselves." See also
Melanchthon CR 22: 224, where Melanchthon sets out "four very important reasons
for criminal punishment," which are, effectively, divine retribution, special deterrence, general deterrence, and education:

> (1) God is a wise and righteous being, who out of his great and proper goodness created
> rational creatures to be like him. Therefore, if they strive against him the order of jus-
> tice [requires that] he destroy them. The first reason for punishment then is the order
> of justice in God. (2) The need of other peaceful persons. If murderers, adulterers, rob-
> bers, and thieves, were not removed, nobody would be safe. (3) [To set an e]xample.
> When some are punished, others are reminded to take account of God's wrath and to
> fear his punishment and thus to reduce the causes of punishment. (4) The importance
> of divine judgment and external punishment, in which all remain who in this life are

not converted to God. As God in these temporal punishments shows that he distinguishes between virtue and vice, and that he is a righteous judge, we are reminded more of this example that also after this life all sinners who are not converted to God will be punished.

See also Martin Bucer, *De Regno Christi* (1550), translated in William Pauck, ed., *Melanchthon and Bucer* (Philadelphia: Westminster Press, 1969), 153, 383: "For the nature of all men is so corrupt from birth and has such a propensity for crimes and wickedness that it has to be called away and deterred from vices, and invited and forced to virtues, not only by teaching and exhortation, admonition and reprimand, which are accomplished by words, but also by the learning and correction that accompany force and authority and the imposition of punishments."

17. See sources discussed in Berman and Witte, "The Transformation," 1635–50. See particularly the discussion of punishment and the uses of law in Johann Oldendorp, *Lexicon Juris* (Marburg, 1546), a standard legal dictionary in Europe throughout the sixteenth and seventeenth centuries.

18. Nicolaus Hemming, *De lege naturae apodicta methodus* (Wittenberg, 1577), 34 ff., and discussion in Krause, *Naturrechtler,* 125 ff.

19. Benedict Wincler, *Principiorum iuris libri quinque* (Leipzig, 1615), chap. 4 and discussion in Krause, *Naturrechtler,* 130 ff.

20. See particularly Johannes Althusius, *Tractatus tres de poenis, de rebus fungibilibus, ac de jure retentionis* (Cologne, 1633).

21. Among the numerous relevant treatises in the seventeenth and eighteenth centuries that had influence in England and America, see, e.g., William Blackstone, *Commentaries on the Laws of England* (1765), ed. Robert M. Kerr (Boston: Beacon Press, 1962), bk. 4, chap. 1.; Hugo Grotius, *On the Law of War and Peace* (1625), trans. Francis W. Kelsey (Indianapolis: Bobbs-Merrill, 1965), bk. 2, chaps. 20, 21; Thomas Hobbes, *De Cive* (1642), ed. Sterling Lamprecht (New York: Appleton-Century-Crofts, 1949), chap. 14; Thomas Hobbes, *Leviathan* (1651), ed. C. B. Macpherson (Harmondsworth, England: Penguin, 1968), chap. 28; Samuel von Pufendorf, *On The Law of Nature and Nations* (1688), ed. W. A. Oldfather (Oceana, N.Y.: Oceana, 1964), bk. 8, chap. 3; Thomas Rutherforth, *Institutes of Natural Law, Being the Substance of a Course of Lectures on Grotius De Jure Belli et Pacis,* 3d. ed. (Philadelphia, 1799), bk. 1, chap. 18; Robert Sanderson, *Bishop Sanderson's Lectures on Conscience and Human Law* (1647) (Lincoln: J. Williamson, 1877), Lect. 8.10–25; John Selden, *De Jure Naturali et Gentium juxta disciplinam Ebraeorum libri septem* (Leipzig, 1695), bk. 1, chap. 4; bk. 4, chap. 11. Excerpts from these and many other early modern sources are included in Andr. Christoph Rosnero, *Thesarus locorum communium jurisprudentiae ex axiomatibus augustini barbosae,* 2d ed. (Leipzig, 1729); Basil Montagu, *The Opinions of Different Authors*

Upon the Punishment of Death, 3 vols. (London: Longman, Hurst, Rees, and Paternoster Row, 1809); L. A. Selby-Bigge, ed., *British Moralists, Being Selections of
Writers Principally from the Eighteenth Century,* 2 vols. (New York: Dover Publications, 1965); D. D. Raphael, *British Moralists 1650–1800* (Oxford: Clarendon
Press, 1969). Among the most critical writings of the later eighteenth and nineteenth centuries are those by Beccaria, Voltaire, Bentham, Romilly, Eden, and others excerpted in Gertrude Ezorsky, ed., *Philosophical Perspectives on Punishment* (Al-
bany. State Univ. of New York Press, 1973), and discussed in W. S. Holdsworth,
A History of English Law, 13 vols. (Boston: Little, Brown, 1938), 11: 556 ff.; J. M.
Beattie, *Crime and the Courts in England, 1660–1800* (Princeton, N.J.: Princeton
Univ. Press, 1986); Leon Radzinowicz, *A History of English Criminal Law and its
Administration from 1750,* 5 vols. (London: Stevens, 1948–86). For discussion of
contemporaneous American writers and developments, see, e.g., Edwin Powers,
Crime and Punishment in Early Massachusetts, 1620–1692 (Boston: Beacon Press,
1966); William E. Nelson, "Emerging Notions of Criminal Law in the Revolu-
tionary Era," *New York University Law Review* 42 (1967): 450–82.

22. For a convenient collection, see Montagu, *The Opinions,* passim.
23. The most valuable such sermons were the "execution sermons" delivered by eminent ministers and/or jurists on the occasion of public executions. For an account
of such sermons, delivered in England and America from the early seventeenth to
the later nineteenth centuries, see J. A. Sharpe, "'Last Dying Speeches': Religion,
Ideology, and Public Execution in England," *Past and Present* 107 (1985): 144–67;
J. S. Cockburn, *A History of English Assizes 1558–1714* (Cambridge: Cambridge
Univ. Press, 1974); Ronald A. Bosco, "Lectures at the Pillory: The Early American
Execution Sermon," *American Quarterly* 30 (1978): 156–76. For English samples,
see George Berkeley, *A Sermon Preached at the Assizes Held at Leicester* (London: J.
Macock, 1686); David Edwards, *Sermons to the Condemned* (London, 1775); Rich-
ard W. Hamilton, *A Sermon Preached at Leeds . . . on Occasion of the Execution of Mr.
Joseph Blackburn, Attorney at Law, for Forgery,* 4th ed. (London: Leeds, 1815). For
American examples, see Increase Mather, *The Wicked Mans Portion, or A Sermon
Preached at the Lecture in Boston in New England . . . 1674* (Boston: John Foster,
1675); Increase Mather, *A Sermon Occasioned by the Execution of a Man Found
Guilty of Murder,* 2d. ed. (Boston: R. Pierce, 1687) (hereafter cited as Mather,
1687 Execution Sermon); Nathan Strong, *A Sermon Preached in Hartford . . . At the
Execution of Richard Doane* (Hartford, Conn.: Elisha Babcock, 1797).
24. For English developments, see the collection of pamphlets and excerpts in
Montagu, *Opinions* 3: 26 ff. For American developments, see David Flaherty, "Law
and the Enforcement of Morals in Early America," in *Law in American History,* ed.
Donald Fleming and Bernard Bailyn (Boston: Little, Brown, 1973), 203–53.

25. See, e.g., Mather, *1687 Execution Sermon*, 13 ("[The Magistrate] is a minister of God, a Revenger to execute wrath upon him that does Evil. Rom. 13.4. Private Reveng[e] is evil; but publick Revenge on those that violate Laws of God, is good. The Magistrate is God's Vice-gerent. As none can give life but God; so none may take it away but God; as such as He has appointed" [italics deleted]); Thomas Hancock, *He is the Minister of God to Thee for Good* (Maidstone, 1735), 12 ("The magistrate . . . must exercise this power [of punishment], in imitation of God, for the good of man."); George Stonestreet, *The Especial Importance of Religious Principles in the Judges and the Advocates of the Courts of Law* (Newport, 1822), 28–29 ("The justice men seek at an earthly tribunal is, when impartially and mercifully administered, both an emblem and an emanation of that essential attribute which we adore in the Almighty . . . the punishments, which at your hands await the workers of iniquity, while they preserve the order of society, serve also to vindicate the moral government of God over His creatures, and to warn men of that heavier vengeance which must hereafter await the impenitent sinner."). See discussion in Randall McGowen, "The Changing Face of God's Justice: The Debates Over Divine and Human Punishment in Eighteenth-Century England," *Criminal Justice History: An International Annual* 9 (1988): 63 ff.

26. Qtd. by A. Bodenheimer, *Recht und Rechtfertigung* (Berlin: Dunker, 1907), 118.

27. See particularly Cesare Beccaria, *On Crimes and Punishments* (1764), trans. Henry Paulocci (Indianapolis: Bobbs-Merrill, 1963); Jeremy Bentham, *The Principles of Morals and Legislation*, in *Works*, ed. John Bowring and William Tait (Edinburgh: W. Tait, 1843), 1–154; Jeremy Bentham, *Theory of Legislation*, trans. E. Dumont, et al. (London: K. Paul, Trench, Trubner, 1904), 272 ff.; Oliver Wendell Holmes, *The Common Law*, ed. M. DeWolfe Howe (Cambridge, Mass.: Belknap Press, 1963), 36 ff.

28. See, e.g., Pufendorf, *On the Law of Nature and Nations*, bk. 8, section 3.9, chapters 11 and 12; Grotius, *On the Law of War and Peace*, bk. 2, section 20.7–9.

29. Qtd. in *Boswell's Life and Letters of Samuel Johnson*, 3 vols. (London: Macmillan, 1906), 2: 447. See also Pufendorf, *On the Law of Nature and Nations*, bk. 8, section 3.11., who emphasizes the value of general deterrence for the victim of a previous crime: "A victim of violence can be secured from that of others, not merely by any form of punishment, but by one that is open and public, and serves as example and warning. That is the reason why executions are usually held not in secluded corners of prisons but in the most frequented places, and with terrifying features [that] may be able to strike fear in the hearts of the common sort."

30. But cf. Immanuel Kant, *The Metaphysical Elements of Justice*, trans. John Ladd (Indianapolis: Bobbs-Merrill, 1965), 100: "Judicial punishment (*poenis forensis*) is entirely distinct from natural punishment (*poenis naturalis*). In natural punishment,

vice punishes itself, and this fact is not taken into account by the legislator. Judicial punishment can never be administered merely as a means to promote some other good for the criminal himself or for civil society, but instead it must in all cases be imposed on him only on the ground that he has committed a crime; for a human being can never be manipulated merely as a means to the purposes of someone else."

31. Sydney Smith, *Elementary Sketches of Moral Philosophy,* 2d ed. (New York: Harper and Brothers, 1860), 252.

32. See particularly Strong, *A Sermon,* 6 ff.

33. Cotton Mather, *The Call of the Gospel Applied Unto all Men in General, and Unto a Condemned Malefactor in Particular,* 2d ed. (Boston: R. Pierce, 1687), 58.

34. A number of early modern jurists spurned retribution as a purpose of punishment on the argument that this was the function of moral law and divine punishment. See, e.g., Grotius, *On the Law of War and Peace,* bk. 2, section 20.4.2. ("One man is so bound to another by ties of common blood that he ought not to do harm to another save for the sake of attaining some good. With God the case is otherwise. . . . For the actions of God can be based upon the right of the Supreme Power, particularly where a man's special desert is concerned, even if they have in view outside themselves."); Blackstone, *Commentaries,* bk. 4, section 1.2 ("As to the *end* or final cause of human punishments. This is not by way of atonement or *expiation* for the crime committed; for that must be left to the just determination of the Supreme Being: but as a precaution against future offences of the same kind."); Beccaria, *On Crimes and Punishments,* 28 ("If God hath decreed eternal punishments for those who disobey His will, shall an insect dare to put itself in the place of Divine justice or pretend to punish for the Almighty who is Himself all sufficient."); Hobbes, *De Cive,* section 3.11; Francis Bacon, *On Revenge* (1597), in *Essays or Counsels Civil or Moral* (London: J. M. Dent, 1902), 11.

35. Henry Fielding, qtd. by Bodenheimer, *Recht und Rechtfertigung,* 177. See also J. Welland, *Difficulties Connected with Punishment as Part of the Divine System of Government* (Calcutta: R. C. LePage, 1864), 12 ("Punishment may be inflicted for some benefit [of] pointing out that sin is not to be regarded as a solitary act, beginning and ending in ourselves, but as an offence and injury to the supreme Law, and so to all, for the law is the life of the community.").

36. See, e.g., Mather, *1687 Execution Sermon,* 10–13, and discussions in Powers, *Crime and Punishment,* 517 and John Witte, Jr., "Blest Be The Ties That Bind: Covenant and Community in Puritan Thought," *Emory Law Journal* 36 (1987): 579, 590 ff. Likewise, Kant argues that a criminal must be punished so that "the bloodguiltiness may not remain upon the people." Qtd. by Graeme R. Newman, *The Punishment Response* (Philadelphia: Lippincott, 1978), 193.

37. James Fitzjames Stephen, *A History of the Criminal Law of England*, 3 vols. (London: Macmillan, 1883), 2: 81. See also A. L. Goodhart, *English Law and the Moral Law* (London: Stevens, 1953), 93 ("If this retribution is not given recognition, then the disapproval may also disappear. A community which is too ready to for~~give the wrongdoer may end up condoning the crime.~~")

38. See, e.g., John Selden, *De Jure Naturali et Gentium*, bk. 1, chap. 4 (in addition to the purposes of deterrence and reformation "we should set another called the end of satisfaction, or purgation, or expiation, as though a deviation from law were made up, as it were, and the consequent inequality of action corrected."). This agitation for confession was a constant refrain of the execution sermons. See examples in Sharpe, "Last Dying Speeches" and Bosco, "Lectures at the Pillory."

39. See the numerous sentiments collected in Montagu, *Opinions*, vols. 2 and 3. On the history of the penitentiary in England and America, see, e.g., Beattie, *Crime and the Courts*, 520 ff.; Radzinowicz, *A History of English Criminal Law*, vol. 5; Michael Ignatieff, *A Just Measure of Pain: The Penitentiary in the Industrial Revolution* (New York: Pantheon Books, 1978); W. J. Forsythe, *The Reform of Prisoners 1830–1900* (London: Croom Helm, 1987). On the important influence of the Quakers on prison reform, see, e.g., Auguste Jorns, *The Quakers as Pioneers in Social Work*, trans. Thomas K. Brown (Montclair, N.J.: Patterson-Smith, 1969), 162.

40. Lance Falconer, qtd. by Walter Moberly, *The Ethics of Punishment* (Hamden, Conn.: Archon Books, 1968), 124. See also the discussion of the penitentiary as "moral hospital" in Isaac Kramnick, "Eighteenth-Century Science and Radical Social Theory: The Case of Joseph Priestly's Scientific Liberalism," *Journal of British Studies* 25 (1986): 1–30.

41. See Sharpe, "Last Dying Speeches"; Bosco, "Lectures at the Pillory."

42. See, e.g., the classification of crimes in Blackstone, *Commentaries*, bk. 4, chaps. 4–17, which begins with "Offenses Against God and Religion," a scheme followed by many English and American writers on criminal law. In the seventeenth and eighteenth centuries, a number of English societies for the reformation of manners and morals emerged, both to promote legislation against various forms of public and private immorality and to catalyze judicial enforcement of these provisions. Radzinowicz, *A History of English Criminal Law* 2: 1–15.

43. 18 Geo. 3, c. 17. Similar sentiments were part of American theories of the penitentiary. See, e.g., *Report of the Board of Inspectors of the Prison for the City and County of Philadelphia* (1791), in Montagu, *Opinions* 3: 284–85: "We have . . . kept in view three principal objects: The public security, The reformation of the prisoners, and Humanity towards those unhappy members of Society . . . The second object we have pursued by moral and religious instruction, by promoting habits of industry, by a separation of the sexes, by the prohibition of spiritous liquors, by

exclusion of improper connexions from without, and by confining the refractory to solitude, low diet, and hard labour. . . . Bibles and other books of practical religion, have been provided for the use of the prison: The clergy of the different denominations in the city and suburbs provide divine service once a week, commonly on Sunday mornings, and other edifying persons have at all times access to the prisoners."

44. Gustave de Beaumont and Alexis de Tocqueville, *On the Penitentiary System in the United States and its Application in France,* trans. Francis Lieber (1833; rpt. New York: A. M. Kelley, 1970), 58–59. See also Zephaniah Swift, *A Digest of the Laws of the State of Connecticut* (New Haven, Conn.: S. Converse, 1823), 260–61 ("It is vain to attempt to reform those who have committed crimes which evidence a total destitution of those moral principles that are the basis of reformation.").

45. On these earlier theories, see particularly, Mary Margaret McKenzie, *Plato on Punishment* (Berkeley and Los Angeles: Univ. of California Press, 1981); Stephan Kuttner, *Kanonistische Schuldlehre von Gratian bis auf die Dekretalen Gregors IX, systematisch auf Grund der handschriftlichen Quellen dargestellt* (Vatican: Biblioteca Apostolica Vaticana, 1935); W. Cole Durham, "Religion and the Criminal Law: Types and Contexts of Interaction," in *The Weightier Matters of the Law,* ed. Witte and Alexander, 193–227.

46. Earlier in this century, retribution had fallen into disfavor—as "a disguised form of vengeance" and a "vestige of man's instinctual past." Jerome Hall, "Justice in the 20th Century," *California Law Review* 59 (1971): 752, 753–54; Jerome Hall, *Studies in Jurisprudence and Criminal Theory* (New York: Oceana Publications, 1958), 242 ff. George Fletcher writes that retribution has returned as a legitimate purpose of criminal punishment, in part because of "disillusionment about deterrence and rehabilitation purposes standing alone." "One way to make an argument for retributive punishment," he writes, "is to focus on the criminal act as the source of the offender's obligation to suffer punishment . . . for his offense creates an imbalance of the benefits and burdens in the society as a whole. Those who obey the law incur burdens that offenders refuse to take upon themselves. To rectify this imbalance the offender must suffer an appropriate punishment. His refusal to conform generates the proverbial 'debt' that must be paid." George Fletcher, *Rethinking Criminal Law* (Boston: Little, Brown, 1978), 416–18. See also Herbert Packer, *The Limits of the Criminal Sanction* (Stanford, Calif.: Stanford Univ. Press, 1968), 38 ff.

47. 18 U.S.C.A. S. 3553(a)(2)(1984).

48. See Johannes Andenaes, *Punishment and Deterrence* (Ann Arbor, Mich.: Univ. of Michigan Press, 1974), 110 ff.; Lon Fuller, *The Morality of Law,* rev. ed. (New Haven, Conn.: Yale Univ. Press, 1969); Joel Feinberg, "The Expressive Function

of Punishment," *The Monist* 49 (1965): 397–423. See also Moberly, *The Ethics of Punishment*, 78 ff.; Walter Moberly, *Legal Responsibility and Moral Responsibility* (Philadelphia: Fortress Press, 1951).

49. See the collection of statements in Sanford H. Kadish and Stephen J. Schulhofer, *Criminal Law and Its Processes*, 5th ed. (Boston: Little, Brown, 1988), 113 ff.

50. For samples of the large body of literature on this point, see Morris R. Cohen, "Moral Aspects of the Criminal Law," *Yale Law Journal* 49 (1940): 987–1026; Patrick Devlin, *The Enforcement of Morals* (London: Oxford Univ. Press, 1965); Joel Feinberg, *The Moral Limits of the Criminal Law* (New York: Oxford Univ. Press, 1984); Thomas C. Grey, *The Legal Enforcement of Morality* (New York: Knopf, 1983); Basil Mitchell, *Law, Morality and Religion in a Secular Society* (London: Oxford Univ. Press, 1972).

51. See, e.g., Harold J. Berman, "The Use of Law to Guide People to Virtue: A Comparison of Soviet and American Perspectives," in *Law, Justice, and the Individual in Society: Psychological and Legal Issues*, ed. June L. Tapp and Felice Levine (New York: Holt, Rinehart and Winston, 1977), 75–84; Hall, *Studies in Jurisprudence and Criminal Theory*, 125–30; Hellmuth Mayer, *Das Strafrecht des deutschen Volkes* (Stuttgart: Enke, 1936), 26 ff.

REFERENCES

Beaumont, Gustave de, and Alexis de Tocqueville. *On the Penitentiary System in the United States and Its Application in France.* Trans. Francis Lieber. 1833. Rpt. New York: A. M. Kelley, 1970.

Beccaria, Cesare. *On Crimes and Punishments.* Trans. Henry Paulocci. 1764. Rpt. Indianapolis: Bobbs-Merrill, 1963.

Blackstone, William. *Commentaries on the Laws of England.* Ed. Robert M. Kerr. 1765. Rpt. Boston: Beacon Press, 1962.

Bodenheimer, A. *Recht und Rechtfertigung.* Berlin: Dunker, 1907.

Boswell's Life and Letters of Samuel Johnson. 3 vols. London: Macmillan, 1906.

Bucer, Martin. *De Regno Christi.* Translated in *Melanchthon and Bucer.* Ed. William Pauck. 1550. Rpt. Philadelphia: Westminster Press, 1969.

Calvin, John. *Institutes of the Christian Religion.* 2 vols. Trans. Ford Lewis Battles and ed. John T. McNeill. 1559. Rpt. Philadelphia: Westminster Press, 1960.

D. Martin Luthers Werke, Kritische Gesamtausgabe. Weimar: Hermann Bohlau, 1883–1979.

Davies, Horton. *The Worship of the English Puritans.* London: Dacre Press, 1948.

Fletcher, George. *Rethinking Criminal Law.* Boston: Little, Brown, 1978.

Grotius, Hugo. *On the Law of War and Peace.* Trans. Francis W. Kelsey. 1625. Rpt. Indianapolis: Bobbs-Merrill, 1965.

Hemming, Nicolaus. *De lege naturae apodicta methodus.* Wittenberg: n.p., 1577.

Kant, Immanuel. *The Metaphysical Elements of Justice.* Trans. John Ladd. Indianapolis: Bobbs-Merrill, 1965.

Mather, Cotton. *The Call of the Gospel Applied Unto all Men in General, and Unto a Condemned Malefactor in Particular.* 2d ed. Boston: R. Pierce, 1687.

Mather, Increase. *A Sermon Occasioned by the Execution of a Man Found Guilty of Murder.* 2d ed. Boston: R. Pierce, 1687.

Melanchthon, Philip. *Werke.* Rpt. in *Corpus Reformatorum.* Ed. G. Bretschneider et al. 88 vols. Leipzig: N. Henschius Nachfolger, 1834–60.

Moberly, Walter. *The Ethics of Punishment.* Hamden, Conn.: Archon Books, 1968.

Montagu, Basil. *The Opinions of Different Authors Upon the Punishment of Death.* 3 vols. London: Longman, Hurst, Rees, and Paternoster Row, 1809.

Pufendorf, Samuel von. *On the Law of Nature and Nations.* Ed. W. A. Oldfather. 1688. Rpt. Oceana, N.Y.: Oceana, 1964.

Smith, Sydney. *Elementary Sketches of Moral Philosophy.* 2d ed. New York: Harper and Brothers, 1860.

Stephen, James Fitzjames. *A History of the Criminal Law of England.* 3 vols. London: Macmillan, 1883.

Stonestreet, George. *The Especial Importance of Religious Principles in the Judges and the Advocates of the Courts of Law.* Newport: n.p., 1822.

Wincler, Benedict. *Principiorum juris libri quinque.* Leipzig: n.p., 1615.

Part IV

Religion and American Political Culture

8. Religion and Liberal Culture: Unconventional Partnership or Unhealthy Co-Dependency

Robert Booth Fowler

There is little doubt that theory about the interaction between religion and our liberal culture in the United States remains scant and underdeveloped. There are signs that a willingness to theorize is emerging, but there is a long road to travel.[1] We have much to do as we work to understand religion and liberalism in America in terms of theory as a means of guiding empirical research in the most fruitful directions. Knowledge of any significance, after all, comes from theory-driven empirical investigation. Tattered theories plumbed from Tocqueville, Max Weber, or Marx still abound. Yet while the "greats" rightly continue to influence our formulations, they are no substitute for theory fashioned in our age.

In this chapter, I want to advance a modest theoretical proposal and then argue it. My purpose is to stimulate discussion, perhaps even debate. Elsewhere I have contended that religion and liberal culture in the United States can best be understood as "unconventional partners," unintentional allies in sustaining our culture as well as much of organized and unorganized religion.[2] Here I want to enlarge this theory in one specific area. In arguing my unconventional-partners thesis, I claimed in passing that the two partners very much need each other.[3] Here I propose to advance this proposition.

Liberal culture and religion in the United States, I will argue, are not mere partners. They are much more than that. They are dependent on each other. They need each other for their respective "health" or "success." Theirs is thus no casual or mundane or accidental partnership. It looks suspiciously integral to each and therefore to understanding each in the contemporary United States.

Whether this relationship is really healthy or is better seen as a destructive co-dependency is a question, however, which I do not intend to confront fully. I have my views and they will not be entirely hidden in what follows. As will be clear, I am not quite sure whether such judgments matter beyond a certain point or, at least, make any practical difference.

I do appreciate that there are those for whom the destructive or unhealthy metaphor is apt. Those who urge us to separate religion and liberal culture are hardly a lonely cohort at the present time.[4] Very often, however, such voices, although acknowledging that religion and liberal culture are currently partners, deny this chapter's thesis that each needs the other. For some critics, liberalism would do well to be free of religion altogether or at least free of activist religion, which seeks to impose its views on the public. For others, religion itself is compromised by its dance with the values and practices of our culture, its materialism, individualism, and metaphysical and moral drift. For them, real religion must attack (or withdraw from) liberal culture, not ratify a corrupt partnership with it.[5]

Two basic definitions must precede my argument. Both *religion* and *liberal culture* are elusive terms. Although not easily definable, still I must explain how I will use them. My conception of religion is phenomenological. By *religion*, I mean what people in this culture consider to be religion. This definition is inclusive and generous, taking in establishment religions and innumerable private religions, the major denominations, other groups such as the Mormons and the followers of Eastern religions, as well as New Age spirituality. By *culture* I mean the beliefs and practices common to any people.[6] In the case of our "liberal" culture, those values most relevant for this study are intellectual skepticism, moral relativism, individualism and individual rights, and democratic pluralism.[7]

LIBERALISM'S NEED FOR RELIGION

Modern liberal political theory is notable for religion's absence in almost any sense. Religion is just not there. It is not in the foreground; it is not in the background. In the hands of its leading theorists at least, modern liberalism does not seem to need religion. Nor does it want religion. A reading of influential modern proponents of liberalism confirms these judgments. John Rawls's *Theory of Justice* makes the most impressive philosophical defense of liberalism in this century. Religion is simply absent there. Robert Dahl continues to be as trenchant a theorist of liberal democracy as there is. Religion is not present in his universe of argument. Richard Rorty now is the center of postmodern liberalism. He is positively scornful of religion and the religious. Even Michael Walzer, something of a liberal (and something of a great many other things), a person who is quite interested in religion, does not grant it a core place in his liberalism.[8]

Such views, which obviously conflict with my theory about the involvement of religion and liberalism in this country, faithfully reflect dominant intellectual opinion in many parts of the United States. Yet I contend they are surprisingly (or perhaps not so surprisingly) remote from the level of social practice and ordinary belief in our culture. At the level of practice, as a culture, a way of life in the United States, my argument will be that liberalism very much needs religion, in fact, depends on it, though this reality is rarely admitted in the culture of liberal theorists.[9]

Liberal culture (i.e., liberalism at the level of practice) needs religion, organized or not, to help fill in the gaps in liberal theory that are so manifest when liberalism comes out of the study and down to earth. The situation is that modern liberalism cannot and does not provide meaning nor a shared morality. It does not do so in principle because its watchwords are skepticism, pluralism, and individualism. Such language is not the vocabulary of foundations or common standards, indeed not of any such standards.

Moreover, in practice, liberal culture increasingly reflects this modern liberal disposition. Individual sovereignty is everywhere more and more the practice. In morality as in art the range of what is acceptable expands steadily as more and more people and perspectives gain their "rights." The only formidable limits today beyond a few prohibitions against acts that flagrantly deny the individual, such as murder, are that we be "sensitive" (honoring pluralism) and not affirm moral absolutes too often or too assertively.

Yet the evidence is widespread that people join religious groups or participate in spiritual experiences in good part because they seek the meaning and morality modern liberalism does not offer either in theory or in practice.[10] True, we are now long past the time where we can accept the assumption that any church's or denomination's growth or decline is correlated neatly with how firm its foundations or morality are. Other things matter in assessing the growth or decline of religious groups. Birth rates, geographical location, the nature of the pastor, plain luck, and a myriad of other factors are often at work. Yet studies are also clear that people are looking for spiritual meaning (not always the same thing as certain truth or values) in religion today. There is no doubt that this goal more than any other attracts people to religious life.

I fashioned this claim from my reading of the many studies cited in *Unconventional Partners*. More recent studies only affirm it. Consider Gallup and Castelli's compilations of the recent data, which include their surveys and those of others.

They report seeing a similar picture. People are looking to religion and churches for spiritual grounds, for meaning and for ethical roots. This is what they join to obtain. These factors are also central to how they evaluate religious organizations. They usually are happy with what they find, but sometimes are dissatisfied. If they are dissatisfied, the controversy usually surrounds the meaning and morality churches do or do not give. This is exactly what we would expect because people turn to religion for just these things. People are involved with religion for its spiritual side and what it might offer them for their practical lives. Thus the issue of whether it delivers is crucial.[11]

Similarly, modern liberalism is notoriously weak in formulating a theory of community. Its skepticism impedes respect for any allegiances beyond the sovereign self, whether family, nation, ethnic group, or church. The same attitude operates in politics, where liberalism views parties with great distaste and interest groups as untrustworthy at best and corrupt at worst.

Almost always, the modern liberal image of community is negative. The fear is that community is hostile to the individual and freedom, if not now then it will be soon. Freedom for the individual and the ideal of community remain an antagonistic dualism in liberal culture even more than in theory. While some liberal thinkers undertake to close the chasm,[12] in society the crime rate goes soaring on, divorce is almost as familiar as marriage, and the list of individual rights, guaranteed, protected, and encouraged against the larger community, expands persistently.

It is no wonder that liberalism in the United States is under such fire from intellectual critics in terms of its theory and practice regarding community. Critics approach from all over the ideological map and with agendas that are often strikingly different. But the cry that liberalism cannot provide enough openness to community for this or any culture is loud. Alasdair MacIntyre compares us unfavorably with the classical world, as does, from quite a contrasting perspective, Allan Bloom. Daniel Bell discusses our missing sense of community, as does Michael Sandel. The list is impressive.[13]

It is in this light that we should evaluate the evidence that religion plays a role as one significant port of welcome for people in search of the community that liberalism and liberal culture know too little about. There is very good evidence that people turn to churches and religion in general for just this purpose, for a sense of sharing closely with others. First, it is no surprise that people think about religion in individualistic America as the appropriate setting to find spiritual community. It is where they expect to join with others in worshipping God. This understanding is, after all, what church and religion have almost always involved. And in some traditions, for example the Roman Catholic, the evidence suggests that the laity is well aware of this definition and supportive of community in this sense.[14]

Community in a second, more social sense is also sought within the world of religion. Put directly, people often join and attend religious groups to obtain social benefits, to participate with others in social interaction and fulfillment. By social, I mean church suppers and after-service coffees, to be sure, but not only this sort of thing. These activities are significant for many people, but I also very much include the vast (as it often is) array of more structured activities in many religious organizations, from the mostly social to the largely spiritual and educational, from scheduled organizational business gatherings to religious education classes and much in between.

The issue is not whether social outlets beyond the worshipping community attract many attendees. They rarely do in comparison with participation in religious services. People do not necessarily participate in coffee hours, much less more serious and demanding church activities. But expectations count. The record is that religious groups which do not address what I would call communal needs can expect to encounter sharp criticism. They will be accused of being cold and unfriendly and can count on alienating present and especially potential congregants.[15]

Yet on the whole, recent data confirm that many religious people, indeed most, are often fairly pleased with the record of churches in terms of community. More than the spiritual community they find, they rate their churches high on scales of both inclusiveness and friendliness. Of course, there are plenty of critics, too, within and outside of organized religion. Either way, the point is that religion and community are linked, whether or not real life fulfills expectations.[16]

My argument, in short, is that religion in the United States helps out liberalism. It covers over liberalism's weaknesses in specific areas. It salves liberalism's wounds and in the process, of course, strengthens it. My conclusion, though, does not imply that there is considerable popular uneasiness over liberalism or of liberal culture. There is scant evidence that those involved in religion generally intend much of a critique. It is one thing to seek out a temporary refuge from the perceived limitations of liberal culture. It is quite another to reject liberalism or dismiss most of our culture. Investment in religion for meaning and community is less an act of rejection than a journey to fulfill what liberalism does not provide. A temporary refuge must not be confused with an intentional revolt.[17]

I concede that I am among those who are sympathetic to a critical stance from a religious standpoint toward aspects of liberal culture. Perhaps what I have argued betrays this inclination. Nonetheless, my point requires no such mood. The gaps in liberalism that religion can address have become obvious over the past thirty years, but how one views them can vary widely. Thus there is also another perspective. Not a few intellectuals have hailed our "openness" and the relentless expansion of individual freedom as a welcome democratic liberation. The absence of much community has ensured social opportunities, and skepticism has allowed innumerable new views and new voices.[18]

Moreover, it is perfectly plausible to maintain that liberalism's unself-conscious use of religion to replace its missing mortar is a sign of liberalism's strength. Rather than faulting liberalism for "depending" on religion for meaning and community in our society, perhaps we should praise liberalism for the flexibility that allows it to adapt and adopt as necessary. It suggests that our liberal culture in its practice is not brittle and is remarkably self-healing. Surely these are virtues. There are a number of possible perspectives. The point I want to make is not that liberalism is "bad," or our liberal culture a wreck, but rather that our culture uses religion and is dependent on it, however one may react to that fact.

The same modulated argument applies to evaluations of how deep the dependence is. It can certainly be exaggerated. In his fascinating recent book, Alan Wolfe shares my assessment that modern liberalism in the United States—and elsewhere—has its lacunae in terms of nonpublic realms of life; his fashionable term is civil society. The bonds and meanings between and among people that neither the market nor government succeed well in fostering are, Wolfe believes, in obvious disarray.

Wolfe's explanation leans heavily on liberal capitalism as the key disintegrative force, though he hardly neglects the role liberal governments play as they try to compensate for the ravages of the market. But whatever his theory, his conclusion is familiar. Liberalism in theory and practice lacks the capacity at present to ensure the community and value which every society needs and which he concludes must be nourished mostly in the private world.[19] At the same time, Wolfe notes that the market and the state are themselves systems of values and both are very much engaged in the promotion of their norms. They are, we might say, one response to the problem they engender. Indeed, they are just one of many instruments with which our society adjusts to what liberalism does not give. This is why religion and religious organizations are only one source for those struggling to obtain meaning, values, and community in our society.

Similarly, Robert Bellah's *Habits of the Heart* notes the persistence of "the second language" of community in many places within our culture. While he deprecates "life-style enclaves," he recognizes that they serve as normative and social moorings for large numbers of citizens.[20] Herve Varenne's classic study of human interactions in modern day life found that even among the most fluid of modern nomads, there is a persistent grasping for norms and community, if often temporary in length and superficial in substance.[21]

How effective religious forces are in the United States as agents of meaning or solidarity for citizens is another matter. My claim is not that religious groups are necessarily doing a good job in directing people in ethical directions nor in building a sense of community. It is hard to estimate how effective religion is in these terms. To measure such an accomplishment in any sure handed fashion would be no easy feat, though it is safe to remark that our culture is no sterling case study of success.

Social unraveling proceeds unabated and role and value confusion are standard. Undoubtedly, religion does not have as much impact as some of its diverse adherents might like for a bewildering variety of reasons. But we cannot ignore the irony of religion serving as a foundation or a community when it is itself so permeated by liberalism. Thinking about American religion as a modifier of the excesses of liberal culture is paradoxical given its pluralism, theological individualism, anti-institutionalism, and devotion to the priesthood of all believers.

Of course, amid the cacophony of religious voices in the United States are plenty that are eager to point the way to their values and their community—many fundamentalists, Catholic bishops, Orthodox Jews, Black Muslims, and so on. But there is also no shortage of groups who have drifted away from such an inclination (captured by the culture, their enemies say). Perhaps much of the modernist laity in mainline Protestantism is in this situation.[22] As James Davison Hunter has argued, to a chorus of controversy, the same fate may lie ahead for evangelical elites.[23]

All these reservations aside, my essential contention remains undisturbed. Liberalism still is much dependent on religion. It uses religion, among other forces, with limited success and indeed with limited support from some elements of contemporary religion, to sustain itself. Religion provides liberal culture with a sometimes shaky foundation and norms, and it is one outlet for many people to find community.

To be sure, such a contribution is needed only by a certain kind of liberalism, but that is the form we live with, so-called modern liberalism—skeptical, pragmatic, individualistic. It is not liberalism in some universalist form and it must be distinguished from classic liberalism. That liberalism had firm roots in religion, sure values, and private community.[24] It was just as needy regarding religion as is our own and was just as dependent on religion, if not more so. The difference— and it is a big difference—was that classic liberal thinkers such as John Locke took that situation as perfectly natural and perfectly appropriate. Liberalism was not born in opposition to religion. Thus perhaps it is no source of wonderment that in our culture liberalism depends on religion. It is not too much to speculate that the prominent evidences of disintegration of our social fabric would grow only more massive if religion and religious institutions left the American scene. That is why defenders of our liberal culture should fear decline in religion. They have no present substitute for what religion, however limply, provides, and no obvious prospects for future substitutes.

RELIGION NEEDS LIBERALISM

Arguments that modern liberal culture needs religion can expect cool receptions. The doyens of liberal culture are not exactly the most ardent supporters of religion or of values closely connected with religion.[25] The converse is also true. Enthusiasm for the idea that religion needs and certainly uses liberalism and liberal culture does not always sit well in elite religious circles. It clashes with the popular agenda across the theological/religious spectrum memorably summarized in H. Richard Niebuhr's phrase "Christ against culture."[26]

We see the message affirmed in pronouncements by mainline Protestant lead- ers about the dangers of American materialism, in evangelical and fundamentalist resistance to secular culture, in the black church's denunciation of drugs, or in Catholic bishops' suspicions about the corruption of capitalist economics. Every- where the theme in vogue is tension between culture and faith, accompanied with considerable unease or outright contempt for liberal culture and its values. Any claims that religious elites in the United States are mere apologists for the status quo is simply out of touch with the reigning theologies and their institutional articulators.

Yet I would make the case that religion does need (again, not necessarily should need) liberalism and makes tremendous use of it. Our liberal culture provides an incredible support system for religion even as liberalism's very limitations as a normative system are, in fact, a great boon for religion. And thus the question arises, who might be the loser if the connection between religion and our liberal order is cut? What might be the consequences if religion really challenges liberalism as some religious leaders so ardently wish?

Consider as my first illustration the matter of religious freedom. It is a precious thing and not especially common in human history, or even in our time. Yet this blessing is very much alive in the United States. There is just no doubt that this gift to religion is nurtured in liberal values. It is an expression of liberalism and is maintained by liberalism. Religion has flourished here on the base of American individualism and interest in freedom, as protected in the First Amendment. The entire story of religion in the United State would be almost unimaginably different had we not had such expansive religious liberty, and this observation bears frequent repetition.

Of course, the diverse nature of religion in the nation has worked interactively with the freedom to play its own role in sustaining that freedom. On the other hand, there have been and are conflicts on the margins between religious freedom and the culture, sometimes ugly or frustrating conflicts. Nor does the Supreme Court, as the final institutional judge of religious liberty, always protect it. The recent decision regarding the use of peyote by members of the Native American church in Oregon may be a case in point for others as it is for me.[27] Yet the weighing of conflicting values and interests is never simple and beneath the moments of temporary alarm, the security of religious liberty in the United States remains unmistakable.

In liberalism's provision of religious liberty (with limits) is implicit a second, closely allied reason that religion in the United States is dependent on liberal values in our culture. Religious diversity has been so common in our culture by no accident. In good part liberalism has supported and often encouraged this diversity in religion as it has in so many other dimensions of life.

We know that this pluralism is truly awesome; the number of denominations is large and the number of independent churches is phenomenal. Highly publicized church unions such as the recently formed Evangelical Lutheran Church of America must not mislead us. The never-ending divisions and subdivisions within American Protestantism go on. American Judaism and Catholicism, in their ways somewhat more cohesive organizationally, have more and more become individualistic religions. People may be Catholic, but they define that Catholicism now in their own terms. Pluralism reigns and grows. Moreover, today there are more religions with more members that fall outside of the traditional Protestant-Catholic-Jewish triad in American life than at any time since European settlement. The Mormons, the Nation of Islam, New Age spirituality, orthodox Islam, Zen, all are part of a formidable list.[28]

Thus we see in religion what we see in all aspects of American society—the spread of liberal individualism and diversity, a movement with few constraints and one which fuels itself with ever-renewing energy. The First Amendment is the symbol that honors, protects, and even celebrates this reality. In making it possible for people to go their individual ways, liberal culture and its symbols also legitimize doing so. Our culture fairly glories in its religious pluralism.

We have traveled a far distance, surely, in our attitudes toward religious pluralism. To a modest degree it was also part of the reality of the late eighteenth century, but the welcome it received was tepid at best. And, as we know, serious conflict throughout the nineteenth century and after was a long chapter in the story of America's religions. Pluralism was the developing reality, but it was far from the living gospel.[29]

Still, the slow triumph of a liberal practice to match the Founders' liberal theory led toward acceptance of religious diversity far beyond what most nations have known, much less approve of. Now both theory and practice stand guard and protect a multitude of religious organizations and spiritual practices. And in their remarkable diversity, they all depend on liberalism for this protection. Perhaps there is no more salient indicator of the strength of this pluralism than the rise of those within the last generation who reject all religion and have organized themselves to promote this belief as a kind of cause. They are as aggressive in their proselytizing as a self-confident and unapologetic religion, which they often resemble. Such groups have become one more part of the interesting life that grows in the extensive fields of religion (and antireligion) in America. Like the rest, these groups have achieved a certain acceptance in the liberal culture.[30]

A third, and perhaps more controversial, reason that religion needs liberal culture is that liberal culture affords organized religion great benefits from the establishment of religion, the present practice in the United States. We do not have the establishment of any single religion or denomination, of course, but we do not have separation of church and state either. The Warren Court may have sometimes respected the "no establishment" clause of the First Amendment. But even then, and since then, there were few determined attempts to abridge the many forms of establishment between religion and government.

To be sure, the definition of legitimate religion has expanded over our history.

Once-hegemonic Protestantism has been joined by Catholicism, and Judaism, and others. Religion, as it is now legally defined, has become broadly inclusive and the direction continues toward more inclusiveness. Yet what this means is that more and more groups are able to take part in the benefits of establishment.

The substance of establishment is everywhere. Church freedom from taxation is the most concrete and in some ways the most significant example, but government aid to "nonprofit" church and religious hospitals, nursing homes, child care facilities, colleges, and so on are hardly to be brushed aside lightly. They are powerful illustrations of establishment. Then there are all the many cultural symbols—from the establishment of Christmas as a holiday to "In God We Trust" on coins to the military and legislative chaplains which are part of public life.

Would other, nonliberal cultures permit establishment? The question is strange, because the answer is self-evident. They have and they do. Would they permit the kind of "multiple" establishment that exists in the United States? We know the answer is that they rarely have or do. Our establishment of religion is very liberal, one that honors the liberal gods of diversity and subjective truth.

Finally, religion benefits considerably from liberalism because of the sustenance it receives as it feeds on liberalism's considerable weaknesses. American religion gains from liberal values' support for religious freedom and diversity. But it also gains from what I have already discussed, from liberalism's silences, from the places where liberalism does not speak or seem to know how to speak. Specifically, this includes modern liberalism's trouble with collective values and value foundations.[31]

Thus the partnership metaphor for the connection between modern liberalism and religion does not imply the two are similar. Modern liberalism is without a cognitive foundation, a reality sometimes bewailed and sometimes celebrated.[32] Either way, no one claims any more that liberalism as we know it rests on strong truth claims. Similarly, there is little evidence of shared norms in our liberal society except the norm of individualism, which in turn suggests the challenge of obtaining agreement on anything else.[33]

In such a setting, it is not possible to make glib predictions about what the future will bring. But it is hardly being bold to predict that intellectual and social structures that claim to facilitate some meaning and order will have their appeal. Again, though, the caveat is in order: I do not suggest that the strength of particular religious groups will be neatly correlated with how absolute their claims are, or how tight their communities are, or anything of the sort.[34]

Nor can we confidently suggest that religion is somehow the natural beneficiary of the modern situation, or that it will be the only one. Among many other factors, what religion looks like in our liberal society will matter. It will matter, for example, whether religion comes in a great range of alternatives as it does in the United States but did not in Sweden or Denmark. And there will, of course, be other sources of meaning and community in every society. Their strengths and weaknesses will also count very much.[35]

Opportunity is the key word, and it is important for religion in modern American culture. Many religious groups are clearly taking it, perhaps mainly because religion in the United States is just the right complement for liberal culture. We are the quintessential liberal Protestant land. Even Catholics and Jews are mostly Protestants.[36] So it is also in the extensive and variegated world of "popular" religion.[37] Everyone has their own God and insists on it. We are liberal Protestant individuals.

American religion is relatively easy for members of our liberal culture to accept because the religious experiences available are so diverse. The pattern is merely an expression of the prevalent "theological" individualism, as everyone can and does have their own God, and their own religious group or church, or faction within a church, or nonchurch.[38]

Discussion about the ethic of niceness in American religion belongs here.[39] This ethic symbolizes how willing much of American religion is to be a partner with liberal culture—even when they are supposedly clashing outlooks. It is the outward sign of the unspoken decision by most American religion to cooperate, not to be assertive in an intense or disruptive fashion. It symbolizes that religion will not really push into the public realm, force choices, or do anything much to disturb liberal culture. Everyone will be "nice" and go their own way. American religion may sometimes decry the liberal world it knows, but on the whole, religion is very nice and it is for nice people.

Religions or religious groups that do not play this game may encounter trouble, though far less in a liberal culture than in any other of which I know. Perhaps the most common "trouble" they may expect is the likelihood of the culture ignoring them. Yet if they become aggressive, or are made to appear so, and set out to convert or coerce the larger culture, they can expect more direct trouble. They can, in fact, count on intense pressure from other societal elements, including religious ones. The late Moral Majority discovered these facts of life very quickly in the 1980s. Operation Rescue does today.[40]

If these same people choose to practice zealously the religious beliefs that fall outside the generous but not completely porous parameters of our loose-bounded society, there will also be trouble. Christian Scientists who have repudiated scientific medical care for their children are an apt illustration.[41] We have a great deal of individualism and pluralism, in short, but part of the unwritten contract of the partnership of religion and liberalism is that religion will be nice.

My conclusion is that (a certain kind of) religion would likely be much weaker in the United States if liberal culture were not dominant. And thus the question: What if liberal culture did not serve as the congenial backdrop to religious life in the United States? To put it more sharply: What if liberal culture began to confront and attack religion?

Here I am not concerned with the scuffling at the edges or the push/pull with impolitic religions or religious groups. This sort of thing is a standard part of political life. My query is, What if there were a full-scale attack on religious freedom, or the withdrawal of most of the benefits of establishment (especially tax freedom), or a direct assault on religious truths and norms? The question must seem absurd, I agree. And that is just my point. American religion and liberal culture are not enemies, and there is no prospect of them becoming enemies. They both need and use each other.

Still, my question lingers. It has its intriguing side. The answer is not so apparent, indeed, cannot be apparent. But I do not perceive why we should think religion or at least religious organizations would, on the whole, do terribly well. Certainly the evidences of religious establishment in the culture would rapidly decline and the numbers of communicants might drop as the practical (cost-free) advantages of religious membership slipped away. Moreover, the sectarian and diverse nature of our religious groups might make them all the more vulnerable to attack and decline.

From another perspective, that which stresses the value of religion as a holy remnant rather than a mass superficiality, religion in the United States might be much better as the result of serious challenge. But why should we assume the result will be a renewed, if smaller, spiritual presence? Czechoslovakia seems to have experienced just such a gain as the result of active persecution, but Sweden suggests a contrasting model. The challenges religion faced there were perhaps more indirect. But nonetheless they proved quite overwhelming and almost fatal to all religious presence.

REFLECTIONS

What I have described as an "unconventional partnership" others have characterized in distinctly less neutral and far more negative terms. We might say they see
a most unhealthy co-dependency between religion and liberal culture in the United
States. They often demand an end to this co-dependency immediately.

One location where we might expect that this cry is the loudest is among those
who claim to have no religion, more than 5 percent of the population, perhaps
toward 10 percent.[42] Certainly we can hear it in the movement of assertive, if tiny,
groups of nonbelievers bent on severing all connections between religion and our
culture. Consider the perfectly titled Freedom from Religion Foundation. Its goal
is to get rid of religion. It is not philosophical in the sense of being primarily
interested in discussions about the truth or falsity of religious claims, nor is it
primarily concerned with fostering the separation of church and state. To be sure,
the foundation delights in arguing against religion and in banishing religious in-
vocations at one or another public school commencement. But its longer run
objective is indicated by the name of the organization. The group seeks the extir-
pation of religion.

It is no accident that its founder, Anne Gaylor, has been much influenced by
libertarian ideas. She views religion as a threat to the proper liberal society. She sees
religion as a rule-providing entity both in theory and in practice. Instead, people
should and can be their own rule makers. Perhaps ironically, perhaps not, the entire
operation enjoys a reputation for being as fanatical as the most ardent religious
follower.[43]

Such militant secularists are often associated with Madalyn Murray O'Hair.
She and her allies have a long record of attacking the religious and urging that their
influence be driven from public life, while working hard to free everyone's private
life of religion. As with the Freedom from Religion Foundation, O'Hair and her
associates have also taken recourse in the courts with mixed results.[44]

Perhaps it is of no value to discuss such secular separatists as if they were
numerous enough to merit attention. Other organizations of greater significance
exist which favor separation of church and state rather than separation of religion
and liberal culture, though the distinction is more sharply drawn in their minds
than in reality. People for the American Way, Norman Lear's organization to
combat religion (or at least politically conservative religion) in American public life
is a noteworthy example. It has received considerable favorable press in its crusade,

and Lear has garnered warm praise from liberal religious figures such as Martin Marty.[45]

Lear's group strives to distinguish itself from anti- or nonreligious separatists. This is reasonable, because the organization and its leadership are hardly hostile toward all religion. On the other hand, People for the American Way is overwhelmingly invested in public disputes with one after another religious group. Its definition of separatism is now very strict, and it is hard to know just where the center of the group's motivational energy now lies.[46]

The litigiousness of such groups as the Freedom from Religion Foundation or the People for the American Way makes headlines, and sometimes it effects change. Yet pressures for ending co-dependency within religious circles, while perhaps less widely known, require consideration also. From within the world of American religion they have potential for real impact and even now sometimes generate significant debate.

The idea of a somehow purer, and, of course, much smaller, gathering of the faithful—the truly faithful—attracts many religious intellectuals, though it is much less apparent who else it beckons. At its heart is the conviction that American religion has somehow sold out to the powers and principalities of this world and become a creature of the corrupt culture. In some versions, this position concentrates on the purified (though this word is rarely used) church that would result if liberalism were truly renounced along with all its cultural associations. The saving remnant is a notion very much alive not only in Protestant fundamentalist realms, but in radical circles, such as those celebrated in *Sojourners* magazine.[47]

This perspective is committed to turning back evil everywhere and convinced that religious faith and liberal culture are enemies.[48] In part this is because liberal culture is said to have lured American religion into its dubious embrace. As Stanley Hauerwas charges, it has domesticated American religious life far too much. By implication, much of American religion has lost its soul.[49]

Do these critics, who represent diverse positions along the religious and political spectra, expect that religion would suffer grievously if it cut its partnership with liberal culture? We know they do not. On the contrary, words such as *renew*, *reborn*, and *restrengthened*, are more commonly used. But I would make a different assessment. I think organized religion would pay an enormous price if it were to become starkly separated from liberal culture, whether willingly or as a consequence of adversarial relations.

Yet there is scant evidence of overall resistance, or outright antagonism, toward the general liberal culture on the part of most of those involved in religion today. There are pockets of intense dissent only, and as I have argued elsewhere, interest in a temporary refuge from liberal culture is quite a different thing than a stance of opposition.[50]

If religion recasts itself, or is forced to do so, in its uneasy relationship with liberal culture toward a stance of opposition, it will find itself apart from the mixed and, yes, "compromised," needs and wants of the ordinary religious person in the United States. It will then start forcing people to choose between religion and their culture in an environment in which liberal cultural norms are ascendant. For many, individualism and pluralism would prove too strong to resist.[51]

The loss could include institutional supports such as freedom from property taxes. Institutional supports do matter, as we know from the early history of Christianity in Europe.[52] I don't lightly dismiss them. Even greater would be the loss of much of the population in a land where today close to three quarters of the people claim membership in a religious organization. The remnant church, or the persecuted church, or the ignored church, without liberalism's blessing and aid might well be the isolated church, pure but irrelevant.

Such discussion, though, is largely empty. It proceeds on the premise that forces for separation, those who for a variety of reasons want the co-dependency they so dislike to die, will make progress toward their aspiration. I don't think they will, at least not in the short run.

It is true that there are ways to argue that secularization is increasingly a reality in American life, even if the case is not self-evident,[53] and thus to conclude that religion faces tough odds in the culture as a whole. But this does not for a moment mean religion and liberal culture may be terminating their partnership. It might better be read as an indication of how the struggle for dominance within the partnership is proceeding.

Meanwhile, matters continue as before. Religion continues to receive, use, and perhaps need liberal culture's preferments, the benefits of liberalism's devotion to freedom. Liberal culture, for its part, continues to depend in part on religion to repair its limitations. Whether the arrangement is judged healthy or unhealthy is in some sense beside the point. It is simply the plane on which religion and liberalism generally deal with each other in our civilization. In my terms, they have been and they remain "unconventional partners," and it is on this reality that an analysis of religion and politics must be based.

NOTES

1. Robert Wuthnow is a welcome example to all of us. See his *Restructuring of American Religion* (Princeton: Princeton Univ. Press, 1988); for a more comparative approach R. F. Inglehart, *Culture Shift in Advanced Industrial Society* (Princeton, N.J.. Princeton Univ. Press, 1990) is a provocative example.

2. Robert Booth Fowler, *Unconventional Partners: Religion and Liberal Culture in the United States* (Grand Rapids, Mich.: Eerdmans, 1989).

3. For my brief original formulation, see Fowler, *Unconventional Partners*, 160–61.

4. Nor when they get right down to it are they always prepared to go all the way with their inclinations. Consider Stanley Hauerwas, "Freedom of Religion: A Subtle Temptation," *Soundings* 82 (1989): 317–39.

5. See, for instance, Franky Schaeffer, *A Time for Anger* (Westchester, Ill.: Crossway Books, 1982) or, from another view, Jim Wallis, *Agenda for a Biblical People* (New York: Harper, 1976), the classic exposition of the *Sojourners'* vision.

6. On culture and its meaning, see Clifford Geertz, *The Interpretation of Cultures: Selected Essays* (New York: Basic Books, 1973); Paul Bohanan, "Rethinking Culture: A Project of Current Anthropologists," *Current Anthropology* 14 (Oct. 1973): 357–65; Marvin Harris, *Cultural Materialism: The Struggle for a Science of Culture* (New York; Random House, 1979); Richard Merelman, *Making Something of Ourselves* (Berkeley and Los Angeles: Univ. of California Press, 1984).

7. For more on liberalism and religion, see Fowler, chap. 1.

8. John Rawls, *A Theory of Justice* (Cambridge: Harvard Univ. Press, 1971); Robert Dahl, *Democracy and Its Critics* (New Haven: Yale Univ. Press, 1989); Richard Rorty, *Contingency, Irony and Solidarity* (Cambridge: Cambridge Univ. Press, 1989); Michael Walzer, *Spheres of Justice: A Defense of Pluralism and Equality* (New York: Basic Books, 1983).

9. A view I first advanced in *Unconventional Partners*.

10. For a discussion of the studies regarding meaning and morality and religion in modern American society, see *Unconventional Partners*, chap. 2.

11. George Gallup, Jr., and Jim Castelli, *The People's Religion: American Faith in the 90's* (New York: Macmillan, 1989).

12. Walzer may be the most impressive example of a community-oriented liberal.

13. I have written a book detailing the breadth of intellectual dissent over liberalism and community that treats these figures and their work in detail. See Robert Booth Fowler, *The Dance with Community* (Lawrence: Univ. Press of Kansas, 1991).

14. David Leege has led the work in this area in Catholicism. See his specific report, *The Parish as Community*, Report no. 10. (Notre Dame: Notre Dame Study of Catholic Parish Life, 1987).

15. See Fowler, *Unconventional Partners,* chap. 3, which presents a fuller argument of the point about community and offers considerable evidence for the claim.

16. Gallup and Castelli, *The People's Religion,* 88–89 and passim.

17. Fowler, *Unconventional Partners,* chaps. 1–3.

18. For example, see Peter Clecak, *America's Quest for the Ideal Self: Dissent and Fulfillment in the 60s and 70s* (New York: Oxford Univ. Press, 1983).

19. Alan Wolfe, *Whose Keeper? Social Science and Moral Obligation* (Berkeley and Los Angeles: Univ. of California Press, 1989).

20. Robert Bellah, Richard Madsen, William Sullivan, Ann Swidler, and Stephen Tipton, *Habits of the Heart: Individualism and Commitment in American Life* (Berkeley and Los Angeles: Univ. of California Press, 1985).

21. Herve Varenne, *Americans Together: Structured Diversity in a Midwestern Town* (New York: Columbia Univ. Press, 1977).

22. Wade Clark Roof and William McKinney, *American Mainline Religion: Its Changing Shape and Future* (New Brunswick. N.J.: Rutgers Univ. Press, 1987).

23. James Davison Hunter, *Evangelicalism: The Coming Generation* (Chicago: Univ. of Chicago Press, 1987).

24. See here Paul Sigmund, "Christianity, Ideology, and Political Philosophy," in *Essays on Christianity and Political Philosophy,* ed. George W. Carey and James V. Schall (Lanham, Md.: Univ. Press of America, 1984); Eldon J. Eisenach, *Two Worlds of Liberalism: Religion and Politics in Hobbes, Locke, and Mill* (Chicago: Univ. of Chicago Press, 1981); John Dunn, *Locke* (Oxford: Oxford Univ. Press, 1984); John Locke, *Two Treatises on Government* (New York: Hafner, 1955).

25. Consider the following studies: Ben Stein, *The View from Sunset Blvd* (New York: Basic Books, 1979); S. Robert Lichter, Stanley Rothman, and Linda S. Lichter, *The Media Elite* (Bethesda: Adler and Adler, 1986).

26. For the classic statement, see H. Richard Niebuhr, *Christ and Culture* (New York: Harper & Row, 1951).

27. The situation was one where members of the Native American Church were fired for using peyote in religious practice and subsequently sought unemployment compensation. The case was *Employment Division* v. *Smith* (1990).

28. I like George Gallup, Jr., and Jim Castelli, *The American Catholic People* (Garden City, N.Y.: Doubleday, 1987) for this theme. Regarding Judaism, Charles Silberman, *A Certain People: American Jews and Their Lives Today* (New York: Summit Books, 1985) brings this point home nicely.

29. See, for example, W. B. Posey, *Religious Strife on the Southern Frontier* (Baton Rouge: Louisiana State Univ. Press, 1965); for a larger view, see Sydney Ahlstrom, *A Religious History of the American People* (Garden City, N.Y.: Doubleday, 1975).

30. See the discussion of such groups as the Freedom from Religion Foundation below.

31. See Fowler, *Unconventional Partners,* chaps. 2 and 3.

32. Examples of those who bewail: Allan Bloom, *The Closing of the American Mind* (New York: Simon & Schuster, 1987); Alasdair MacIntyre, *After Virtue: a Study in Moral Theory* (Notre Dame: Univ. of Notre Dame Press, 1981); and of those much happier: Charles W. Anderson, *Pragmatic Liberalism* (Chicago: Univ. of Chicago Press, 1990); Don Herzog, *Without Foundations* (Ithaca, N.Y.: Cornell Univ. Press 1983)

33. On this point, see Bellah et al., *Habits of the Heart.*

34. As opposed to the common interpretation of the stimulating work, Dean Kelley, *Why Conservative Churches are Growing* (New York: Harper & Row, 1972); see Dean R. Hoge and David R. Roozen, eds., *Understanding Church Growth and Decline* (New York: Pilgrim Press, 1979).

35. See Bellah et al., *Habits of the Heart;* Varenne, *Americans Together;* and Theodore Caplow et al., *All Faithful People: Change and Continuity in Middletown* (Minneapolis: Univ. of Minnesota Press, 1983).

36. See, for example, Andrew Greeley, *American Catholics since the Council* (Chicago: Thomas More, 1985); and Silberman.

37. For "popular" religion, see Peter W. Williams, *Popular Religion in America: Symbolic Change and the Modernization Process in Historical Perspective* (Englewood Cliffs, N.J.: Prentice-Hall, 1980).

38. A good source book on Catholicism is Gallup and Castelli, *The American Catholic People.*

39. See, for example, John Murray Cuddihy, *No Offense: Civil Religion and Protestant Taste* (New York: Seabury, 1979); and Hauerwas, "Freedom of Religion: A Subtle Temptation."

40. On the Moral Majority, see these three collections: David G. Bromley and Anson Shupe, eds., *New Christian Politics* (Macon, Ga.: Mercer Univ. Press, 1984); Robert C. Liebman and Robert Wuthnow, eds., *The New Christian Right* (New York: Aldine, 1983); Richard J. Neuhaus and Michael Cromartie, eds., *Piety and Politics: Evangelicals and Fundamentalists Confront the World* (Washington, D.C.: Ethics and Public Policy Center, 1987); Robert Booth Fowler, "The Failure of the New Christian Right" (Paper presented at the Ethics and Public Policy Center, Washington, D.C., 1990).

41. See David Margolick, "Death and Faith, Law and Christian Science," *New York Times,* 8 Aug. 1990, p. 1 and 9.

42. See Roof and McKinney, *American Mainline Religion,* 16 and 255.

43. Though it operates nationally, the Freedom from Religion Foundation is located in Madison, Wisconsin. Its activities are a constant source of controversy and stimulation on the local scene. The founder and head, Anne Gaylor, has spoken to my class on her views and her group is a frequent participant on Madison's Channel 4, Access Cable, from which I have my information on same.

44. See, for instance, "God's in His Heaven? Don't Talk About It at this Convention," *New York Times,* 1 May 1984, p. 1 and ff; Madalyn Murray O'Hair, *Freedom Under Siege: The Impact of Organized Religion on Your Liberty and Your Pocketbook* (Los Angeles: J. Tarcher, 1974); also see her publication *The American Atheist.*

45. See, for example, Martin Marty, "A Profile of Norman Lear: Another Pilgrim's Progress," *Christian Century* (21 Jan. 1987): 55–58.

46. What is the People for the American Way about? Three recent essays on this query: "People for the American Way, D.C. Conference," *Library Journal* 33 (May 1987): 10–11; "People for the American Way," *American Spectator* 20 (June 1987): 16–18; "By the Dawn's Early Light," *National Review* 34 (22 Jan. 1990): 17–18.

47. No doubt this perspective pervades fundamentalism but also fits in much of liberation theology. Both are very taken with the small communities of the faithful. For another distinctly nonfundamentalist Protestant approach that is sympathetic, see William R. Hutchinson, ed., *Between the Times: The Travails of the Protestant Establishment in America* (Cambridge: Cambridge Univ. Press, 1989).

48. This is the philosophy of *Sojourners* magazine, though like liberation theology it can be seen as having a good deal of the "purer" church model also. See Jim Wallis, *The Call to Conversion* (New York: Harper & Row, 1981); Robert Booth Fowler, *The New Engagement: Evangelical Political Thought 1966–1976* (Grand Rapids, Mich.: Eerdmans, 1982).

49. See Hauerwas, "Freedom of Religion;" for a fuller discussion, I strongly recommend his *A Community of Character: Toward a Constructive Christian Social Ethic* (Notre Dame: Univ. of Notre Dame Press, 1981).

50. Fowler, *Unconventional Partners.*

51. In assessing the views and values of the American people the evidence is, obviously, complicated. For the best short discussion of the data in concrete application as interpreted by a number of different views, I heartily recommend Gerald Pomper, ed., *The Election of 1988: Reports and Interpretations* (Chatham, N.J.: Chatham House, 1989).

52. See, for example, Ramsay MacMullen, *Christianizing the Roman Empire* (New Haven, Conn.: Yale Univ. Press, 1984).

53. See Rodney Stark and William Sims Bainbridge, *The Future of Religion: Secularization, Revival and Cult Formation* (Berkeley and Los Angeles: Univ. of California Press, 1985), chap. 1.

REFERENCES

Bellah, Robert, Richard Madsen, William Sullivan, Ann Swidler, and Stephen Tipton. *Habits of the Heart: Individualism and Commitment in American Life.* Berkeley and Los Angeles: Univ. of California Press, 1985.

Dahl, Robert. *Democracy and Its Critics.* New Haven, Conn.: Yale Univ. Press, 1989.

Fowler, Robert Booth. *Unconventional Partners: Religion and Liberal Culture in the United States.* Grand Rapids, Mich.: Eerdmans, 1989.

Gallup, George, Jr., and Jim Castelli. *The People's Religion: American Faith in the 90's.* New York: Macmillan, 1989.

Hunter, James Davison. *Evangelicalism: The Coming Generation.* Chicago: Univ. of Chicago Press, 1987.

Rawls, John. *A Theory of Justice.* Cambridge: Harvard Univ. Press, 1971.

Roof, Wade Clark, and William McKinney. *American Mainline Religion: Its Changing Shape and Future.* New Brunswick, N.J.: Rutgers Univ. Press, 1987.

Rorty, Richard. *Contingency, Irony and Solidarity.* Cambridge: Cambridge Univ. Press, 1989.

Varenne, Herve. *Americans Together: Structured Diversity in a Midwestern Town.* New York: Columbia Univ. Press, 1977.

Walzer, Michael. *Spheres of Justice: A Defense of Pluralism and Equality.* New York: Basic Books, 1983.

Wolfe, Alan. *Whose Keeper? Social Science and Moral Obligation.* Berkeley and Los Angeles: Univ. of California Press, 1989.

Politics and Eternity:
The Voice of Religion
in Political Discourse

Clarke E. Cochran

> Political philosophy . . . is the consideration of the relation between politics
> and eternity. The end in politics is conceived to be the deliverance of a man
> observed to stand in need of deliverance. . . . We may, then, enquire of any
> political philosophy conceived on this plan, whether the gift of politics to
> mankind is, in principle, salvation itself, or whether it is something less, and
> if the latter, what relation it bears to salvation.
>
> —Michael Oakeshott[1]

We are all too familiar today with the debasement of civil discourse. Offensive
language and images permeate popular culture, in music, art, television, and movies.
Popular speech often seems founded on the frequent repetition of a limited number
of sexual and scatological terms. Manipulation and cheap shots overwhelm political
campaigns. What good would it do to mix religious language with such a brew?
Would the yeast of, say, Christian vocabulary leaven the whole mass of civil discourse? Or would the vulgarity of popular culture simply debase religious imagery?
Even worse, would the resulting mixture produce a poisonous concoction of religious intolerance and tyranny? There is enough evidence for these dangerous results, both in our country and around the world, to give pause to anyone who wants
to contend, as I do, that religious and political language should interact in civil
discourse. So I commence to make my case with some trepidation.

Religion is a constant reminder of the unity of public and private life, but also
of the boundary between them. Private and public life need each other, but they
are different realms. The validity and the distinctive character of each contributes
to a healthy society. Religion affirms the public/private distinction but also the need
to meet at the boundary. In this chapter I describe these boundary tensions in both
general and specific terms.[2]

THE BOUNDARIES OF RELIGION AND POLITICS

As a system of belief, behavior, and emotion relating to a reality beyond human control or attainment, religion suggests to the sensitive participant in culture just what is at stake in public/private border controversies. Culture is first of all public; its beliefs, customs, traditions, stories, and emotions are the common possession willy-nilly of citizens who need share no significant private life. Culture's material and spiritual goods attract and (sometimes, perhaps often) repel, just because they are part of a deeply ingrained heritage.

Because religion suggests that ingrained culture is not divine (at the most, it is the direct will and creation of the divine), religion more directly than other systems of value insinuates the tension between culture and something higher than culture. Although religion is linked to culture and frequently coopted by it, religions with reflective traditions emphatically suggest tension with culture. The inherent dynamic of religion's orientation to a transcendent source of being, independent of human control, opens the path toward cultural conflict. As much as culture takes upon itself divine color, it cannot hide its human roots.

Though the tension between the divine and the mundane sometimes manifests itself as stress between private and public life, the individual, where the competing attractions of culture and the sacred intersect, is the true locus of tension. Machiavelli, for example, denouncing Christianity's public effects, clearly understood that the strain was not between private religion (Christianity) and the public good (the republic) but between the different public demands of Christianity and the republic. The unique perspective of religion reveals the person as a field of cross-cutting tensions between the divine and culture in private and public life.

Political and economic conditions can pose a threat to spiritual and mental health. The converse also holds. Spiritual conditions can threaten political and economic health. These threats have no fixed source. Their origin may lie in private life or in public, in particular individuals or in culture itself. Martin Marty expresses well this private and public dynamic:

> Religion in the western world delicately balances its private and public faces. The impetus of biblical thought is to keep the two in tension. People will not respond to the sacred or be faithful to what they experience as the divine if they do not find their inmost needs addressed. . . .

The religion that has predominated in the West, however, . . . has always seen that purely private faith is incomplete. Worse than that, because it serves only the purpose of those who hold it and comes under no scrutiny of judgment, it can easily become idolatrous.[3]

We must go beyond Marty's insight, however, to see that these are not separable concerns, for the demands for private meaning and public interchange take place in the same persons and the same religious institutions. Private sorrows and public conflicts compete for attention in the same hearts, as do religious principles and economic realities. Religion furnishes distinctive insight into these tensions.

Although I emphasize cross-cutting tensions within the human heart, I do not mean to suggest an individualism focused on how persons experience and cope with such tensions. Groups too, such as families, associations, neighborhoods, businesses, legislatures, and courts, experience these tensions and seek collective resolutions. Surprisingly, as sensitive as he is to the interrelatedness of public and private, Michael Walzer misses this point. Although his book *Spheres of Justice* is remarkable in explicitly considering divine grace in a theory of justice, Walzer devotes only six pages to grace and seems to regard its place as (theoretically) simple.[4] Walzer's realm of grace is a purely autonomous sphere, and he invokes the metaphor of the wall of separation. This sphere is autonomous because he regards it as a matter of freedom, of individual choice. Therefore, as I read him, the realm of religion is purely private.

Walzer recognizes that parents try to pass grace to their children, and this fact is for him the proof of its privacy, for sons and daughters often choose not to believe. But religion is not simply the private choice of belief or unbelief, acceptance or rejection of grace. It comprises as well the consequences, private and public, of belief and unbelief. Moreover, other spheres of life affect religion, shaping the content and manner of belief and unbelief. To say that grace is purely private is to ignore religions like Islam in which the idea of purely individual or familial grace would be quite foreign. Moreover, even in religions like evangelical Christianity that tend strongly toward privatized grace, such grace often has been a primary motivator to public action. Indeed, public action can seem demanded if the individual is to remain in a state of grace.

Because religion touches (sometimes unconsciously) the core of a believer's character, it bears upon the moral boundaries of public and private life. The role of politics in creating social peace and justice depends upon personal interior peace and justice. Government and politics can contribute, but cannot bring men and women to virtuous living or inner tranquility, for they cannot prescribe all virtuous action or proscribe all vice. Moreover, political life cannot bring final beatitude.

Because it influences moral virtue and individual well-being, therefore, religion can powerfully assist the state by inculcating and nourishing a moral foundation for culture. Yet this role is easily misunderstood and often converted into either theocracy or civil religion.

One final general consideration is in order at this point. Although I have stressed the intersection of religion and public life, religion, nevertheless, fundamentally reminds us of the limits of politics and of the nonequivalence of politics and public life. Because religion intends transcendence, it relativizes and thereby limits all other spheres of activity, including politics. Religion points to a sovereignty beyond state sovereignty.[5] In the American tradition, for example, the Bible has reminded us that "public spirit will always be opposed by private interest," that law and coercion must supplement public virtue and participation, and that "the larger the political society, the greater the tension between body and spirit, private feelings and public duties."[6] Religion need not disdain interests. It might, rather, elevate interests. For example, Jesus makes "you shall love your neighbor as yourself" the second great commandment. Self is not denied, but the interests of the neighbor are to be elevated to the same level of intensity that we innately feel for our own. The elevation transforms them. Thus, religion can recognize self-interest in politics, but work to transform it. There is an analogy here to Tocqueville's comments about "interests rightly understood" in an educated democracy.

Interests elevated or transformed do not equal salvation. Religion tells us that public problems and their solutions are not entirely political. Glenn Tinder puts the point this way:

> It is characteristic of boundary situations . . . that they not only bring us to the edge of worldly security but leave us, so to speak, with nothing between ourselves and eternity. For using power and violence, there is no full justification on earth. Officials with faith thus face not only the moral dilemma imposed by their responsibilities but also God, whose commands can guide human beings when rules fail and whose forgiveness can justify them when they themselves fail.[7]

Indeed, the distinctive contribution of religion to public and private life, to individuals and to culture is to refer them to what is beyond politics. The following

pages discuss some of these things beyond politics—sin, evil, death, tragedy, forgiveness, promise, and trust—and how they appear on the border between public
and private life.

This reference beyond politics constitutes a challenge to political discourse to
look beyond its natural pre-occupation with interests and compromise. Indeed, it
is this role of challenge to politics that seems to me to be religion's distinctive
contribution to political discourse. (I believe also that politics has a contribution
to make in challenging the pretensions of religion, but that is another topic.)

SIN AND EVIL IN PUBLIC AND PRIVATE LIFE

A persistent delusion in contemporary culture, an emanation of Philip Rieff's "therapeutic society,"[8] makes obsolete sin and evil, and therefore guilt. The delusion
pervades the contention that education and counseling, plus appropriate doses of
technology and money, can cure major social and psychic ills. AIDS, teenage
pregnancy, urban decay, drug abuse, joblessness and homelessness, crime, and racial
and sexual discrimination could be cured or greatly alleviated if society, and the
particular individuals most concerned, could only receive appropriate education
and compassionate counseling and if enough money and high technology were
devoted to solutions. Or so it is said.

By labeling as delusions such approaches to social and personal problems, I do
not contend that education, counseling, technology, and material resources are
irrelevant. Rather, I insist that we acknowledge, privately and publicly, the role of
sin in creating and perpetuating what are as much evils as ills. Attacking them
requires methods suitable to combating sin as well as the methods for fighting
ignorance, psychic disturbances, and lack of material resources.

What we call something reveals our sense of its causes and suggests how we
think it might be attacked. To speak of social disturbances or crises as ills suggests
medical and psychological causes and the ministrations of science, technology, and
counseling. The language of problems suggests rational solutions. To speak of
them as evils suggests religious or philosophical perspectives, and to speak of crimes
suggests legal, penal, and coercive approaches. I submit that to understand and
attack social ills-problems-evils-crimes requires all these perspectives. No single
approach suffices, certainly not the rationalistic educational-technological.

Religion reminds us of the role of human volition, and the sins and crimes stemming from it, in creating and perpetuating personal and social evil. There is a clear connection between this point and the role of religion in promoting the morality necessary for public peace and justice.

I do not argue that all religions stimulate the sense of sin or that they do so in the same ways or to the same degree. But certainly Judaism, Islam, Christianity, Hinduism, and Buddhism recognize the deep roots of sin in the orientations of the human heart, and they contain stories explaining its origin, accounts of how to resist it, and rituals and disciplines for cleansing the soul.[9] Some methods are more passive than active, but the point is that private sin is recognized, as are its public consequences, and that public sin is also recognized with its private consequences. These religions discern not only "moral man and immoral society," but the reverse as well.

Guilt effectively links public and private life. To acknowledge guilt is to make contact with a world outside one's own delusions. Guilt ties the agent to the world through admission of the consequences of choice. What is true of individual guilt holds for nations and other public bodies. Religious sensitivity to guilt can call the public, especially politics, to awareness of responsibility vis-à-vis citizens and to surrender illusions of innocence or grandeur. Such constitutes the public role of religious prophets. The prophet as public critic parallels the priest in the private world. (It is dangerous, however, to reverse the two roles. The priest in public underwrites the regime; the prophet in private becomes a cynic.)[10]

Because religion has a special link to guilt and sin, the public, through the state, may profitably use religious institutions to address public problems such as crime and drug abuse particularly involving guilt and shame. It should not do so by making such things matters of public sin or involving religion directly in the definition of crimes or by making the struggle against crime or drug addiction religious crusades. Rather, the proper role of religion lies in rehabilitation efforts, service to victims of crime and drug abuse, and preventative education programs. I have specifically in mind here public employment of chaplains in prisons, youth detention centers, drug abuse treatment programs, and the like. I also have in mind public funding, on the same basis as nonreligious programs, of private religious youth programs, detoxification and recovery programs, counseling centers, halfway houses, and literacy and job-training programs.

The general point is that religious institutions function best in addressing public ills as part of the "third sector," the nonprofit organizations that are neither wholly public nor private. Nongovernmental organizations (NGOs), many of them religious, perform the same role in international development. Small, flexible, and independent, NGOs and domestic nonprofits may more creatively adapt to local conditions affecting their program concerns than top-heavy bureaucratic public agencies, such as the Department of Health and Human Services and the Agency for International Development.

FEAR OF DEATH

If the public, especially political, significance of religion for the sense of sin is crucial, the importance of religion in the face of death is doubly so. Evil may be accounted for, and even dismissed, in a variety of ways, but death is more difficult to deny, though we try in many subtle ways.[11] Few deny that religion does and should deal with death, but it should do so privately, by helping individuals and families face death and its fears. What relevance does this have for politics?

Public life and death are not unacquainted. Think of the public funerals of heads of state or major public figures such as Gandhi, Robert Kennedy, and Martin Luther King, Jr. These are occasions, heavily laden with religious and political symbolism, in which the public ritually and collectively confronts death. Even more pointedly, think of the significance of the public display of Lenin's corpse.

These illustrations pale, however, before the fact, not simply that polities hold the power of life and death but that they claim legitimately to hold it. In the modern world at least, only the political order is allowed, legitimately, to take life through capital punishment and to wage war. This latter involves not simply ordering citizens to risk their lives but to take life. Moreover, polities have the responsibility to insure that citizens are guarded as much as possible against the threat of death from starvation, drought, disease, and natural disaster.

The end of the Cold War, paradoxically, brought closer to home the connection between death and politics, first in the Persian Gulf War, in which the taking of life came easily. Even more to the point, the question of whether the western nations should enter militarily into the nationalist and religious wars of the Balkan peninsula brought home the dangers of the religion and politics connection. Finally, American participation in the United Nations' effort to end massive death by starvation in Somalia revealed yet another dimension in the way politics encounters death. In each of these cases religion was important. In the Persian Gulf War, application of just-war theory was prominent; in the Balkans, religious passions; and in Somalia, public assistance to NGOs long involved in starvation relief.

Recognition of the link between death and politics and, therefore, of the connection through religion between private and public life is not unknown in the history of political theory, but lately has been rarely expressed. Plato, of course, saw these connections, beginning and ending the *Republic* with the theme of justice and death. Hobbes recognized how problematic is the sovereign's power of death. Therefore, the little-read second half of *Leviathan* on the Kingdoms of Light and Darkness binds the book's whole argument. According to Hobbes, successful political order requires readiness to die, but self-interest cannot motivate such willingness. Only religious belief can.[12]

This insight into the links between death, politics, and religion deepens earlier points about morality and sin. Reflections on public and private life apart from religion could help explain the importance of character and virtue and even motivate citizens toward them, but what about death? How, apart from religion, motivate a person to die?[13] Religion does deal with the private and public meanings of death, so every society, every public order, must have a religious component of some sort, for every society must deal with both dimensions of death. Natural reason and political history need, in the face of death, sacred history and supernatural religion. Hence, the excitement and the risk of religion and politics. They seek to instruct us in death.

It might be objected that this argument is merely a subtle rationalization of the utility of religion to politics. Religion is useful because it provides a way to justify a regime's life taking. Hobbes's account is certainly open to this objection, as is mine up to this point. My response is two-fold. First, I have not yet said anything about how religion must interact with politics. Some ways of interaction certainly do improperly make religion the servant of politics. Mine does not. Second, I reject civil religion's reduction of religion to utility.

Given this concern with life and death, religion must challenge politics precisely in those matters most directly related to life and death. I have in mind particularly questions of war and peace, abortion, and capital punishment. Religion plays a creative role in political discourse when it points out that abortion is about more than tissue and choice. It is about the gift of life and the right to take life. Although I recognize the dangers of the politics of abortion, I also believe that it is vital for American society's health that abortion be seriously debated among citizens. That is happening now, thanks in large measure to religious voices that challenged the easy acceptance of legal abortion.

That challenge accomplished, what seems most critical at the present public policy juncture is whether religious forces can be part of a creative compromise to break the stalemate between pro-life and pro-choice forces. Though the two political parties appear stuck on the extremes, the nation may very well be ready for compromise. The vast majority of Americans are not radically pro-life or radically pro-choice. They do not like abortion and believe that it is wrong, but they are not ready for government to forbid it. They are ready, however, for restrictions such as waiting periods, informed consent, parental and spousal notification, and limits on late-term abortions.

Political and moral pressure (and civil disobedience), much of it from the side of religion, have made abortions more difficult to obtain and more stigmatized. Religious groups have issued the challenge, but it is now time for politics to exert its expertise—compromise.[14] If the political parties can move toward a centrist position reflecting the desire of Americans to permit abortion, but to discourage it under many circumstances, then both religious and political forces will have played a creative role. Moreover, it would be a role that allows the moral and political debate to continue and for adjustments to be made over time if ideological rigidities soften.

War and capital punishment present similar opportunities for religious and political dialogue. Each involves the taking of life. Religious voices have been prominent in debates on both issues. Religious groups and actors were leaders in the anti–Vietnam War movement and in opposition to capital punishment today. When public opinion can swing rapidly between pro and anti on war and the death penalty, it is important that religion remind us of the morally troubling and tragic consequences of the positions we adopt.

Other end-of-life issues present similar challenges to both religion and politics. If the state reserves to itself monopoly over death, then can it allow physician-assisted suicide or other forms of euthanasia? As Daniel Callahan persuasively argues, health care costs at the end of life cannot effectively be controlled or resources freed for providing basic care to all unless cultural attitudes toward life and death, and the desire to take complete control over each, become more realistic.[15] Religion certainly must become involved in profound cultural debate about such fundamental matters of public policy.

Religion can keep liberal societies aware of death and, therefore, of human limitation. Thus for liberal society to succumb to the temptation to relegate religion to the private sphere is to support its ready tendency to deny death. This denial unleashes liberal society's most negative inclinations. Though it might be argued that reason can substitute for religion to address the problem of death, this solution will not work. The sources of our fear of death are too deep for rational analysis.[16]

Moreover, if liberal rationalism cannot legitimate the power of life and death, pseudo-religious ideologies are only too ready to step in. Replacing the sacred with the trans-human value of the nation, history, the race, or a utopia, they seek to justify death in the present in the name of these values. The proportion of believers in a society is always large and relatively constant. When they cease to believe in the gods, they make gods of what they believe in. The horrible costs of this route in human life and dignity are only too well known. The desire of ideologies to become substitute religions is nowhere more powerful than in the encounter with death. The political role of religion might be justified for no other reason than to guard against totalitarianism. Yet religion itself has been put to the services of totalitarian and authoritarian justification of regimes of death. This service usually takes the form of theocracy or an oppressive civil religion.

THE FRAILTY OF PUBLIC/PRIVATE LIFE

Civic bonds are more frail than we like to admit. Betrayal, violence, and rampant self-interest rend polities as well as marriages. One of the most striking things of the 1992 political season, as indeed the early 1990s, generally, was a widespread rage that threatened public unity. Most obviously, that rage was demonstrated in the Los Angeles riots. By midcampaign, however, that rage had faded to be replaced by the anger of American citizens over politics and politicians. People were angry about political corruption, about political cowardice, and about their own uncertain economic future. Moreover, this rage is not confined to political life or to black anger at discrimination and intolerable living conditions. Many ordinary citizens go through each day "fed up to here" and on the verge of exploding into random, anomic violence. One of the most challenging tasks of politics today is to understand this rage and to try to devise responses that draw upon our best political traditions. But it may also need to call upon the resources of religious institutions.

The brokenness represented by anger is not unusual in public life. What is unique is the position of religion among the fragments. Just as religion provides understanding of death, it explains the fragility of human relationships. Used to dealing with frailty, its picture of the moral order has a place for fragility and broken relationships. It can channel anger and hostility, point to new possibilities within the shards, reconcile and forgive hurts, and supply justification for retaliation.

Hannah Arendt discusses movingly the brittleness of public space and how the uncertainty and irreversibility of action undermine it. Only the human capacity for forgiveness and promising overcome this frailty. Although Arendt emphasizes the secular sides of these experiences, she acknowledges their religious origins.[17] Justice, too, is prone to fall short. Self-interest, human weakness, natural calamities, and differential individual capacities, needs, and desires upset the temporary balances of justice, producing injustice and demands for a new balance.

In the midst of the conflict, often the violence, spawned on the private/public border and in political life by the failures of justice, often only admission of guilt, with corresponding forgiveness and promises of reform, can defuse violence and work political reconciliation. Although it is certainly possible to offer forgiveness and to make promises from nonreligious motives, historically speaking religion, especially the religions of Judaism and Christianity, have introduced forgiveness and promise (covenant) to the public stage.

The question of how, when, and in what form forgiveness may be introduced to the public stage is difficult. Appeals to forgiveness may be masks for self-interest. These appeals are also most open to rebuttals from the perspective of justice, the principal political virtue. To forgive a wrong or to give up enforcement of a contract, it is argued, will be unjust to the wronged or to the other party to the contract. Moreover, it will encourage the same old behavior that created the situation in the first place. There is no abstract answer to such objections. Sometimes justice must take precedence. Forgiveness is not always the appropriate response to a political problem. Nevertheless, appeals to forgiveness can be powerful, and they can be healing. The difficulty of making any fixed "rules for forgiveness" is illustrated by three highly publicized instances: amnesty for Vietnam-era draft evaders, forgiveness of massive Third World debt, and the question of whether a senator like Robert Packwood can ask for forgiveness of sexual harassment and continue to serve, or whether politics excludes such forgiveness.[18]

Often admissions of guilt, forgiveness, and promises are smokescreens for continued pursuit of self-interest. But this fact does not detract from the deep necessity in political life of genuine forgiving and promising. Indeed, all-too-familiar deceptions generate the need for sacred support to forgiving and promising. Without such roots, trust too easily gives way to cynicism. The pains of public life—conflicting interests, false promises, and false images of ourselves and others—are only too real. It is precisely the surprising power of the gift of forgiveness when it is offered and of the promise when it is kept that make it possible to keep forgiving and trusting in the face of so much evidence to the contrary. Here, according to Gilbert Meilaender, is the role for religion. "The churches and other communities of virtue do not 'possess a moral superiority' so much as they witness to the gift-like character of the good."[19]

EARTH, DREAMS, AND DESTINY

Finally, let me simply allude to a few additional important substantive questions under debate today in which religion's voice can and should make a contribution to political discourse. I cannot give them as full a treatment as I have the issues above, but they do deserve at least a mention.

A whole set of environmental issues in the last few decades has awakened us to the fragility of the planet itself. It seems not out of place that religions, which often have creation myths at their heart, might have some wisdom to contribute. In particular, the idea of stewardship found in Christian thought can challenge the "use it up; throw it away" mentality of American politics and culture.

Similarly, religion is deeply concerned with human dreams and aspirations, with communication about what ultimately might satisfy the longings of the human heart. It is not unthinkable then that, with politics so frequently concerned with greed, prosperity, and material affluence, the voices of religion might give us pause in our headlong pursuit of a quick economic fix.

Finally, this same concern with human dreams and aspirations gives religion a fundamental concern with human destiny, with the value of the individual and the community. Thus the voices of religion might legitimately be found in discussions of fundamental human rights and in ways to combat the terrible denials of rights in so many parts of the world.

CONCLUDING REFLECTIONS

I have spoken thus far of the vital importance of religion to public and political life. Religion uniquely deals with sin, death, and the fragility of public life. It supports and sustains the continuation of politics when evil, death, and broken promises threaten to overwhelm public life and transform it into coercion, violence, or simple self-interested manipulation. It is now time to address even more explicitly the ways in which religion and politics can interact creatively in tension on the border between private and public life. Martin Luther King, Jr., argued that the goal of nonviolent resistance is to set up a creative tension necessary for growth.[20] That kind of creative tension should characterize the interaction of religion and politics.

Two or more forces pulling in different directions define a tension. Sometimes its stress holds things together—as with, for example, a rubber band. But sometimes it causes things to break apart, as when a spring snaps from being wound too tightly. To understand the religion/politics tension, we must define the directions in which each pulls. We must also show how tension between them permits each to work better.

Religion brings politics to awareness of the highest, lowest, and most mysterious features of life, especially of the lofty and mysterious. Politics, better acquainted with the lowest, brings religious passion and self-assurance to awareness of the middle ground between the highest and the lowest; that is, it teaches religion the necessity and the art of compromise. Moreover, some of the highest and lowest things are already at home in politics—honor, bravery, lust for power, and the passions of blood and soil. Politics can make religion alert to these, and to their danger.

Religion pulls toward the transcendent, toward principles, virtues, ideals, and perfection. Unrestrained by tension, this religious dynamic produces fanaticism. Religious passion finds it difficult to compromise, to acknowledge how striving after perfection founders on human weakness. Politics, however, demands compromise, for the key fact of politics, especially of participatory public life, lies in confrontation with the ideas and the interests of others, with the mosaic of human frailty and plurality.

Just as religion would avoid compromise, politics would avoid righteousness. Politics pulls toward the vague middle ground, toward indifference and cynicism. Left to itself, politics seeks the easy, painless way. High principles make for difficult political choices, for it is painful to confront higher things, to acknowledge the possibility of something better and to accept the discipline necessary to reach it. Religion in public life can teach politics about the higher things and stimulate, even embarrass, politicians and citizens to discover them.

The tension produced by these conflicting natural tendencies defines their relationship as both competitive and cooperative. The danger of misunderstanding the relationship between religion and politics comes when we forget that it must include both cooperation and competition. When the tension is lost, the two either fly apart or, worse, collapse together. The latter is the world's too-frequent condition.

Such a collapse of religion and politics, at least in the American experience, may be described as "ideological capture." By this I mean the interpretation of faith through the lens of liberalism, conservatism, socialism, or any other ideology. Instead of assessing politics, policy, and ideology through the lens of faith, the opposite takes place. In addition, because political ideology also carries the danger of being wholly action oriented, it leaves little room for reflection, prayer, doubt, and ambiguity. Because it wants results and believes it has the simple key needed to get results, ideology refuses to wait on God's time.[21]

Particularly dangerous is the ideology of Americanism, or American Civil Religion, which posits the notion that the United States has the right and destiny to be the greatest nation in the world. This form of ideological capture produces inflated expectations, hopes, and dreams about America's place in history. Not surprisingly, North American political rhetoric seems most concerned with putting our nation back in first place—economically, culturally, and politically. But what warrant do we have to claim such a position? A religion that avoids capture by ideological movements must be acutely sensitive to the sins of pride and ambition and to the limits of nations, and must be ready to challenge such pretensions.

Proponents of politics might object that religion should be allowed a role only where shared secular premises do not settle an issue. Secular argument takes pride of place. This objection, however, must fail. Political language does have its own dimensions, value, and validity. Therefore, it must possess a very wide scope, and this scope is properly politics and public policy. Thus it is fitting, especially in liberal democracy, that secular, political discourse be the ordinary language of public life. This priority keeps religion muted in political debate, taming its dangerous political tendencies.

Nevertheless, despite the fact that political argument may be most common, the border area between religion and politics still must be the scene of very lively discussion and debate. But that discussion and debate will be conducted at the border, not at the political center; that is, the religious voice must enter the realm of policy debate, not the central political experiences of candidate or party endorsement. Precisely because of its distance from the center, religious belief will have the opportunity to challenge conventional, secular perspectives and to present alternatives not otherwise available.[22]

The tensional model of religion and politics provides a way in which liberal democracy can achieve tolerance. As the different participants seek common ground, they begin to discover the participatory virtues of the public realm in a new way. All will not be sweetness and light. Not all religious persons will adhere to civil discourse. Not all political actors adhere to civility. Yet the value of the preceding argument is to show not only that religious and political language can properly interact but that there are some kinds of issues on which religious language gives a perspective unavailable to purely public reason.

Moreover, there is a way in which religion, as part of our cultural heritage, may become a repository of principles and traditions from that heritage that otherwise might be neglected. Sometimes those principles are needed to call politics to account when it might ride roughshod over important principles. There is, in short, an entirely proper role for religious language to be the language of challenge to dominant political forces. When that happens, the religious language looks like an invader from across the public-private border. But that border is not rigidly defined; moreover, religion can speak a language neglected, but not forgotten, in the political realm. It must be willing in turn to learn from politics political ways of speaking, even as it challenges dominant political forces.

The role for religion in political discourse that I have outlined suggests one more challenge, this one a challenge for religion itself. There is a tension between religion's political activity to protect itself from the public and its challenge to the public. Legitimate though protection might be, as in free exercise cases, religion can become just another political voice, one of many with no distinctive authority, if it focuses on self-defense, protection of institutional interests, or ideological stances.

Indeed, the voice of religion may become strident, rather than prophetic, if its challenge to politics is self-righteous. For example, it weakens the voice of religion if it calls for protection of the fundamental rights of workers, but at the same time asks for exemptions from labor laws covering workers in religious institutions. The voice of religion must be as quick to challenge its own unjust institutions as it is those of the public realm. Here is perhaps the most difficult task for religion in political discourse, to be one of the few voices that is capable of self-criticism.

NOTES

1. "Introduction" to *Leviathan,* by Thomas Hobbes (Oxford: Basil Blackwell, 1946), lxiv.
2. For the extended version of my argument, see *Religion in Public and Private Life* (New York: Routledge, 1990), which this essay draws upon and expands.
3. Martin E. Marty, "Foreword," in *Religion in American Public Life,* ed. Robin W. Lovin (New York: Paulist, 1986), 1.
4. Michael Walzer, *Spheres of Justice* (New York: Basic, 1983), chap. 10.
5. Peter Berger, "Religious Liberty and the Paradox of Relevance," *The Religion & Society Report* 5 (Jan. 1988): 1–2.
6. Wilson Carey McWilliams, "The Bible in the American Political Tradition," in *Political Anthropology, III: Religion and Politics,* ed. Myron J. Aronoff (New Brunswick, N.J.: Transaction, 1984), 19.
7. Tinder, *The Political Meaning of Christianity: An Interpretation* (Baton Rouge: Louisiana State Univ. Press, 1989), 146. It is for this reason that Tinder can say that "politics is properly spiritual" (199).
8. Philip Rieff, *The Triumph of the Therapeutic* (New York: Harper Torchbooks, 1968).
9. Religions have more than didactic teachings on these subjects. The exemplary lives of saints in many religious traditions provide models of outstanding lives, often in tension with ordinary cultural norms and expectations. See John Stratton Hawley, ed., *Saints and Virtues* (Berkeley and Los Angeles: Univ. of California Press, 1987).
10. It is precisely the tension between religion and public life that draws the prophet to the public realm to challenge its complacency. This same tension frightens the priest away or drives him to collapse the two realms together.
11. See the profound meditations of Ernest Becker, *The Denial of Death* (New York: Free Press, 1973). Becker's account of how repression of the knowledge of death distorts individual life suggests the necessity of considering how the public denial of death distorts public life.

12. See Eldon J. Eisenach, *The Two Worlds of Liberalism* (Chicago: Univ. of Chicago Press, 1981), esp. 13–17, 47–50, 57.

13. Philosophy, of course, may do so. Nothing in my discussion of religion rules out philosophy, and I explicitly do not assimilate philosophy to religion. Although politics could itself never perform the special functions of religion considered in this chapter, philosophy might. Hence, the tension between Athens and Jerusalem. Nevertheless, philosophy seems unlikely to play a significant public role in regard to death. Ideology is another matter, and I address it below.

14. See Christopher Wolfe, "The Case for Political Compromise," *First Things* 24 (June/July 1992): 22–29.

15. Daniel Callahan, *What Kind of Life? The Limits of Medical Progress* (New York: Simon & Schuster, 1990).

16. On the idea of religion as an antidote to liberal individualism, see Robert Booth Fowler, *Unconventional Partners: Religion and Liberal Culture in the United States* (Grand Rapids, Mich.: Eerdmans, 1988).

17. Hannah Arendt, *The Human Condition* (Garden City, N.Y.: Doubleday Anchor, 1959), 212–23.

18. Amitai Etzioni has called for secular, political counterparts of religious rituals of atonement and rehabilitation, which he argues would reinforce a morally sensitive community life. See "Roads to Repentance," *The Responsive Community* 2 (Spring 1992): 10–13.

19. In *Virtue—Public and Private,* ed. Richard John Neuhaus (Grand Rapids, Mich.: Eerdmans, 1986), 73.

20. See, "Letter from Birmingham City Jail," in *Why We Can't Wait,* by Martin Luther King, Jr. (New York: Harper & Row, 1964).

21. See Tinder, *The Political Meaning of Christianity,* for the importance of waiting. I refer in the text to the capture of religion by ideology. The opposite is also possible, and may indeed be the case in some Islamic nations today, but the American temptation is the reverse.

22. The position that I have articulated seems to opt for religion's "witness" over its possible political "effectiveness." See the excellent discussion of this issue in Allen Hertzke, *Representing God in Washington: The Role of Religious Lobbies in the American Polity* (Knoxville: Univ. of Tennessee Press, 1988). It is indeed the role of religion to witness, to call issues and forgotten perspectives to attention. Ultimately, religion can only be effective in civil discourse if its themes are picked up by ordinary actors and tried in the furnace of electoral politics and legislative compromise.

REFERENCES

Arendt, Hannah. *The Human Condition.* Garden City, N.Y.: Doubleday Anchor, 1959.

Berger, Peter. "Religious Liberty and the Paradox of Relevance." *The Religion & Society Report* 5 (Jan. 1988): 1–2.

Callahan, Daniel. *What Kind of Life? The Limits of Medical Progress.* New York: Simon & Schuster, 1990.

Cochran, Clarke E. *Religion in Public and Private Life.* New York: Routledge, 1990.

Eisenach, Eldon J. *The Two Worlds of Liberalism.* Chicago: Univ. of Chicago Press, 1981.

Etzioni, Amitai. "Roads to Repentance." *The Responsive Community* 2 (Spring 1992): 10–13.

Hobbes, Thomas. *Leviathan.* Oxford: Basil Blackwell, 1946.

King, Martin Luther, Jr. *Why We Can't Wait.* New York: Harper & Row, 1964.

Marty, Martin E. "Foreword." In *Religion in American Public Life.* Ed. Robin W. Lovin. New York: Paulist Press, 1986.

McWilliams, Wilson Carey. "The Bible in the American Political Tradition." In *Political Anthropology, III: Religion and Politics.* Ed. Myron J. Aronoff. New Brunswick, N.J.: Transaction, 1984.

Neuhaus, Richard John, ed. *Virtue—Public and Private.* Grand Rapids, Mich.: Eerdmans, 1986.

Rieff, Philip. *The Triumph of the Therapeutic.* New York: Harper Torchbooks, 1968.

Tinder, Glenn. *The Political Meaning of Christianity: An Interpretation.* Baton Rouge: Louisiana State Univ. Press, 1989.

Walzer, Michael. *Spheres of Justice.* New York: Basic Books, 1983.

Wolfe, Christopher. "The Case for Political Compromise." *First Things* (June/July 1992): 22–29.

Conclusion:
The Religion Puzzle

James W. Skillen

The preceding chapters succeed in demonstrating once again the complexity of America's struggle to legalize religion. At the surface of the dominant public ideology, everything seems simple and uncontentious: church and state have been separated throughout the United States; thus, the free practice of diverse faiths flourishes apart from governmental interference while politics and the processes of making law unfold as nonreligious practices, free of ecclesiastical bondage and unhindered by religious warfare.

But that is not reality. Reality begins to appear when we stop for just a moment to ask about the nature of religion and about the multiple disputes over its legal place in the American polity. The only thing that seems clear and simple is that most Americans—going all the way back to Madison and Jefferson—admit that there are different expressions of religion. Few if any religious people practice "religion" in general; rather, they practice Christianity, Judaism, Islam, Secularism, Mormonism, or some other faith. With respect to the inner nature and living character of these different religions, the legal and political debates in the United States actually tell us very little. The word *religion* is actually used most often in public discourse not to say anything about the nature of different religions but to debate the legal place of diverse religious practices. In other words, the public debate over religion is, for the most part, a debate about how the political order should recognize—and either approve or disapprove—various practices of different religions.

This may seem like a simple and obvious point to make, but it is highly important, because a number of the preceding essays seem to assume that the word *religion* is capable of bearing more weight than it actually does. Having not given sufficient attention to the origin and character of diverse religious practices in America, some of the authors in this book simply assume that religion is a clearly recognizable subject in its own right that can be distinguished clearly from other subjects such as secular activities, public life, liberal culture, the state, politics, and so forth. But precisely because American citizens practice different religions in different ways, the assumption that there is an isolable generality called religion will not work. The complexity and diversity of religious life will not yield to the unilateral imposition of a simple schema that divides life between religious and nonreligious spheres.

This is why Carl Esbeck's chapter is so valuable at the start. By paying close attention both to the reality of American life as well as to the dilemmas created in the course of the U.S. Supreme Court's rulings on religious affairs, Esbeck is able to show at least six different views of the political order and of how it should relate to religious life. And, at bottom, he argues, the resolution of disagreements will require honesty in facing up to the fundamentally different views of life (not just of religion in a narrow sense) that we Americans hold:

> At its root, one's view of church-state relations is dependent in large measure on one's theological or philosophical world view. Rightly or wrongly, historical events are cited [by different people], if at all, as make weight in support of a position held for other reasons. Only when this is admitted can we start being honest about why American views on the appropriate relationship of church and state are as varied as our religious and philosophical allegiances.[1]

Esbeck's point is supported by Harvard Law professor Mary Ann Glendon and Raul F. Yanes in a recent article in which, among other things, they criticize the "relatively low priority" of religious freedom among lawyers who hold "a widely accepted set of assumptions about religion" that make it difficult for them "to attend to the associational, institutional, and ecological dimensions of Religion Clause cases."[2] Part of the "cognitive problem that is pervasive in contemporary legal culture," say Glendon and Yanes, is that it is "geared only to the individual, the state, and the market" and is thus unable to perceive "the social dimensions of human personhood, and of the social environments that individual human beings require in order to fully develop their potential."[3] One's cognitive preconceptions (fundamental world view) structure what one sees and fails to see.

Owning up to the honesty that Esbeck demands, I must admit from the start, therefore, that my own view of life and of these matters fits essentially under Esbeck's fourth categorization—that of the "structural pluralists."[4] The comments that follow demonstrate some of the consequences of that viewpoint as well as my relative discomfort with the arguments of those authors in this book who seem not to have reflected sufficiently on their taken-for-granted assumptions about the nature of religion and the political order.

Neal Riemer's reexamination of James Madison seems to substantiate rather than clear up both men's equivocation about the subject of religion and politics. Riemer writes as if phrases such as *church and state* can, rather easily, be used interchangeably with *religion and state, spiritual and secular domains, religious groups and secular activities.* But—to start with Madison—did that founding father really make a case for the disestablishment of the church on the basis of a world view that assumes a sharp distinction between what is religious and what is secular? Didn't Madison, instead, much more than Riemer, recognize the possibility that religions may extend themselves differently into various areas of life? When for example, Madison (according to Riemer) objected to Patrick Henry's bill of 1776 because it stood in opposition to "the equal right of every citizen to the free exercise of his Religion according to the dictates of conscience," wasn't Madison recognizing that conscience might lead different people to greater or lesser exertions in the practice of their religions, and that the state should not be allowed to decide ahead of time what is and what is not religious?[5] Doesn't the faith of many Jews, Muslims, and Christians entail conscience-bound patterns of family life, education, business, and even politics, and not just of church life? How then may any person (or state or federal constitution) presume ahead of time that there is a clearly recognized "nonreligious" domain? Surely Riemer and others should not confound the institutional distinction between church and state with the dichotomy between the religious and the secular, the spiritual and the mundane, religion and so-called secular life. Riemer's world view drives him, nonetheless, to precisely that confounding.

Riemer believes that Madison would agree with him that "governmental financial aid to parochial schools" should not be legally permitted, but that "equal and non-discriminatory treatment for people or religious organizations" in matters such as police and fire protection should be allowed.[6] But what is the basis for this distinction other than Riemer's view of the proper confines of religion over against a secular state? And why should Riemer's world view be accepted as the proper interpretive framework for the Court's rulings or for legislation? It seems to me that one could as easily make the case—on grounds established by Charles Emmerich, Daniel Dreisbach, and Frank Guliuzza—that Madison's strong case for religious freedom would permit "equal and non-discriminatory treatment for people and religious organizations" when the "dictates of conscience" drive them to educate their children in ways consistent with their religions. What could justify the state's usurpation of a conscientious right at this juncture? What could possibly justify the state's discriminatory treatment of its citizens by paying only for the schooling of those children whose parents' view of education is sufficiently secularized?

My aim here is not to try to prove that Riemer's distinction between religion and secularity is mistaken, though I believe it is, but rather to show that his convictions about these matters are precisely what require justification as the basis for the just legal treatment of diverse religious practices. The historical record, as illuminated by several other chapters in this book, shows that Riemer's assumptions cannot be taken for granted and are by no means universally held by Americans.

Emmerich argues, for example, that the "anticlerical and privatized conception of religion advanced by [U.S. Supreme Court] Justice Rutledge in *Everson* cannot account for America's long and rich heritage of religious liberty. Nor is it an outlook that Madison would endorse."[7] Emmerich goes on to expose a deeper problem with the presumed religious-secular dichotomy, namely, its implication of state sovereignty over all of the so-called secular areas of life: "Modern scholars and courts invariably address religious freedom issues from the perspective of statism, that is, they assume the sovereignty of the state over virtually all areas of life and then ask, to what extent if at all must the state tolerate religious practices that impinge upon its authority."[8]

In truth, should we not, on the basis of the historical record, move in just the opposite direction and argue that the United States is itself grounded not in secularism but in a deistic form of Christian religion? As Dreisbach demonstrates, Jefferson grounded religious freedom and even governmental authority in the fact that "Almighty God hath created the mind free" and willed that "free it shall remain."[9] Human rights, including the right to self-government, are rooted, at least to some extent, in the Creator, from Jefferson's point of view.

Or if not in deism, perhaps America's roots can be found in Calvinism, or in Reformed Protestantism generally. John Witte makes the strong case in his essay that American criminal law cannot be accounted for apart from the Reformation. According to Witte, the fact that contemporary jurists no longer recognize the moral and even theological foundations of criminal law says more about their errors and forgetfulness than about the full reality of contemporary laws and the state. Julia Stronks says of those who hold the judicial conviction that "religion can be and must be excluded from the public sphere" actually ignore "the all-encompassing nature of religion. Many faiths," she explains, "articulate a worldview in which religion has a necessary impact on the public arena—including schooling of children, employment decisions, and the use of money such as tax funds."[10]

Dreisbach's criticism of William Lee Miller is relevant at this point. Miller's book *The First Liberty* (1986), according to Dreisbach, gives great attention to Jefferson's Virginia Bill No. 82 for establishing religious freedom, but practically ignores the larger context of Jefferson's reasoning in four companion bills that show a more accommodating view of religion.[11] Part of Miller's difficulty, it seems to me, is due to his inattention to the diverse ways in which the word (and the reality of) *religion* shows up in both early America and today.

In Roger Williams's day, as Miller correctly points out, religion was not a "separated compartment . . . divorced from the great issues of politics, government, and the shaping of institutions." To the contrary, "religion provided the all-embracing terms in which the great issues were debated."[12] Toward the end of the book, in examining some Supreme Court decisions, Miller argues that religion is not exactly parallel to race, or color, or sexual preference, or national origin. Rather, he affirms, religion is "part of the substance" to which a human being "has an inner, changing, substantive relationship, and which, individually and communally, provides the frame to guide and shape conduct and define the great issues of living. . . . Religion is culture not nature; belief not biology; mind and spirit not ethnicity."[13] From a historical point of view, Miller writes, one simply must recognize that even the "bare bones of republicanism" and the very emergence of this country "have not been disconnected . . . from 'religion,' even in its less spacious definitions." America's institutions "have underpinnings in the Christian religion."[14]

To write about religion in this way simply does not permit its confinement in church institutions or in a separable compartment that can then be set over against a variety of other separable functions and activities of human life, which are then judged to be nonreligious or secular. Certainly the political and legal realms cannot be thus separated from religion, as Miller himself shows. And yet in the Foreword of his book, Miller states that the new American idea of separating church and state implied "that there did not have to be any link between religion and the state, between ultimate convictions and the power of the law."[15] Miller's book never takes up a critical examination of this highly equivocal use of the term *religion*.

The chapters by Booth Fowler and Clarke Cochran exhibit a similar kind of oversight. Fowler admits at the start that religion is an elusive term but says he will use the word to mean "what people in this culture consider to be religion."[16] But, in fact, throughout his chapter (and throughout his book *Unconventional Part-*

ners[17]), Fowler simply assumes that religion is a self-standing subject that can stand alongside "liberal culture" as a distinguishable if congenial partner. Not all people in this culture use *religion* in the way Fowler does, however.

Such a simple dichotomy between religion and liberal culture, it seems to me, is inadequate to get at the diverse categories that Esbeck has enumerated, and it leaves unexamined these two sociological abstractions that Fowler works with. Even if Fowler's assumptions are the same as those of the majority of Americans, his way of approaching the matter does not allow a critical penetration to the fundamental problems in those very assumptions. Among other things, his approach hides from view what Witte, Stronks and Miller have touched on, namely, the *religious* character of much of American (liberal) culture. Not all religions stand in contrast to liberal culture; not all of this so-called liberal culture is nonreligious in character. In fact, the very framework of religion/culture is a product of the Enlightenment, and it represents a modern, nonneutral world view equivalent to other encompassing religious ways of life. In describing the intimate interdependence of what he calls religion and liberal culture in America, I believe that Fowler is describing an integral way of life—the "American way of life." But not all Americans follow this way of life even if it is dominant in our society. Moreover, the American way of life is neither unreligious nor nonreligious; it is, rather, a contrasting competitor with other ways of life such as orthodox Judaism, wholehearted Islam, systematic secularism, consistent Thomism, and others. Without entering into a critical examination of the problematic assumptions that ground his entire argument, Fowler cannot, it seems to me, even begin to resolve the First Amendment quandaries we now face.

For Cochran, religion also appears to be a readily distinguishable sphere of life. In its reference to transcendence, religion "relativizes and thereby limits all other spheres of activity, including politics."[18] At the same time, however, Cochran wants to overcome any hardened separation between religion and politics by introducing the idea of "border areas." In the public arena, political argument must play the major role, says Cochran, but religious argument may legitimately join in combat on the edges. Despite the fact, says Cochran, that

> political argument may be primary, the border area between religion and politics will be the scene of very lively discussion and debate. But that discussion and debate will be conducted at the border, not at the political center; that is, the religious voice must enter policy debate, not the central political experiences of candi-

date endorsement and interest-group lobbying. Precisely because of its distance from the center, religious belief will have the opportunity to challenge conventional, secular perspectives and to present alternatives not otherwise available.[19]

Perhaps my difficulty here arises because of Cochran's heavy reliance on spatial analogies. But what are these abstract subjects of religion and politics that interact in space? Who controls the "border area" if not either political or religious institutions? Why may religion not engage itself at the political "center"? Or to ask it in another way, what in fact does exist at the center of political debate today if not a conflict among the different religiously deep world views—the views of deists, secularists, Christians, Jews, New Agers, and more? How does religious belief in general challenge conventional, secular perspectives if "it" is not engaged at the same point and on center stage with those perspectives?

The truth is that American views range widely from one extreme, at which religion is seen as something to which the supposedly secular state should grant a small separable space, to the other extreme, at which the entire political and legal order is seen as depending on one or another religion or at least on an accommodating truce or overlap among contending religions. The preceding chapters illuminate this diversity of convictions ranging from those of secular statists to those held by people who see the all-embracing character of religion. But although most Americans have no difficulty admitting that religious convictions and practices are highly diverse, few are willing to grant that the basis for legalizing religion can remain politically splintered or forever be called into legal dispute. The difficulty, however, is in finding common political/legal agreement about the just treatment of diverse religious ways of life expressed in the activities of churches, schools, daycare centers, employment practices, families, friendships, and countless professional and voluntary organizations.

Today, in fact, disagreements over the manner in which the Constitution and government should recognize and respect diverse religious practices seem to be stronger than ever before. The U.S. Supreme Court's decisions in this field have been judged to be incoherent and in disarray, as several of the authors note. Both Guliuzza and Stronks illustrate the extent to which that incoherence exists. And I believe that Guliuzza points us in the right direction to discover the possibility of achieving coherence when he argues that the First Amendment requires of government an evenhanded treatment of diverse religious practices now that Christian churches have been disestablished from their former, politically privileged positions.[20] The point of the mandate in the Constitution's First Amendment, then, is not to separate the state from religion but to separate one or another church from a position of politically established privilege. This also is Glendon's and Yanes's reading of the First Amendment:

> The provisions dealing with religious freedom were placed first among this group, followed by the familiar protections for speech, the press, and the right of the people to assemble and to petition for redress of grievances. The structure of the amendment suggests that the subject of protection in the first participial phrase is religious freedom, just as freedom of speech, press, assembly, and petition are the subjects of protection in the following two phrases. If the two religion provisions are read together in the light of an overarching purpose to protect freedom of religion, most of the tension between them disappears. They are complementary provisions, both in the service of the same fundamental right. They bar Congress from abridging religious freedom in one specific way (by legislation "respecting an establishment of religion"), and in general ("or prohibiting the free exercise thereof").[21]

Stronks's question at the end of her chapter is, therefore, the one that requires our return with utmost seriousness to the issue of "legalization." No matter how religion is defined, says Stronks, "in some cases the public authorities will be required to limit the individual's expression of religion. If a religion's precepts hurt children or prevent citizens from participating in the defense of a country or deceive the public or discriminate against women, how is the state to balance the importance of freedom of expression?"[22] Glendon and Yanes put the same challenge this way:

> Free exercise, like any other right, cannot be unlimited. Institutional, associational, and individual free exercise rights, like other rights, will sometimes be in tension with each other and with other important constitutional values. The major interpretive challenge for the future, we believe, will be to accord as much scope as possible to the constitutional guarantee of free exercise in its personal, associational, and institutional dimensions, while respecting the freedom of conscience of nonbelievers and without preferring one religion to another. A virtue of a structural approach to that formidable task is that it points toward addressing problems of fairness to all Americans, whatever their beliefs, through considering the complex interplay among free exercise, free speech, and equal protection principles, rather than through rigid, mechanical separationism.[23]

The question or challenge put this way is not first of all whether we will ever be able to come up with a uniform definition of religion that will thereafter always allow clear and happy adjudication of all religious rights claims. Rather, the question is this: In recognizing that Americans practice diverse religions, which are not reducible to a lowest common denominator, what then is the legitimate reach of government's authority for the purpose of protecting the common public life of all citizens while it acknowledges their prior right to practice their religions according to the dictates of conscience?

To answer this question, we need not—in fact, we must not—first seek a constitutionally established, sacred/secular world view by which to force all religions into one predefined box. Rather, we should concentrate on clarifying the nature of government's responsibility to protect the life and public space of its citizens who, we must presume, should be free to live by their religious (and other deepest) dictates of conscience. Clearly the task of clarifying the nature of political responsibility will remain a very difficult one. But our aim will be to try to resolve our disagreements about the nature of governmental responsibility rather than to try to arrive at a politically uniform definition of religion. The latter is not a political or legal necessity.

In seeking to propose an answer to the question about government's responsibility—an answer that will comport with Guliuzza's and Stronks's suggestions— my contention is that a properly constituted government should be responsible to protect and encourage the life, shared public space, and equal opportunities of all its citizens, but not to decide how people may or may not practice their religions. Civil and criminal laws as well as constitutional guarantees should require of government the protection of its citizens' lives no matter how those lives might be threatened. Certainly this will entail, for example, that private citizens and groups of citizens in the United States may not put other people—including children— to death. Such a restriction arises not from government's authority to interfere with (or intrude into) a particular religion based on the government's prior right to define acceptable religion. Rather, to protect life and to punish life takers inheres in government's responsibility as civil authority in contrast to that of every other institution. In protecting the life of children from a child-sacrificing cult, for example, the government does not unfairly intrude on a religious group's freedom; rather, government hereby enforces a civic rule of life protection that is violated by any person or group that threatens human life—whether that person or group be a thieving murderer, a polluting industrial enterprise, a health-threatening food processor, or a child-sacrificing religious cult.

Of course, one may legitimately ask where I get my view of the state to back up this argument. And I, then, will have to make my necessarily religiously grounded case for a constitutionally limited state that ought to recognize the independence of people who are always more than citizens and who ought to be allowed to live out their lives in a plurality of institutions and communities ranging from families and schools to churches and business enterprises. I will have to explain in some detail why I believe that people living under such a constitution ought to have the civil right of practicing their religions not only in churches but in the ways they organize their families, educate their children, conduct their businesses, and so forth. All of this, I will want to show, can be done with the full and equitable support of government as long as government is fair and evenhanded in its treatment of all citizens.

Church and state should be recognized as distinct institutions, in this view, but so also should families, schools, business enterprises, and a host of other organizations and associations. Religions, however, should be free to flourish wherever the "dictates of conscience" lead them in all areas of life. If government funds fire departments, those departments should protect all properties whether belonging to Christians or to atheists. If government chooses to fund schooling, those funds should extend proportionately to all school-age children whether they attend schools of one faith or another.[24] If the American government ever chooses to ensure the health of all its citizens through a variety of freely chosen health-care companies, the government's insurance ought to flow to Christian as well as Muslim health-care companies, to secularized as well as religiously ecumenical companies.

Diverse religions should be free to flourish as widely as religious citizens want to practice them. With Madison I agree that "the right to practice one's religion in accordance with conscience" is so fundamental that civil rules lack authority "to interfere with it unless the state's survival" is clearly at stake.[25] Government's authority, then, is not to predefine religion or the realm of religion, but to operate consistently within the constitutional limits that call it to do justice to citizens and to assure the state's survival. A religiously diverse school system no more threatens the state's survival than does a religiously diverse ecclesiastical arrangement. A religiously diverse health-care system no more threatens the state's survival than does a religiously diverse arrangement of publishing houses. Religiously diverse families no more threaten the survival of the state than do religiously diverse members of the House of Representatives or the Senate in Washington, D.C.

Threats to human life, on the other hand, no matter whence those threats arise, do endanger the survival of the state. Attempts by one group of citizens (whether a church or a business enterprise or a school) to monopolize the public commons is a threat to the state's survival. A government's unfair, disproportionate, or inequitable treatment of its citizens (by establishing one church over others, or by funding one system of schools to the disadvantage of others, or by supporting government-run hospitals while refusing to aid others) can indeed endanger the state. Thus, the state ought to attend carefully to its proper business, which is to protect the life of all citizens and to give fair and equitable treatment to every institution created by those citizens, to the extent that the state's survival and the survival of its citizens is not threatened. Or to put the matter positively, in order for the state to enhance its survival as a community of public justice, it not only ought to protect the life of every citizen but should also encourage the sense of fairness among citizens by treating them equitably in all their activities.

Does this view of the state conflict with other views? Of course it does, and that is precisely what we citizens should be arguing about. But let us be honest and lift up our different views of the state (the political community) to a full, critical discussion. One reason I have hope with regard to achieving the full protection of religious freedom in a healthy pluralistic polity is that most of us already agree that religions are diverse and that none should be established or given special privilege. What we disagree about is the nature of the state and how it ought to allow widespread religious freedom without reverting to a religious establishment or endangering its own survival. I believe that the real dangers to the survival of the United States today come from efforts to further restrict religious practice and to solidify the state's imagined secularity. To overcome these dangers we need to return to the debate about the nature of a political order that will uphold religious freedom in all of life. And for that debate I believe we need to consider very carefully the case for structural and confessional pluralism.

NOTES

1. Carl H. Esbeck, "A Typology of Church-State Relations in Current American Thought," this volume, chap. 1.

2. Mary Ann Glendon and Raul F. Yanes, "Structural Free Exercise," *Michigan Law Review* 90 (Dec. 1991): 546.

3. Ibid.

4. For background to the argument that follows, see James W. Skillen and Rockne M. McCarthy, eds., *Political Order and the Plural Structure of Society*, Emory Univ. Studies in Law and Religion, No. 2 (Atlanta: Scholars Press, 1991); James W. Skillen, *The Scattered Voice: Christians at Odds in the Public Square* (Grand Rapids, Mich.: Zondervan, 1990); Skillen, "Going Beyond Liberalism to Christian Social Philosophy," *Christian Scholar's Review* 19 (Mar. 1990): 220–30; Skillen, "What Does Biblical Obedience Entail for American Political Thought?" in *The Bible, Politics, and Democracy*, ed. Richard John Neuhaus, Encounter Series No. 5 (Grand Rapids, Mich.: Eerdmans, 1987), 55–80.

5. Neal Riemer, "Madison: A Founder's Vision of Religious Liberty and Public Life," this volume, chap. 2.

6. Ibid.

7. Charles J. Emmerich, "The Enigma of James Madison on Church and State," this volume, chap. 3.

8. Ibid.

9. Daniel L. Dreisbach, "In Pursuit of Religious Freedom: Thomas Jefferson's Church-State Views Revisited," this volume, chap. 4.

10. Julia K. Stronks, "The Courts' Definition of Religious Activity: Protection of Diversity or Imposition of a Majority View?" this volume, chap. 5.

11. Dreisbach, "In Pursuit of Religious Freedom," this volume, chap. 4.

12. William Lee Miller, *The First Liberty: Religion and the American Republic* (New York: Knopf, 1986), 170–71.

13. Ibid., 320.

14. Ibid., 346.

15. Ibid., vii.

16. Robert Booth Fowler, "Religion and Liberal Culture: Unconventional Partnership or Unhealthy Co-Dependency," this volume, chap. 8.

17. Fowler, *Unconventional Partners: Religion and Liberal Culture in the United States* (Grand Rapids, Mich.: Eerdmans, 1989).

18. Clarke E. Cochran, "Politics and Eternity: The Voice of Religion in Political Discourse," this volume, chap. 9.

19. Ibid.

20. Frank Guliuzza, "The Supreme Court, the Establishment Clause, and Incoherence," this volume, chap. 5.
21. Glendon and Yanes, "Structural Free Exercise," 541.
22. Stronks, "The Courts' Definition of Religious Activity," this volume, chap. 5.
23. Glendon and Yanes, "Structural Free Exercise," 549.
24. My argument, developed in detail with respect to equal educational opportunity, can be found in James W. Skillen, "Religion and Education Policy: Where Do Go From Here?" *The Journal of Law and Politics* 6 (Spring 1990): 503–29; Skillen, "Changing Assumptions in the Public Governance of Education: What Has Changed and What Ought to Change," in *Democracy and the Renewal of Public Education,* ed. Richard John Neuhaus, Encounter Series No. 4 (Grand Rapids, Mich.: Eerdmans, 1987), 86–115; and Rockne M. McCarthy, James W. Skillen, and William A. Harper, *Disestablishment a Second Time: Genuine Pluralism for American Schools* (Grand Rapids, Mich.: Eerdmans with the Christian Univ. Press, 1982).
25. Qtd. in Emmerich, "The Enigma of James Madison," this volume, chap. 3.

REFERENCES

Fowler, Robert Booth. *Unconventional Partners: Religion and Liberal Culture in the United States.* Grand Rapids, Mich.: Eerdmans, 1989.

Glendon, Mary Ann, and Raul F. Yanes. "Structural Free Exercise." *Michigan Law Review* 90 (Dec. 1991): 477–550.

McCarthy, Rockne M., James W. Skillen, and William A. Harper. *Disestablishment a Second Time: Genuine Pluralism for American Schools.* Grand Rapids, Mich.: Eerdmans with the Christian Univ. Press, 1982.

Miller, William Lee. *The First Liberty: Religion and the American Republic.* New York: Knopf, 1986.

Skillen, James W., and Rockne M. McCarthy, eds. *Political Order and the Plural Structure of Society.* Emory Univ. Studies in Law and Religion, No. 2. Atlanta: Scholars Press, 1991.

‖ Selected Bibliography

Adams, Arlin M., and Charles J. Emmerich. "A Heritage of Religious Liberty." *University of Pennsylvania Law Review* 137 (1989): 1559–1671.

————. *A Nation Dedicated to Religious Liberty: The Constitutional Heritage of the Religion Clauses*. Philadelphia: Univ. of Pennsylvania Press, 1990.

Alley, Robert S., ed. *James Madison on Religious Liberty*. Buffalo: Prometheus Books, 1985.

————. *The Supreme Court on Church and State*. New York: Oxford Univ. Press, 1988.

Andenaes, Johannes. *Punishment and Deterrence*. Ann Arbor, Mich.: Univ. of Michigan Press, 1974.

Barth, Karl. *Ethics*. Trans. R. Dietrich Braun. New York: Seabury Press, 1981.

Beaumont, Gustave de, and Alexis de Tocqueville. *On the Penitentiary System in the United States and Its Application in France*. Trans. Francis Lieber. 1833. Rpt. New York: A. M. Kelley, 1970.

Bellah, Robert. *Beyond Belief: Essays on Religion in a Post-Traditional World*. New York: Harper and Row, 1970.

Bellah, Robert, Richard Madsen, William Sullivan, Ann Swidler, and Stephen Tipton. *Habits of the Heart: Individualism and Commitment in American Life*. Berkeley: Univ. of California Press, 1985.

Berman, Harold J. *The Interaction of Law and Religion*. Nashville, Tenn.: Abingdon Press, 1974.

Berman, Harold J., and John Witte Jr. "The Transformation of Western Legal Philosophy in Lutheran Germany." *Southern California Law Review* 62 (1989): 1573–660.

Beth, Loren. *The American Theory of Church and State*. Gainesville, Fla.: Univ. of Florida Press, 1958.

Bohatec, Josef. *Calvin's Lehre von Staat und Kirche*. Aalen: Scientia, 1961.

————. *Calvin und das Recht*. Graz: H. Boeklaus, 1934.

Bowers, Claude G. *The Young Jefferson, 1743–1789*. Boston: Houghton Mifflin, 1945.

Bonhoeffer, Dietrich. *Ethics*. Trans. Neville H. Smith. Ed. Eberhard Bethge. New York: Macmillan, 1955, 1965.

Boyd, Julian P., ed. *The Papers of Thomas Jefferson*. Vol. 2. Princeton: Princeton Univ. Press, 1950.

Bradley, Gerard V. *Church-State Relationships in America*. New York: Greenwood Press, 1987.

Brant, Irving. *James Madison: Commander in Chief, 1812–1836*. Indianapolis: Bobbs-Merrill, 1961.

———. *James Madison: Father of the Constitution, 1787–1800*. Indianapolis: Bobbs-Merrill, 1950.

———. *James Madison: The Nationalist, 1780–1787*. Indianapolis: Bobbs-Merrill, 1948.

———. *James Madison: The President, 1809–1812*. Indianapolis: Bobbs-Merrill, 1956.

———. *James Madison: Secretary of State, 1800–1809*. Indianapolis: Bobbs-Merrill, 1953.

———. *James Madison: The Virginia Revolutionist, 1751–1780*. Indianapolis: Bobbs-Merrill, 1941.

Buckley, Thomas E. *Church and State in Revolutionary Virginia, 1776–1787*. Charlottesville: Univ. Press of Virginia, 1977.

Cobb, Sanford H. *The Rise of Religious Liberty in America*. New York: Macmillan, 1902.

Cochran, Clarke E. *Religion in Public and Private Life*. New York: Routledge, 1990.

Cord, Robert L. *Separation of Church and State: Historical Fact and Current Fiction*. New York: Lambeth Press, 1982.

Corwin, Edward. "The Supreme Court as National School Board." *Law and Contemporary Problems* 14 (1948): 3–22.

Cunningham, Noble E., Jr. *In Pursuit of Reason: The Life of Thomas Jefferson*. Baton Rouge: Louisiana State Univ. Press, 1987.

Curry, Thomas J. *The First Freedoms: Church and State in America to the Passage of the First Amendment*. New York: Oxford Univ. Press, 1986.

"Developments—Religion and the State." *Harvard Law Review* 100 (1987): 1606–1781.

Devlin, Patrick. *The Enforcement of Morals*. London: Oxford Univ. Press, 1965.

Drakeman, Donald L. "Religion and the Republic: James Madison and the First Amendment." *Journal of Church and State* 25 (1983): 427–45.

Dreisbach, Daniel L. *Real Threat and Mere Shadow: Religious Liberty and the First Amendment*. Westchester, Ill.: Crossway Books, 1987.

Dumbauld, Edward. *Thomas Jefferson and the Law*. Norman: Univ. of Oklahoma Press, 1978.

Dunn, Charles W., ed. *Religion in American Politics*. Washington, D.C.: Congressional Quarterly Press, 1989.

Eckenrode, Hamilton James. *Separation of Church and State in Virginia: A Study in the Development of the Revolution*. Richmond: Davis Bottom, 1910.

Estep, William. *The Anabaptist Story*. Grand Rapids, Mich.: Eerdmans, 1975.

———. *Revolution Within the Revolution: The First Amendment in Historical Context, 1612–1789*. Grand Rapids, Mich.: Eerdmans, 1990.

Ezorsky, Gertrude, ed. *Philosophical Perspectives on Punishment*. Albany: State Univ. of New York Press, 1973.

Feinberg, Joel. *The Moral Limits of the Criminal Law*. New York: Oxford Univ. Press, 1984.

Fletcher, George. *Rethinking Criminal Law.* Boston: Little, Brown, 1978.

Fleming, Donald, and Bernard Bailyn, eds. *Law in American History.* Boston: Little, Brown, 1973.

Ford, Paul Leicester, ed. *The Writings of Thomas Jefferson.* 10 vols. New York: G. P. Putnam's Sons, 1899.

Fowler, Robert Booth. *Unconventional Partners: Religion and Liberal Culture in the United States.* Grand Rapids, Mich.: Eerdmans, 1989.

Fuller, Lon. *The Morality of Law.* Rev. ed. New Haven, Conn.: Yale Univ. Press, 1969.

Geertz, Clifford. *The Interpretation of Cultures.* New York: Basic Books, 1973.

Glendon, Mary Ann, and Raul F. Yanes, "Structural Free Exercise." *Michigan Law Review* 90 (Dec. 1991): 477–550.

Goodhart, Arthur L. *English Law and the Moral Law.* London: Stevens, 1953

Greenawalt, Kent. *Religious Conviction and Political Choice.* New York: Oxford Univ. Press, 1988.

Grey, Thomas C. *The Legal Enforcement of Morality.* New York: Knopf, 1983.

Guliuzza, Frank. "The Practical Perils of an Original Intent Based Judicial Philosophy: Originalism and the Church-State Test Case." *Drake Law Review* (forthcoming).

Gurley, James Lafayette. "Thomas Jefferson's Philosophy and Theology: As Related to His Political Principles, Including Separation of Church and State." Ph.D. diss., Univ. of Michigan, 1975.

Hall, Jerome. *Studies in Jurisprudence and Criminal Theory.* New York: Oceana Publications, 1958.

Hamilton, Alexander, John Jay, and James Madison. *The Federalist.* (1787–88). New York: Modern Library, n.d.

Handy, Robert T. *A Christian America: Protestant Hopes and Historical Realities.* Oxford: Oxford Univ. Press, 1984.

Healey, Robert M. *Jefferson on Religion in Public Education.* New Haven: Yale Univ. Press, 1962.

Hening, William Waller, ed. *The Statutes at Large: Being a Collection of all the Laws of Virginia, From the First Session of the Legislature, in the Year 1619.* 12 vols. Richmond: J. & G. Cochran, 1823.

Henry, Carl F. H. *Twilight of a Great Civilization.* Westchester, Ill.: Crossway Books, 1988.

Herbert, Jerry, ed. *America, Christian or Secular?* Portland: Multnomah Press, 1984.

Hertzke, Allen. *Representing God in Washington: The Role of Religious Lobbies in the American Polity.* Knoxville: Univ. of Tennessee Press, 1988.

Howard, A. E. Dick. "The Supreme Court and the Establishment of Religion." In *James Madison on Religious Liberty.* Ed. Robert S. Alley. Buffalo: Prometheus Books, 1985.

Howe, Mark DeWolfe. *The Garden and the Wilderness: Religion and Government in American Constitutional History.* Chicago: Univ. of Chicago Press, 1965.

Hunter, James Davison. *Culture Wars: The Struggle to Define America.* New York: Basic Books, 1991.

Hunter, James Davison, and Os Guinness, eds. *Articles of Faith, Articles of Peace: The Religious Liberty Clauses and the American Public Philosophy.* Washington, D.C.: Brookings Institution, 1990.

Inglehart, Ronald F. *Culture Shift in Advanced Industrial Society.* Princeton: Princeton Univ. Press, 1990.

Isaac, Rhys. *The Transformation of Virginia, 1740–1790.* Chapel Hill: Univ. of North Carolina Press, 1982.

"Jefferson and the Church-State Wall: A Historical Examination of the Man and the Metaphor." *Brigham Young University Law Review* 1978 (1978): 645–74.

Kauper, Paul G. *Religion and the Constitution.* Baton Rouge: Louisiana State Univ. Press, 1964.

Kessler, Sanford. "Locke's Influence on Jefferson's 'Bill for Establishing Religious Freedom.'" *Journal of Church and State* 25 (1983): 231–52.

Ketcham Ralph L. *James Madison: A Biography.* New York: Macmillan, 1970.

Koch, Adrienne. *Madison's "Advice to My Country."* Princeton, N.J.: Princeton Univ. Press, 1966.

Koch, Adrienne, and William Peden, eds. *The Life and Selected Writings of Thomas Jefferson.* Modern Library Series. New York: Random House, 1944.

Laycock, Douglas. "'Nonpreferential' Aid to Religion: A False Claim About Original Intent." *William and Mary Law Review* 27 (1986): 875–923.

———. "The Remnants of Free Exercise." *The Supreme Court Review* (1990): 1–68.

Levy, Leonard W. *The Establishment Clause: Religion and the First Amendment.* New York: Macmillan, 1986.

Linder, Robert, and Richard Pierard. *Twilight of the Saints: Biblical Christianity and Civil Religion in America.* Downers Grove, Ill.: Inter-Varsity Press, 1978.

Lindsay, Thomas. "James Madison on Religion and Politics: Rhetoric and Reality." *American Political Science Review* 85 (1991): 1321–37.

Lipscomb, Andrew A., and Albert Ellery Bergh, eds. *The Writings of Thomas Jefferson.* 20 vols. Washington, D.C.: Thomas Jefferson Memorial Association, 1905.

Littell, Franklin Hamlin. "The Basis of Religious Liberty in Christian Belief." *Journal of Church and State* 6 (1964): 132–46.

McCarthy, Rockne, James W. Skillen, and William A. Harper. *Disestablishment a Second Time: Genuine Pluralism for American Schools.* Grand Rapids, Mich.: Christian Univ. Press, 1982.

McConnell, Michael W. "Free Exercise Revisionism and the Smith Decision." *University of Chicago Law Review* 57 (1990): 1109–53.

———. "The Origins and Historical Understanding of Free Exercise of Religion." *Harvard Law Review* 103 (1990): 1409–517.

McGowen, Randall. "The Changing Face of God's Justice: The Debates Over Divine and Human Punishment in Eighteenth-Century England." *Criminal Justice History: An International Annual* 9 (1988): 63–98.

McLoughlin, William, ed. *Isaac Backus on Church, State and Calvinism: Pamphlets, 1754–1789*. Cambridge: Belknap Press of Harvard Univ. Press, 1968.

———. *New England Dissent, 1630–1833: Baptists and the Separation of Church and State*. Cambridge: Harvard Univ. Press, 1971.

Madison, James. *The Papers of James Madison*. Ed. William T. Hutchison and William M. E. Rachal, vols. 1–7. Ed. Robert A. Rutland and William M. W. Rachal, vols. 8–10. Chicago: Univ. of Chicago Press, 1962–77.

Malbin, Michael. *Religion and Politics: The Intentions of the Authors of the First Amendment*. Washington, D.C.: American Enterprise Institute for Public Policy Research, 1978.

Malone, Dumas. *Jefferson the Virginian*. Boston: Little, Brown, 1948.

Mead, Sidney. *The Lively Experiment*. New York: Harper & Row, 1963.

Miller, William Lee. *The First Liberty: Religion and the American Republic*. New York: Alfred A. Knopf, 1986.

Mitchell, Basil. *Law, Morality and Religion in a Secular Society*. London, New York: Oxford Univ. Press, 1972.

Moberly, Walter. *Legal Responsibility and Moral Responsibility*. Philadelphia: Fortress Press, 1951.

———. *The Ethics of Punishment*. Hamden, Conn.: Archon Books, 1968.

Morgan, Richard E. *The Supreme Court and Religion*. New York: Free Press, 1972.

Neuhaus, Richard John, ed. *Democracy and the Renewal of Public Education*. Grand Rapids, Mich.: Eerdmans, 1987.

Niebuhr, H. Richard. *Christ and Culture*. New York: Harper, 1951.

Noll, Mark, Nathan Hatch, and George Marsden. *The Search for Christian America*. Westchester, Ill.: Crossway Books, 1983.

Perry, Michael J. *Love and Power: The Proper Role of Religion and Morality in American Politics*. New York: Oxford Univ. Press, 1991.

Peterson, Merrill D. *The Jefferson Image in the American Mind*. New York: Oxford Univ. Press, 1960.

———. *Thomas Jefferson and the New Nation*. New York: Oxford Univ. Press, 1970.

———, ed. *James Madison: A Biography in His Own Words*. New York: Newsweek, 1974.

Peterson, Merrill D., and Robert C. Vaughan, eds. *The Virginia Statute for Religious Freedom: Its Evolution and Consequences in American History*. New York: Cambridge Univ. Press, 1988.

Plöchl, Willibald M. "Thomas Jefferson, Author of the Statute of Virginia for Religious Freedom." *Jurist* 3 (1943): 182–230.

Randall, Henry S. *The Life of Thomas Jefferson.* 3 vols. New York: Derby and Jackson, 1858.

Reichley, A. James. *Religion in American Public Life.* Washington, D.C.: Brookings Institution, 1985.

Report of the Committee of Revisors Appointed by the General Assembly of Virginia in MDCCLXXVI. Richmond: Dixon & Holt, 1784.

Riemer, Neal. "Religious Liberty and Creative Breakthroughs: The Contributions of Roger Williams and James Madison." In *Religion in American Politics,* ed. Charles W. Dunn. Washington, D.C.: Congressional Quarterly Press, 1989.

Roof, Wade Clark, and William McKinney. *American Mainline Religion: Its Changing Shape and Future.* New Brunswick, N.J.: Rutgers Univ. Press, 1987.

Rutland, Robert. "How Involved Was Madison in Framing the Constitution and the Bill of Rights?" In *The Political Theory of the Constitution,* ed. Kenneth W. Thompson. Lanham, Md.: Univ. Press of America, 1960.

Rutland, Robert A., and William M. E. Rachal, eds. *The Papers of James Madison.* Vol. 8. Chicago: Univ. of Chicago Press, 1973.

Sandler, S. Gerald. "Lockean Ideas in Thomas Jefferson's Bill for Establishing Religious Freedom." *Journal of the History of Ideas* 21 (1960): 110–16.

Sanford, Charles B. *The Religious Life of Thomas Jefferson.* Charlottesville: Univ. Press of Virginia, 1984.

Schachner, Nathan. *Thomas Jefferson: A Biography.* 2 vols. New York: Appleton-Century-Crofts, 1951.

Singleton, Marvin K. "Colonial Virginia as First Amendment Matrix: Henry, Madison, and Assessment Establishment." *Journal of Church and State* 8 (1966): 344–64.

Skillen, James W. "Religion and Education Policy: Where Do We Go From Here?" *The Journal of Law and Politics* 6 (Spring 1990): 503–29.

———. *The Scattered Voice: Christians at Odds in the Public Square.* Grand Rapids, Mich.: Zondervan, 1990.

Skillen, James W., and Rockne M. McCarthy, eds. *Political Order and the Plural Structure of Society.* Emory Univ. Studies in Law and Religion, No. 2. Atlanta: Scholars Press, 1991.

Stark, Rodney, and William Sims Bainbridge. *The Future of Religion: Secularization, Revival and Cult Formation.* Berkeley: Univ. of California Press, 1985.

Stephen, James Fitzjames. *A History of the Criminal Law of England.* 3 vols. London: Macmillan, 1883.

Stokes, Anson Phelps. *Church and State in the United States.* 3 vols. New York: Harper and Brothers, 1950.

Stonestreet, George. *The Especial Importance of Religious Principles in the Judges and the Advocates of the Courts of Law.* Newport: n.p., 1822.

Tinder, Glenn. *The Political Meaning of Christianity: An Interpretation.* Baton Rouge: Louisiana State Univ. Press, 1989.

Tushnet, Mark. *Red, White, and Blue: A Critical Analysis of Constitutional Law.* Cambridge: Harvard Univ. Press, 1988.

Vallauri, Luigi L., and Gerhard Dilcher, eds. *Christentum, Säkularisation und modernes Recht.* Baden-Baden: Nomos Verlagsgesellschaft, 1981.

Weber, Paul J. "Strict Neutrality: The Next Step in First Amendment Development?" In *Religion in American Politics,* ed. Charles W. Dunn. Washington, D.C.: Congressional Quarterly Press, 1989.

Witte, John Jr., and Frank S. Alexander, eds. *The Weightier Matters of the Law: Essays on Law and Religion.* Atlanta: Scholars Press, 1988.

Wolfe, Alan. *Whose Keeper? Social Science and Moral Obligation.* Berkeley: Univ. of California Press, 1989.

Wuthnow, Robert. *The Restructuring of American Religion.* Princeton: Princeton Univ. Press, 1988.

|| Contributors

CLARKE E. COCHRAN (Ph.D., Duke University) is Professor of Political Science at Texas Tech University. He is the author of several publications, including *Character, Community, and Politics* (University of Alabama Press, 1982) and *Religion in Public and Private Life* (Routledge, 1990).

DANIEL L. DREISBACH (D. Phil., Oxford University; J.D., University of Virginia School of Law) teaches in the School of Public Affairs at American University. He is the author of *Real Threat and Mere Shadow: Religious Liberty and the First Amendment* (Crossway Books, 1987).

CHARLES J. EMMERICH (J.D., University of Idaho College of Law) is Research Consultant at the University of Pennsylvania Law School and teaches constitutional law at Wheaton College (Illinois). He is coauthor, with former U.S. Court of Appeals Justice Arlin Adams, of *A Nation Dedicated to Religious Liberty: The Constitutional Heritage of the Religion Clauses* (University of Pennsylvania Press, 1990).

CARL H. ESBECK (J.D., Cornell Law School) is Professor of Law at the University of Missouri School of Law. He teaches courses on constitutional law and church-state relations and has published articles in a variety of law reviews on such topics as tort claims against religious organizations and clerics, church autonomy under the establishment clause, and the *Lemon* test.

ROBERT BOOTH FOWLER (Ph.D., Harvard University) is Professor of Political Science at the University of Wisconsin, Madison. He is the author of various books, including *A New Engagement: Evangelical Political Thought, 1966–1976* (Eerdmans, 1982), *Religion and Politics in the United States* (Scarecrow Press, 1985), and *Unconventional Partners: Religion and Liberal Culture in the United States* (Eerdmans, 1989).

FRANK GULIUZZA (Ph.D., Notre Dame) is Assistant Professor of Political Science at Weber State University. Among his works in progress is *Beyond Incoherence: Making Sense of the Church-State Debate.*

LUIS E. LUGO (Ph.D., University of Chicago) is Professor of Political Science at Calvin College. He has served as managing editor of *Ethics: An International Journal of Social, Political, and Legal Philosophy.*

NEAL RIEMER (Ph.D., Harvard University) is Andrew V. Stout Professor of Political Philosophy, Emeritus, at Drew University. He is the author of several books, including *James Madison: Creating the American Constitution* (Congressional Quarterly Press, 1986) and *The Future of the Democratic Revolution: Toward a More Prophetic Politics* (Praeger, 1984).

JAMES W. SKILLEN (Ph.D., Duke University) is Executive Director of the Association for Public Justice and the Center for Public Justice in Washington, D.C. His most recent book on religion and politics is *The Scattered Voice: Christians at Odds in the Public Square* (Zondervan, 1990).

JULIA K. STRONKS (J.D., University of Iowa) is a doctoral candidate in the Department of Government and Politics at the University of Maryland.

JOHN WITTE, JR. (J.D., Harvard Law School) is currently Assistant Professor at Emory University School of Law and director of its Law and Religion Program. He has published numerous articles in law review journals and is coeditor of *The Weightier Matters of the Law: Essays on Law and Religion* (Scholars Press, 1988).

‖ Index